China's Belt and Road Initi

This volume assesses China's Belt and Road Initiative (BRI) as it approaches its tenth year in operation. The programme has gone through a difficult transition since its inception in 2013, with an environment developing in a way utterly unanticipated by Chinese decision-makers. Despite pragmatic adjustments to the BRI, the lack of a firm empirical base has impeded the BRI and led to its demise in many countries.

With the accumulation of nearly ten years of project and economic data, it is possible to make an in-depth assessment of the BRI. For this purpose, the study examines the infrastructure component of the BRI in 39 countries, stretching from the Americas to Oceania and, finally, South Asia. The study finds a strong relationship between a country's progress in improved governance and the quality of its infrastructure. Countries that have benefited from the BRI have simultaneously achieved progress in governance areas, such as the rule of law and control of corruption. By not emphasizing improved governance structures, China condemns many of its partners to failure.

Researchers, students, and economic development specialists from Latin America to South Asia and Oceania will find this study a useful departure from the volumes of anecdotal BRI assessments.

Robert E. Looney is a Distinguished Professor Emeritus in the National Security Affairs Department at the Naval Postgraduate School, Monterey, California, USA. He specializes in issues relating to economic intelligence and economic development in the Middle East, Latin America and Africa. He has published 22 books and is currently the editor of the Routledge series Europa Emerging Economies. Professor Looney is on the board of editors of the *International Journal of World Peace* and the *Journal of Third World Studies*. He has published over 300 articles in numerous professional journals and is a regular contributor to the *Milken Institute Review* and the *World Politics Review.*

Europa Introduction to...

The Focus titles in this series build on the unparalleled worldwide coverage of The Europa World Year Book and its associated regional surveys: Africa South of the Sahara; Central and South-Eastern Europe; Eastern Europe, Russia and Central Asia; The Far East and Australasia; The Middle East and North Africa; South America, Central America and the Caribbean; South Asia; The USA and Canada; and Western Europe, also available online at www.europa-world.com. Books in the series provide students, postgraduates, academics, professionals and researchers with up-to-date, balanced, authoritative and concise introductions to topics in the Europa core areas of country-specific contemporary politics and economics, and regional and international affairs. Volumes in the series, authored by experts, present a factual overview in a concise format, offering readers the opportunity rapidly to research current issues.

Italy's Contemporary Politics
James L. Newell

Economic Transformation in Sub-Saharan Africa: The Way Forward
Donald L. Sparks

China's Belt and Road Initiative at Ten: Country Experiences in the Americas, Oceania and Asia
Robert E. Looney

China's Belt and Road Initiative at Ten

Country Experiences in the Americas, Oceania and Asia

Robert E. Looney

Routledge
Taylor & Francis Group

LONDON AND NEW YORK

First published 2023
by Routledge
4 Park Square, Milton Park, Abingdon, Oxon OX14 4RN

and by Routledge
605 Third Avenue, New York, NY 10158

Routledge is an imprint of the Taylor & Francis Group, an informa business

British Library Cataloguing in Publication Data
A catalogue record for this book is available from the British Library

Library of Congress Cataloging-in-Publication Data
A catalog record has been requested for this book

ISBN: 978-0-367-47123-1 (hbk)
ISBN: 978-1-032-38469-6 (pbk)
ISBN: 978-1-003-34522-0 (ebk)

DOI: 10.4324/b23227

Typeset in Times New Roman
by Taylor & Francis Books

For Pamela

Contents

Illustrations

About the Author

Robert E. Looney is a Distinguished Professor Emeritus in the National Security Affairs Department at the Naval Postgraduate School, Monterey, California, USA. He received his PhD in Economics from the University of California, Davis. He specializes in issues relating to economic intelligence and economic development in the Middle East, Latin America and Africa. He has published 22 books, including *Economic Policymaking in Mexico: Factors Underlying the 1982 Crisis*, Duke University Press (1985), and *Iraq's Informal Economy: Reflections of War, Sanctions and Policy Failure*, the Emirates Center for Strategic Studies and Research (2007). He has also edited six Routledge handbooks: *Handbook of US-Middle East Relations* (2009), *Handbook of Oil Politics* (2012), *Handbook of Emerging Economies* (2014), *Handbook of Transitions to Energy and Climate Security* (2017), *Handbook of International Trade Agreements* (2018) and *Handbook of Caribbean Economies* (2021). He is currently the editor of the Routledge Europa Emerging Economies series. Professor Looney is on the board of editors of the *International Journal of World Peace* and the *Journal of Third World Studies*. In addition, he has published over 300 articles in numerous professional journals and is a regular contributor to the *Milken Institute Review* and the *World Politics Review*. As an international consultant, Professor Looney has advised the governments of Iran, Saudi Arabia, Japan, Mexico, Panama and Jamaica, as well as the World Bank, the International Monetary Fund, the International Labour Office, the Inter-American Development Bank, SRI International and the RAND Corporation.

Preface

The last ten years have seen the People's Republic of China's Belt and Road Initiative (BRI) go through a difficult transition. First, there has been pushback from several recipients over concern of falling into a 'debt trap' because of projects not generating sufficient funds for debt servicing. Second, in some countries an 'anti-Chinese' environment festers, making it difficult even to complete existing projects. Third, China is finding that several Western countries such as the United States, Japan, Australia and India are becoming increasingly concerned about China's growing influence in their traditional spheres of influence and are mounting counter-campaigns of projects and assistance.

Fourth, there has been a slowdown in the Chinese economy as it transitions from primarily an export-based economy to one more focused on the domestic economy. This transition has also been fraught with increasing domestic debt levels and the potential for widespread bankruptcies in the country's substantial real estate market. Fifth, the US–China trade war served to compound this problem as it triggered investor concern and the departure of some Western companies. Sixth, the coronavirus COVID-19 pandemic struck, throwing many member countries into sharp contractions, with work on BRI projects halted or severely slowed. Seventh, in attempting to stabilize their economies during the pandemic, many BRI countries saw their budget deficits drive debt levels into dangerous ranges. Finally, when many countries appeared to be prepared to restart their BRI projects in the post-pandemic period, the Russian Federation invaded Ukraine, disrupting trade flows, causing energy price spikes, and further complicating the debt situation of many emerging economies. While the ramifications of this event are still unclear, there is little doubt that it will have a profound effect on the way China pursues the BRI, and the extent to which member countries will continue to implement their memorandums of understanding with China.

With these developments in mind, the chapters that follow attempt to assess BRI at ten by examining a series of country experiences in the Americas, the Pacific and Asia. What commonalities exist across this geographic span, what characteristics set each region apart and what is the path forward?

Acknowledgements

Clearly, a book of this scope and sheer length could not have come to completion without the contributions of many individuals. A special thanks to my colleagues at the Naval Postgraduate School, whose help and encouragement proved invaluable. Students in my seminars on the Political Economy of Latin America have provided invaluable critiques of the Caribbean, Central America and South America chapters, together with perceptive insights from their own experiences in the region.

Thanks to Peter Passel at the Milken Institute for permission to draw on several articles published in the *Milken Institute Review.* Thanks also go to Judah Grunstein for giving me permission to draw on several articles appearing in *World Politics Review.* Jackie West at Routledge kindly let me draw on my essay on the Belt and Road Initiative in Latin America (2022) for *South America, Central America and the Caribbean,* while Juliet Love did the same for my essay on the Belt and Road Initiative in East Asia and the Pacific for *The Far East and Australasia* (2020).

Greta E. Marlatt, head research librarian at the Naval Postgraduate School Knox Library, went far beyond the call of duty to keep me informed of the latest BRI developments through her invaluable 'Greta's Links'.[1] Meanwhile, Jason Altwies, also at the Naval Postgraduate School, provided invaluable research assistance. Also, special thanks to Alison Phillips for her professionalism and stellar efforts in preparing the manuscript for publication.

Most of all, thanks go to Cathy Hartley, Europa Commissioning Editor, who conceived the original study, supplied ongoing guidance, and provided good cheer and positive encouragement throughout the project.

Note

1 Greta E. Marlatt, 'Greta's Links', https://gretaslinks.blogspot.com/.

1 Introduction

When the People's Republic of China introduced its Belt and Road Initiative (BRI) in 2013, many observers hailed the massive trade and infrastructure project as a 21st-century Silk Road that would eventually link East Asia with Europe and Africa.[1] [2] The initiative represented much more to the capital-starved developing and emerging nations that lined its route: a modern-day version of the post-World War II US Marshall Plan, but this time backed by a pledge of US $1 trillion in Chinese funding.[3]

Many of the early BRI participants had 'junk' credit ratings, so the initiative offered an alternative source of funding for much-needed investment, mainly in infrastructure and especially in transport-related projects such as railways, ports and roads.[4] And unlike Western aid and loans from multilateral sources such as the Asian Development Bank, Chinese funding did not come with inconvenient demands for improvements in governance or the business environment.[5]

China and other BRI advocates touted the initiative as a finely orchestrated plan that would create new supply chains for China, facilitate regional economic integration and job creation, and lead to higher economic growth rates for participating countries.[6] In contrast, detractors warned that the initiative was a scheme to extend Chinese hegemony over much of the developing world, despite Chinese claims that the BRI had no geopolitical, ideological or military objectives.[7] A middle view contended that the BRI was simply a vision that lacked a coherent strategy.[8] Nearly ten years later, the jury is still out. While the BRI achieved some stunning successes, it has also left some devastated economies in its wake.

These positions appear at length in many popular and professional books and journals. However, most of these studies generalize in a non-quantitative fashion from a few individual projects, countries or regions. That is only natural given the dearth of data on BRI programmes. China does not even maintain a public list of BRI projects,

DOI: 10.4324/b23227-1

let alone data that would facilitate calculations such as return rates, making it almost impossible to establish standards for individual countries or evaluate their BRI progress.[9]

The present study attempts to overcome these limitations in several ways. First, it assesses in some detail the BRI activities using a large sample of BRI countries from diverse regions. Second, it looks at the national economic/political context in which BRI programmes occur. Has economic growth slowed? Are government budgets over-extended? Are sound governance structures in place?

Third, it attempts to establish a method for assessing situations in which BRI infrastructure programmes are likely to produce a significant and positive impact on infrastructure quality and those where improvements might be more difficult to achieve. Fortunately, the World Bank publishes a Logistics Performance Index (LPI) across 160 countries every two years, the most recent being 2018. One component of the LPI is transport infrastructure quality.[10] The statistical analysis presented in Appendix A shows a close, statistically significant relationship between the country governance levels measured by the World Bank and the LPI.

On the assumption that the quality of transport infrastructure is a proxy for the quality of the overall infrastructure, countries can attain improved infrastructure quality through better governance – for example, a lesser degree of corruption results in improved project selection. Or they can achieve enhanced infrastructure quality through BRI projects – perhaps even some combination of the two.

The statistical results in Appendix A suggest that the relationship between infrastructure and governance also stabilizes over time, with imbalances in earlier periods initiating corrective changes over time in infrastructure quality to restore the infrastructure quality/governance balance. For example, suppose a country overachieved in an earlier period – with infrastructure quality significantly greater than that which the country's governance/infrastructure pattern might predict. In such a case, the country will probably have difficulty maintaining the same level of infrastructure quality. BRI programmes will be less effective in improving infrastructure quality owing to offsetting factors such as the inability of the government to maintain existing facilities because of low levels of government effectiveness (a dimension of governance). These patterns suggest situations in which BRI programmes are likely to produce significant gains for infrastructure quality and those where less success is more likely to occur.

The following chapters assess the BRI experience of thirty-nine countries. The groupings follow geographic lines, although each region appears to have unique characteristics that set its BRI experience apart from the others. Starting with the region least critical to China's interests, the Caribbean, subsequent chapters examine groupings of roughly increased importance to China – Central America, South America, Oceania, South-East Asia, the Mekong countries, South Asia and finally Central Asia. The concluding chapter summarizes the lessons learned and speculates about the BRI's future.

Notes

1 The paragraphs that follow draw heavily on Robert Looney, 'China's Belt and Road', *Milken Institute Review*, 3 January 2019. www.milkenreview. org/articles/chinas-belt-and-road.
2 Jonathan E. Hillman, 'How Big Is China's Belt and Road?' Center for Strategic and International Studies, 3 April 2018. www.csis.org/analysis/ how-big-chinas-belt-and-road.
3 Iris Pang, 'China's Belt and Road: Bigger Than the Marshall Plan?' ING Think, 20 July 2018. https://think.ing.com/articles/china-belt-and-road-big ger-than-the-marshall-plan/.
4 Wade Shepard, 'How China's Belt and Road Became a "Global Trail of Trouble"', *Forbes Magazine*, 10 December 2021. www.forbes.com/sites/wa deshepard/2020/01/29/how-chinas-belt-and-road-became-a-global-trail-of-t rouble/?sh=3b950318443d.
5 Martin Raiser and Michele Ruta, 'Managing the Risks of the Belt and Road', World Bank Blogs, 20 June 2019. https://blogs.worldbank.org/easta siapacific/managing-the-risks-of-the-belt-and-road.
6 Frank Holmes, 'China's Belt and Road Initiative Opens Up Unprecedented Opportunities', *Forbes Magazine*, 29 June 2021. www.forbes.com/ sites/greatspeculations/2018/09/04/chinas-belt-and-road-initiative-opens-up -unprecedented-opportunities/#35ed9a813e9a.
7 FPA Administrator, 'The Belt and Road Initiative: Shaping the Narrative of a China Story', Foreign Policy Blogs, 16 August 2018. https://foreignp olicyblogs.com/2018/08/16/the-belt-and-road-initiative-shaping-the-narrati ve-of-a-china-story/.
8 Lee Jones, 'China's Belt and Road Initiative Is a Mess, Not a Master Plan', *Foreign Policy*, 9 October 2020. https://foreignpolicy.com/2020/10/ 09/china-belt-and-road-initiative-mess-not-master-plan/.
9 Jonathan E. Hillman, 'China's Belt and Road Is Full of Holes', Center for Strategic and International Studies, 4 September 2018. www.csis.org/ana lysis/chinas-belt-and-road-full-holes.
10 The World Bank, Logistics Performance Index. https://lpi.worldbank.org/ (accessed 27 April 2022).

2   The BRI in the Caribbean

Introduction

Initially, the People's Republic of China considered the Caribbean and much of Latin America beyond the scope of the Belt and Road Initiative (BRI).[1] This position changed in 2017, and in mid-2018 Trinidad and Tobago joined the programme. Subsequently, Antigua and Barbuda, Barbados, Dominica, Grenada, Guyana, Jamaica, and Suriname joined. As BRI late joiners, the Caribbean countries have benefited from learning from past mistakes and controversies associated with the programme in other parts of the world.

As the BRI is a recent phenomenon in the region, the following country experiences illustrate why and how the BRI unfolded in member countries and the constraints that they faced. The countries selected are those in which projects are already underway or in which Chinese firms are engaged in pre-BRI activities that could provide insights into how new BRI projects may fare.

The countries fall into two groupings. The first, including Cuba, Jamaica, Trinidad and Tobago, the Dominican Republic, and Guyana, are those for which data drawn from the World Bank's Logistics Performance Index (LPI) is available. The second set, including Barbados, Suriname, and Antigua and Barbuda, lack LPI data, and thus are assessed in more general terms. The chapter omits Haiti because it is not a BRI member, nor has the country received any BRI-type financing or projects.

Despite being located in the same geographic region, the growth experiences of the four countries under consideration vary considerably (Figure 2.1). Because of its oil, Trinidad and Tobago rapidly led the way in regional per capita incomes during the commodity super-cycle of the late 1990s and early 2000s. Still, the economy has declined in recent years. The most dynamic economy continues to be

DOI: 10.4324/b23227-2

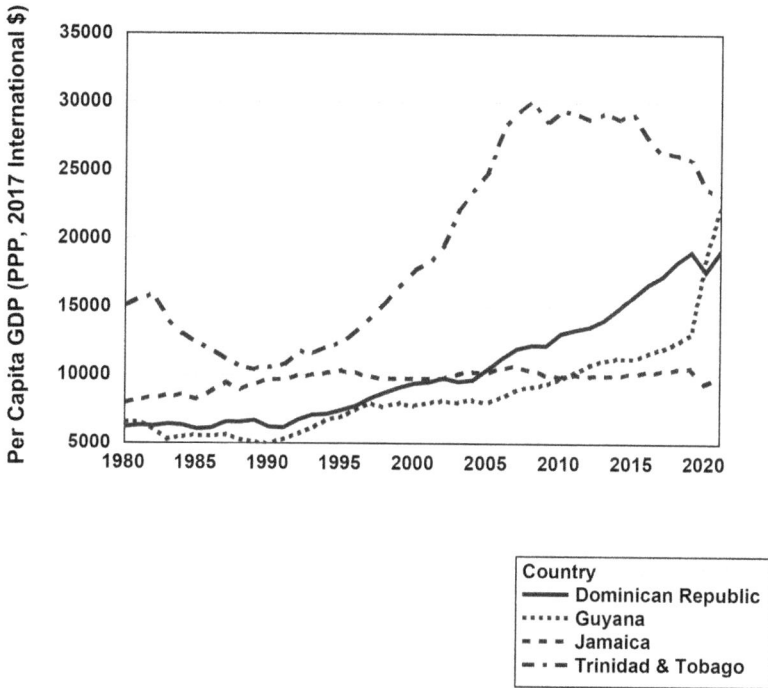

Figure 2.1 Per Capita Income Growth in the Caribbean, 1980–2021
Source: International Monetary Fund, World Economic Outlook Database,
October 2021.

the Dominican Republic, but Guyana may soon have the highest per capita income owing to its recent oil discoveries.

The Jamaican economy has been relatively stagnant since the late 1970s, but is showing signs of achieving a steady expansion because of stabilization programmes that have significantly reduced government indebtedness (Figure 2.2). With the exception of Jamaica, public debt levels are not excessive, although those of the Dominican Republic and Trinidad and Tobago are reaching 60 per cent of gross domestic product (GDP).

Jamaica and Trinidad and Tobago have relatively high levels of governance, although those of Trinidad and Tobago have declined since the early 2000s while those of Jamaica have risen gradually (Figure 2.3). Levels for Guyana and the Dominican Republic lag, but those in the Dominican Republic have grown steadily since 2010. Cuba's governance levels consistently lag, although there has been a slight improvement since around 2005.

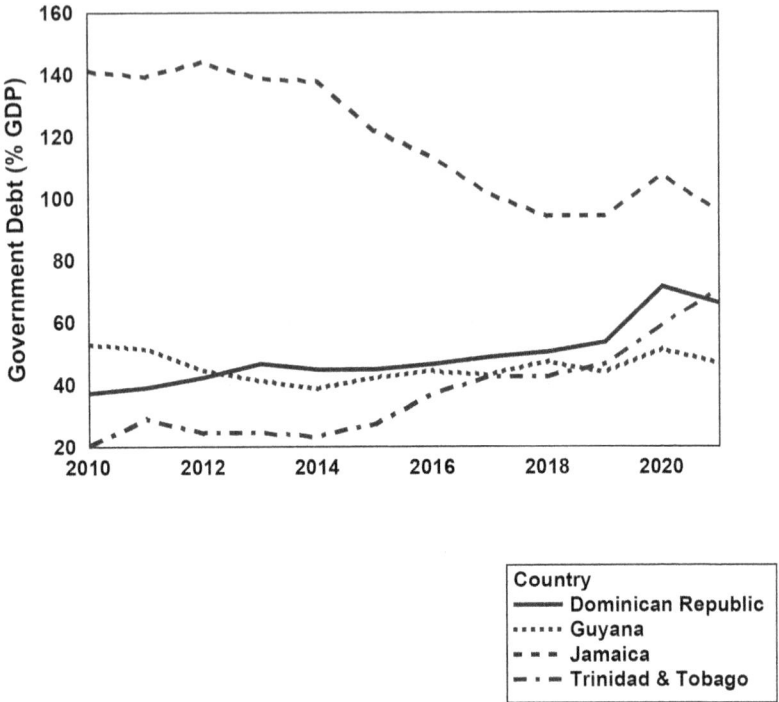

Figure 2.2 Government Debt as a % of GDP in the Caribbean, 2010–21
Source: International Monetary Fund, World Economic Outlook Database:
October 2021.

Transport infrastructure quality compared with the sixteen Latin
American and Caribbean (LAC) countries for which data are available
suggests that all the countries in this group, with the exception of the
Dominican Republic, are underachievers (Figure 2.4). Specifically, at
their level of governance, the quality of their transport infrastructure
is lower than expected. The gaps for Jamaica and Guyana are the
highest, followed by Trinidad and Tobago, and Cuba.

Cuba

Cuba opted to join the BRI in 2019.[2] China has been active in the
country for many years and, to a certain extent, is replacing some of
the country's lost assistance following the demise of the Soviet Union
and, more recently, Venezuela.

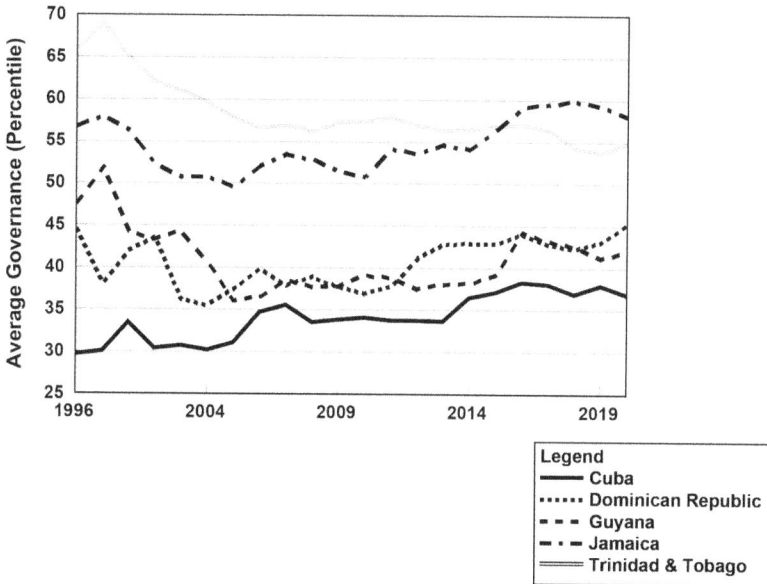

Figure 2.3 Governance Levels in the Caribbean, 1996–2020
Note: Governance is the average of its components: voice and accountability, political stability and absence of violence/terrorism, government effectiveness, regulatory quality, rule of law and control of corruption.
Source: World Bank, Worldwide Governance Indicators Database.

To date, China has three projects totalling US $740m. in Cuba. The American Enterprise Institute (AEI) considers that two of these BRI projects have a total value of $240m.[3] The first project undertaken in 2005 by China's Minmetals invested $500m. in partnership with Cuba's Cubapetroleo (Cupet) to produce 68,000 metric tons of ferro-nickel per year in eastern Cuba.

In recent years China has forgiven around $5,000m. of Cuba's debt, with new finance limited to several projects, one undertaken for $100m. by the China Communications Construction in 2014 and the other for $140m. launched in 2018 by Power Construction Corp (Power China).[4] However, the relationship between the two countries was strengthened after Cuba joined the BRI.

Chinese companies are examining opportunities in Cuban biomedicines and renewable energy with the prospect of establishing operations in the Mariel Special Development Zone.[5] China is also facilitating the country's transition from analogue to digital television as well as assisting in expanding the country's mobile broadband

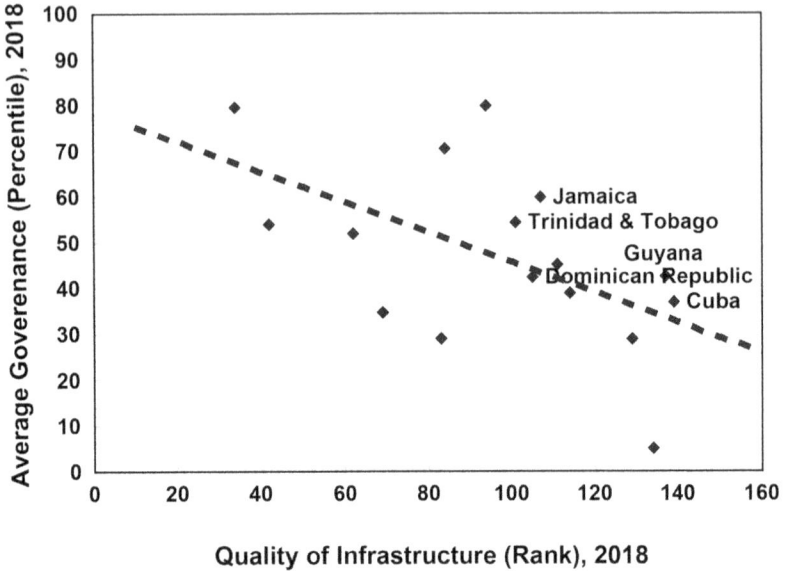

Figure 2.4 Governance/Transport Infrastructure Quality Relationship, Caribbean, 2018

Source: Governance: World Bank, Worldwide Governance Indicators Database; Infrastructure: World Bank, Logistics Performance Index Database.

coverage. In other activities, China has helped to upgrade the country's rail transport through the donation of some train carriages. Meanwhile, the Chinese company Gran Muralla is assisting in the country's offshore oil exploration efforts.[6]

While China is stepping up its efforts in Cuba, it is unlikely to devote anywhere near the same level of resources as those provided by the Russian Federation or Venezuela. Instead, Chinese efforts are likely to assist the country in utilizing its human capital to develop new exports and become a regional distribution hub.

Cuba's economy will not be attractive to Chinese BRI projects and other investments for some time. The economy suffered a sharp contraction in per capita income of around 10.9% in 2020, and GDP is unlikely to return to pre-COVID-19 pandemic levels until at least 2024.[7] The slow recovery stems from the inflationary effects of the country's recent currency reform (the dual currency system was abandoned in January 2021 and the 'official' exchange rate, which valued the convertible peso at par with the US dollar, was removed from circulation and replaced by a single exchange rate). The imposition of US sanctions and a stop-start recovery in tourism will directly affect investment and trade and indirectly affect government revenue, thus limiting the authorities' ability to inject stimulus and engineer a rapid recovery.[8]

Cuba's low ranking (135th) in transport infrastructure quality is consistent with its low governance levels (36.8th percentile in 2020). However, this ranking is a little lower than predicted (at around 120th position) by the region's governance/infrastructure model. This underachieving suggests some scope for improvement under a BRI programme. However, without supporting improvements in governance, it is unlikely that even an expanded BRI programme would prove capable of significantly boosting the economy.

Despite the government's claims of economic reforms, the economy remains highly repressed, with little change from the mid-1990s.[9] Given the country's financial situation, governance reform, including better rule of law, lower corruption, higher regulatory quality, and improved government effectiveness, holds the best prospect for improving the country's infrastructure.

Jamaica

For decades, the Jamaican economy has declined, with average annual growth rates falling from 2.3% in the 1980s to 1.3% (1990s), 0.9% (2000s) and 0.1% from 2010–21. Government budget deficits averaged 2.7% in the 1990s, 5.8% in the 2000s and 0.2% from 2010–21. Government debt as a share of GDP averaged 91.8% in 2000, increasing to 141.4% in 2010, but with stabilization programs in place, it declined to the still dangerous level of 95.8% in 2021.

Jamaica joined the BRI in April 2019.[10] The Jamaican government expected that the agreement would cause Chinese financing to flow into infrastructure, logistics, manufacturing and connectivity.[11] At the signing, China was already quite involved in the economy with investments in bauxite, sugar and industrial parks. Jamaica is the largest recipient of Chinese projects in the Caribbean at $2,680m., with six significant Chinese investments, four of which are BRI-type and total $2,540m.[12]

Despite some pushback on the deepening relations with China from some concerned groups within the country, there has been a consensus at the political level that the relationship is beneficial to Jamaica.[13] The most controversial project is the $600m. toll road that runs from Kingston in the south to Ocho Rios on the north coast.[14] From the start, the project encountered criticism because of its lack of transparency and highly overgenerous terms. The Chinese reserved, without explanation, a fifty-year concession on the highway. Corruption involving a large payment to a Jamaican government minister was also a concern. The project also did not provide many jobs for Jamaicans, although many were as qualified, or indeed more so than the Chinese workers.

The most recent BRI project in Jamaica commenced in 2017 and involved PowerChina in a $760m. energy undertaking. This may be the last BRI project in the country for some time. In November 2019 the government announced that it would not take on any more loans from China.[15] This mortarium is unusual for a BRI signatory, as governments usually take advantage of Chinese credit to finance development projects. The Jamaican government's decision stems from a need to continue reducing the country's public debt stock, which stood at 94.3% of GDP in 2019 before increasing to 107.4% in 2020. By 2021 it had fallen back to 95.8%.

Jamaica's governance has been improving in recent years. After bottoming at the 50th percentile in 2005, it rose to the 58th percentile by 2020. The most significant gains occurred in government effectiveness, which rose from the 52nd percentile in 2005 to the 68th percentile in 2020. This improved governance has created a sizeable gap of underachievement. In 2018, for example, the quality of Jamaica's transport infrastructure ranked 107th, albeit that the usual governance/ infrastructure pattern would have supported a ranking of around 60th.

The country, therefore, has a dilemma. Should it attempt a rapid increase in infrastructure quality with more borrowing from China or proceed at a much slower pace through continued improvements in governance? The International Monetary Fund (IMF) has praised the government's Fiscal Responsibility Law, which has seen government debt as a percentage of GDP falling dramatically.[16] The Fund expects a further decline to 87.2% in 2022 and to 62.9% by 2026. If this reduction stays on track, it may open the scope for additional BRI financing without fear of a 'debt trap' jeopardizing further economic expansion.

Trinidad and Tobago

Trinidad's economy has experienced a severe decline in the past decade. After averaging a GDP growth rate of only 0.9% from 2010–15, the economy contracted at an average annual rate of 3.1% from 2016–21. During this latter period government deficits averaged 6.0% of GDP, with government debt increasing from 20.3% of GDP in 2010 to 37.1% in 2015 and to 70.4% by 2021.

Despite its oil wealth, the government's chronic budgetary difficulties made Chinese low interest loans attractive. Trinidad and Tobago joined the BRI in May 2018, becoming the first country in the Eastern Caribbean to become a member.[17] Trinidad and Tobago, together with China, see the agreement leading to increased cooperation in the financing of infrastructure investment, industrial parks and tourism.

China has been involved in construction and investment in Trinidad and Tobago for many years, starting with Jiangsu International's $180m. education construction project in 2008. China financed six BRI-type projects totalling $930m. between December 2014 and June 2020.[18] Projects involved the development of the 133-acre Phoenix Park Industrial Estate at Point Lisas. In May 2019 the Shanghai Construction Group and China Railway agreed to the building of a $160m. general hospital in Port of Spain.

However, the quality of Trinidad and Tobago's transport infrastructure significantly underperforms. By 2018 Trinidad and Tobago's infrastructure quality ranking, 101st in 2018, was lower than expected (low 70s) based on the country's level of governance (55th percentile). The China-Trinidad connection dates back many years and has spawned many controversies and charges of corruption and malfeasance. The country's governance has experienced a long-term decline, dropping from the 69th percentile in 1998 to the 57.5th percentile in 2010. As with many oil economies, corruption is a significant problem, with the country's World Bank ranking in terms of control of corruption declining from the 80th percentile in 1996 to the 51st percentile in 2020.

Poor governance and increasing corruption have resulted in Chinese loans and construction activity attracting considerable criticism. One of the more visible Chinese projects was the construction of the National Academy for the Performing Arts (NAPA) in Port of Spain. NAPA, built by the Shanghai Construction Company, opened in 2009.[19] Little in the way of transparency surrounded the project. There were no competitive bids. Structural flaws resulted in the closure of the building in 2015, pending millions of dollars in repairs. However, Chinese companies remain involved because of corruption despite past problems in other infrastructure projects, and local companies cannot undertake large infrastructure projects.

In 2019 corruption concerns over non-transparency and presumed overgenerous terms awarded to the Chinese company forced Trinidad and Tobago's government to terminate its $71.7m. project between the Housing Development Corporation (HDC) and China's Gezhouba Group International Engineering Company.[20]

The next few years may see limited Chinese activity because of the country's fiscal situation and high debt levels. The IMF predicts that government debt will increase to 82.1% by 2026.[21] With debt levels in this range, a significant expansion of BRI lending is risky, particularly given the unpredictability of oil markets. A more prudent course of action would stress governance reforms, focusing on reining in corruption.

The Dominican Republic

The Dominican Republic has also become one of the fastest-growing economies in Latin America, with annual growth averaging 4.5% between 1980 and 2021, compared with the regional (LAC) average of 2.5%. Economic growth showed stability during this period, averaging 3.8% in the 1990s, 5.0% in the 1990s, 4.3% in the 2000s and 5.0% from 2010–21.

Despite the sustained growth of the economy, there are several concerns over its future growth. Owing to its extensive trade links with the United States, the Dominican Republic's economy moves in unison with that country's business cycle, mainly outside the control of domestic monetary and fiscal policy. Other risks to the economy include the lingering effects of the pandemic on tourism and remittances, adverse fluctuations in oil and gold prices, drug-related crime, natural disasters, particularly hurricanes and earthquakes, and instability in neighbouring Haiti.

In May 2018 the Dominican government formally announced its switch of diplomatic recognition from the Republic of China (Taiwan) to China, with the Chinese reportedly offering $3,100m. in loans and investments.[22] The Dominican government justified the move as part of its efforts to facilitate greater commercial links with China for Dominican businesses. Many observers expect that there will be increased investment and stronger trade links between the two countries in the coming years. It is likely that China will offer capital and expertise to improve Dominican infrastructure and increase the capacity of its tourism and manufacturing sectors.

In September 2018 the Dominican government contacted China Civil Engineering Construction (CCECC) with a list of projects that might interest the company.[23] These included the construction of a railway connecting the Dominican Republic with Haiti; a series of dams on the Boba-Baquí rivers; a port modernization; and new wastewater and sewage systems. CCECC showed an interest in the projects with the possibility of loans at concessional rates.

Because of the diplomatic shift away from Taiwan, the Dominican Republic is now on the list of Chinese government-approved destinations for Chinese tourists.[24] It hopes to attract Chinese visitors to diversify markets for its booming tourism sector. The two governments have signed a framework for an aviation agreement, which could lead to flights between the two countries by Chinese airlines.

The quality of infrastructure in the Dominican Republic is nearly in line with its level of governance. Governance improved steadily from the 35th percentile in 2004 to the 45th percentile by 2020. However, during this period corruption increased, and the country dropped from the 33rd percentile to the 21st percentile by 2010. However, since then, corruption levels have improved to the albeit still low 27th percentile. Continued improvements in governance may pay high dividends in infrastructure quality.

In the near future, governance improvements may be the prime driver of infrastructure quality. The country's debt situation may warrant restraint on BRI projects. The fiscal response to the pandemic, plus exchange rate depreciation and the pre-financing of part of the 2021 budget (by 1.6% of GDP), led to a sharp increase in public debt, to 66.1% of GDP at the end of 2021, up from 44.9% in 2015.[25] However, the government's debt profile mitigates risks, given that it is primarily long-term debt held by official creditors. The IMF expects debt to decline, albeit gradually, to 58.0% of GDP with growth recovering and fiscal stimulus measures being lifted.[26]

Guyana

China's extensive economic links to Guyana began with that country's first foreign aid project, a clay brick factory built in the 1970s.[27] Guyana joined the BRI in July 2018. Projects discussed included a road running from Guyana's coast to Brazil and a deep-water port.[28] Chinese firms have been active in infrastructure projects in the country for years, with China Harbour Engineering involved in the expansion of Cheddi Jagan airport in 2011. In 2012 the China Railway First Group began work on a hydroelectric plant at Amalia Falls. From 2009–21 eight major Chinese construction and investment projects totalled $2,750m., with four BRI projects coming to $1,830.[29] Chinese financing of these projects amounted to $2,750m. with the largest, valued at $930m., made in May 2018 by China National Off-Shore Oil (CNOOC).

In the past, Guyana has endured periods of high external debt, acting as a constraint on the country's infrastructure development.

That situation is changing dramatically due to the discovery of at least 4,000m. barrels of oil off its coast. With its investment of $930m. in 2018, the Chinese oil firm CNOOC now has a 25% share in Exxon-Mobil's Stabroek block.

Guyana's experience with Chinese investment has provoked considerable criticism.[30] Chinese firms often pick up proposed projects without an open bidding process. Companies often import Chinese contract workers as their primary labour force. Guyanese business executives often claim that Chinese state-owned enterprises are pushing out local businesses with little benefit for the country's workers. There is also concern that China leverages its size to gain unfettered access to natural resources, which risks the exploitation of Guyana's vast virgin rainforests.[31] Finally, there are doubts about whether Chinese investment has laid the foundation for sustained economic growth.

Guyana's improved governance in recent years is encouraging. In 2016 Guyana's overall governance began to improve, reaching the 44th percentile, up from the 36th percentile in 2005, before slipping back to the 42nd percentile in 2020. Control of corruption also improved. Starting at the 26th percentile in 2016, the country reached the 49th percentile in 2020. However, setbacks occurred in the critical area of government effectiveness, where the country dropped from the 57th percentile in 1998 to the 38th percentile by 2020.

These patterns suggest that some problems that have undermined past infrastructure efforts remain. Still, the quality of the country's infrastructure at the 137th percentile is below that expected, at around the 120th percentile, given its overall level of governance. With careful monitoring, Chinese BRI projects could significantly upgrade much of the country's infrastructure by providing expertise, investment and technology.

Barbados

Barbados joined the BRI in 2019 and in 2021 replaced HM Queen Elizabeth II by declaring itself a republic. While many observers see the two developments as interrelated, Barbados's move to a republic is symbolic for all intents and purposes.[32] The country has been independent of the United Kingdom for fifty-six years, with the Queen essentially a ceremonial head of state. Despite becoming a republic, Barbados remained a member of the Commonwealth. Many factors lie behind the move, including vast support within Barbados for the Black Lives Matter (BLM) movement.[33] However, before China entered the picture, a serious debate over becoming a republic had been ongoing for at least forty years, with the country close to approving a referendum in 2007.[34]

However, there is no evidence to support the contention that China's focus on Taiwan extends to undermining the British Commonwealth. That is not to say that China has not extensively lent to Commonwealth members. China has invested about $667m. in roads, homes, sewers and a hotel in Barbados over the past sixteen years. As of mid-2022, China had undertaken three BRI-type projects totalling $420m. Two were in the tourism sector, and a third initiated in March 2017 involved the Grantley Adams International Airport.

Still, many rumours surround China's activity in the country. Discussions with China over the redevelopment of the national stadium have summoned up comparisons with Chinese activity in other countries.[35] The Chinese takeover of the Hambantota Port in Sri Lanka or, more recently, the control of Uganda's sole international airport sparked speculation that the country's Grantley Adams International Airport and the Bridgetown Port had been leased to a Chinese entity.[36] Government officials and airport authorities deny both allegations.[37]

The amount of debt owed to China is only around 2.5% of Barbados's total indebtedness, and the country was in severe debt distress long before its involvement with China.[38] Data from the IMF show that debt as a share of GDP averaged 132.5% of GDP (60% is deemed risky) from 2010–19, jumping to 156.8% in the pandemic year of 2020.[39] The country's debt burden has stifled growth, with the economy contracting at an average annual rate of 0.1% from 2010–19, and capped off by a contraction of a further 18% in 2020.

Barbados's significant challenges include revitalizing the tourism sector and managing the aforementioned high debt levels.[40] At slightly less than 140% of GDP in 2021, the public debt stock is the highest in the region and is not sustainable. Public support for reducing the debt burden appears firm, but years of fiscal consolidation (austerity) under continued IMF programmes will be necessary to reduce the ratio to more sustainable levels.[41] With debt at this level, it is problematic how much additional debt, even if it were available, might China be able to assume.

Suriname

Suriname joined the BRI in July 2018, hoping that membership could lead to 'enhanced cooperation in the fields of infrastructure construction, agriculture, forestry, fishing, law enforcement, human resources, and public health'.[42] However, the standard AEI database of Chinese enterprises lists no projects, BRI or non-BRI, for Suriname.[43] Initially, Chinese companies were to be involved in the modernization of the national Johan Pengel Airport, although there are ongoing delays stemming from the COVID-19 pandemic. Other priority areas that may receive Chinese interest involve improved transport infrastructure, especially the country's rail and road networks.

Suriname's situation is likely to improve. Recent oil discoveries suggest that the country has recoverable oil resources of nearly 2,000m. barrels.[44] A scenario similar to that playing out in Guyana may develop with China, making significant BRI investments in oil exploration and supporting transport facilities.

Antigua and Barbuda

In June 2018 Antigua and Barbuda were the first to sign up for China's BRI in the eastern Caribbean.[45] Tourism is the most promising area for investment in Antigua and Barbuda. The government invited the CCECC to participate in the development of tourism infrastructure.[46] The company also won a $90m. contract to construct a cargo port and cruise ship harbour. China's Export-Import Bank of China (China EXIM Bank) supplies the financing.

However, Chinese investment on the island has generated considerable controversy.[47] One particular investment, the Yida project initially conceived in 2014, came with great expectations.[48] Its design included the creation of a manufacturing hub and the generation of several hundred jobs. However, the project has incurred significant costs in terms of environmental degradation and increased vulnerability to hurricane damage.

The Yida project illustrates the problem that many of the smaller Caribbean islands face in negotiating BRI projects.[49] China often plays one country off against another to produce a more favourable treatment for its investors. Here, the developers established a seafood harvesting company with claims on 90% of the profits. The Yida development was also free of taxes, and investors buying in for more than $400,000 were eligible for Antiguan citizenship.

Assessment

The Caribbean will probably remain a tangential region for the BRI. The region has limited natural resources, mainly oil, gas and aluminium. For this reason, Guyana and perhaps Suriname may receive the bulk of Chinese attention. The debt situation in Cuba, Jamaica, Trinidad and Tobago, and Barbados makes additional borrowing difficult. The Dominican Republic will be unwilling to jeopardize its relationship with the United States by stepping up its engagement with China. China also has interests elsewhere, and if the number of BRI programmes contract because of Chinese economic difficulties, the Caribbean is likely to be the first to be significantly affected.

Notes

1 Pepe Zhang, 'Belt and Road in Latin America: A Regional Game Changer?' *Belt and Road in Latin America: A Regional Game Changer?* Atlantic Council, 17 October 2019. www.atlanticcouncil.org/in-depth-research-rep orts/issue-brief/belt-and-road-in-latin-america-a-regional-game-changer/.
2 Johannes Werner, 'Cuba Officially Joins Belt and Road Energy Initiative', *Cuba Standard*, 18 October 2021. www.cubastandard.com/cuba-officially-joins-belt-and-road-energy-initiative/.
3 American Enterprise Institute, 'China Global Investment Tracker'. www. aei.org/china-global-investment-tracker/ (accessed 27 April 2022).
4 Kenneth Rapoza, 'China Has Forgiven Nearly $10 Billion in Debt. Cuba Accounts for over Half', *Forbes Magazine*, 11 January 2021. www.forbes. com/sites/kenrapoza/2019/05/29/china-has-forgiven-nearly-10-billion-in-de bt-cuba-accounts-for-over-half/?sh=359b5fd615ba.
5 Marc Frank, 'Cuba Grants Vietnamese Company Concession at Special Development Zone', Reuters, 30 March 2018. www.reuters.com/article/ cuba-vietnam-investment/cuba-grants-vietnamese-company-concession-at-special-development-zone-idUSL1N1RC09Z.
6 Gustavo Arias Retana, 'China Looks to the Caribbean to Strengthen Its Presence and Exploit Cuban Oil', *Diálogo Américas*, 7 April 2022. https:// dialogo-americas.com/articles/china-looks-to-the-caribbean-to-strengthen-i ts-presence-and-exploit-cuban-oil/.
7 The World Bank, 'Cuba'. https://data.worldbank.org/country/CU (accessed 27 April 2022).
8 Helen Yaffe, 'Day Zero: How and Why Cuba Unified Its Dual Currency System', LSE Latin America and Caribbean blog, London School of Economics and Political Science ,10 February 2021. https://blogs.lse.ac.uk/ latamcaribbean/2021/02/10/day-zero-how-and-why-cuba-unified-its-dual-c urrency-system/.
9 The Heritage Foundation, '2022 Index of Economic Freedom: Cuba'. www.heritage.org/index/country/cuba (accessed 27 April 2022).
10 *Pride News*, 'Jamaica Becomes Latest Caribbean Country to Sign on to China's Belt and Road Initiative', 12 April 2019. http://pridenews.ca/2019/ 04/12/jamaica-latest-caribbean-country-sign-chinas-belt-road-initiative/.
11 The Caribbean Council, 'Jamaica Joins China's Belt and Road Initiative'. www.caribbean-council.org/jamaica-joins-chinas-belt-and-road-initiative/ (accessed 27 April 2022).

12 American Enterprise Institute, 'China Global Investment Tracker'.
13 Bradley J. Murg and Rasheed J. Griffith, 'An Ignored Canary in an Unknown Coal Mine: The Caribbean's Economic Engagement with China', *The Diplomat*, 14 December 2020. https://thediplomat.com/2020/12/an-ignored-canary-in-an-unknown-coal-mine-the-caribbeans-economic-engagement-with-china/.
14 Sandra Laville, 'Beijing Highway: $600M Road Just the Start of China's Investments in Caribbean', *The Guardian*, 24 December 2015. www.theguardian.com/world/2015/dec/24/beijing-highway-600m-road-just-the-start-of-chinas-investments-in-caribbean.
15 *Jamaica Gleaner*, 'No New Loans from China, Says PM', 10 November 2019. https://jamaica-gleaner.com/article/news/20191110/no-new-loans-china-says-pm.
16 International Monetary Fund, 'Jamaica Works to Maintain Its Hard-Won Economic Stability', IMF Country Focus, 22 February 2022. www.imf.org/en/News/Articles/2022/02/18/cf-jamaica-works-to-maintain-its-hard-won-economic-stability.
17 *Trinidad and Tobago Government News*, 'T&T and China Strengthen Cooperation'. www.news.gov.tt/content/tt-and-china-strengthen-cooperation (accessed 27 April 2022).
18 American Enterprise Institute, 'China Global Investment Tracker'.
19 Andre Bagoo, 'National Academy for the Performing Arts Tragedy', Trinidad and Tobago News blog, 15 March 2010. www.trinidadandtobagonews.com/blog/?p=2698.
20 Shaliza Hassanali, 'Faris: Why the Fuss over Axed HDC, Chinese Project', *Trinidad Guardian*, 10 September 2019. www.guardian.co.tt/news/faris-why-the-fuss-over-axed-hdc-chinese-project-6.2.930666.72f6050de1.
21 International Monetary Fund, World Economic Outlook Database, October 2021. www.imf.org/en/Publications/WEO/weo-database/2021/October (accessed 29 April 2022).
22 S. D., 'Why Are Taiwan's Friends Vanishing?' *The Economist*, 27 July 2018. www.economist.com/the-economist-explains/2018/07/27/why-are-taiwans-friends-vanishing.
23 Valeria Castillo, 'Dominican Republic Warms to China', *Dialogo Chino*, 14 February 2019. https://dialogochino.net/en/trade-investment/22177-dominican-republic-warms-to-china/.
24 Ibid.
25 International Monetary Fund, World Economic Outlook Database, October 2021.
26 Ibid.
27 Kaieteur News, 'Clay Brick Factory, 46 Acres of Prime Lands Up for Sale', 24 April 2021. www.kaieteurnewsonline.com/2021/04/24/clay-brick-factory-46-acres-of-prime-lands-up-for-sale/.
28 Department of Public Information, 'Guyana Signs onto China's "Belt and Road" Initiative', 28 July 2018. https://dpi.gov.gy/guyana-signs-onto-chinas-road-and-belt-initiative/.
29 American Enterprise Institute, 'China Global Investment Tracker'.
30 Jared Ward, 'Guyana Is Proof of the Pitfalls of Chinese Aid and Investment in the Caribbean', *World Politics Review*, 9 November 2016. www.worldpoliticsreview.com/articles/20410/guyana-is-proof-of-the-pitfalls-of-chinese-aid-and-investment-in-the-caribbean.

31 Kevin Edmonds, 'Guyana: Colonialism with Chinese Characteristics?' NACLA, 26 June 2013. https://nacla.org/blog/2013/6/26/guyana-colonia lism-chinese-characteristics.

32 BBC News, 'Barbados to Remove Queen Elizabeth as Head of State', 16 September 2020. www.bbc.com/news/world-latin-america-54174794.

33 Michael Safi, 'Nelson, BLM and New Voices: Why Barbados Is Ditching the Queen', *The Guardian*, 29 November 2021. www.theguardian.com/ world/2021/nov/29/nelson-blm-and-new-voices-how-barbados-came-to-cut -ties-to-crown.

34 BBC News, 'Bajans to Vote on Republic Status', 26 November 2007. http s://www.bbc.co.uk/caribbean/news/story/2007/11/printable/071126_bajanre p.shtml.

35 *Barbados Today*, 'China to Focus on Loan to Rebuild Stadium', 14 July 2021. https://barbadostoday.bb/2021/07/14/china-to-focus-on-loan-to-rebui ld-stadium/.

36 Maria Abi-Habib, 'How China Got Sri Lanka to Cough up a Port', *New York Times*, 25 June 2018. www.nytimes.com/2018/06/25/world/asia/china -sri-lanka-port.html.

37 *Stabroek News*, 'CEO Denies Barbados Airport Leased to China', 26 November 2021. www.stabroeknews.com/2021/11/26/news/regional/barba dos/ceo-denies-barbados-airport-leased-to-china/.

38 Kareem Smith, 'Story on China-Barbados Link "Based on Falsehoods and Innuendo", *Barbados Today*, 26 November 2021. https://barbadostoda y.bb/2021/11/26/story-on-china-barbados-link-based-on-falsehoods-and-in nuendo-persaud/.

39 International Monetary Fund, World Economic Outlook Databases. www. imf.org/en/Publications/SPROLLs/world-economic-outlook-databases#sor t=%40imfdate%20descending (accessed 4 May 2022).

40 Yajaira Archibald, 'What's Next for Barbados' Tourism Industry?' *Caribbean Development Trends*, 8 April 2021. https://blogs.iadb.org/caribbea n-dev-trends/en/whats-next-for-barbados-tourism-industry/.

41 International Monetary Fund, 'IMF Staff Concludes Virtual Visit to Barbados', Press Release 22/32, 11 February 2022. www.imf.org/en/News/Arti cles/2022/02/11/pr2232-barbados-imf-staff-concludes-virtual-visit.

42 Chris Devonshire-Ellis, 'China's Belt & Road: The Caribbean & West Indies', *Silk Road Briefing*, 13 June 2019. www.silkroadbriefing.com/news/ 2019/05/24/chinas-belt-road-caribbean-west-indies/.

43 American Enterprise Institute. "China Global Investment Tracker'.

44 Tsvetana Paraskova, 'TotalEnergies Announces Major Oil Discovery Offshore Suriname', OilPrice.com, 21 February 2022. https://oilprice.com/La test-Energy-News/World-News/TotalEnergies-Announces-Major-Oil-Disco very-Offshore-Suriname.html.

45 Esther Jones, Carseen Greenidge and Richie Ferrol. 'The Caribbean Engages the Belt and Road Initiative', *Caribbean Investigative Journalism Network*, 17 August 2020. www.cijn.org/the-caribbean-engages-the-belt-a nd-road-initiative/.

46 Robert Soutar and Maryan Escarfullett, 'Chinese Tourism Investments Flow into Antigua and Barbuda despite Risks', *China Dialogue*, 14 May 2020. https://chinadialogue.net/en/nature/10568-chinese-tourism-investmen ts-flow-into-antigua-and-barbuda-despite-risks/.

47 Gemma Handy, 'Antigua: Sprawling "Chinese Colony" Plan across Marine Reserve Ignites Opposition', *The Guardian*, 20 June 2019. www.theguardian.com/world/2019/jun/20/antigua-yida-project-chinese-colony-controversy.
48 Ibid.
49 Ibid.

3 The BRI in Central America

Introduction

For centuries, historical and geographical circumstances have deeply embedded Central America in the United States' sphere of influence. During the past few decades, the region was also the world's most Republic of China (Taiwan)-friendly region. However, in recent years, these historical relationships began to break down owing to the growing influence of the People's Republic of China in the area. Most obvious is the dramatic diplomatic shift away from Taiwan towards China. Panama led the way, followed by El Salvador and Nicaragua. China is also expanding its trade with the region, often displacing longstanding markets for US firms.[1]

Four countries, Panama, El Salvador, Costa Rica and Nicaragua, are now members of China's Belt and Road Initiative (BRI). The BRI activities have played out differently in each of these countries. However, the extent to which BRI membership has affected their diplomatic decisions is problematic. China has given these countries a new set of economic options.

Central America's BRI countries fall into two groups – the economically successful, Panama and Costa Rica, and those not so successful, El Salvador and Nicaragua. Per capita income growth has been highest in Panama, followed by Costa Rica, with El Salvador and Nicaragua falling further behind (Figure 3.1). Debt levels rose rapidly after 2010, with government debt as a share of gross domestic product (GDP) reaching dangerous ranges, especially in El Salvador, Costa Rica, and to a lesser extent Panama and Nicaragua (Figure 3.2).

BRI programmes in the region's four countries pose new challenges for the United States; however, they have provided greater opportunities for additional sources of financing. However, the scope for expanded BRI programmes differs significantly from country to country.

DOI: 10.4324/b23227-3

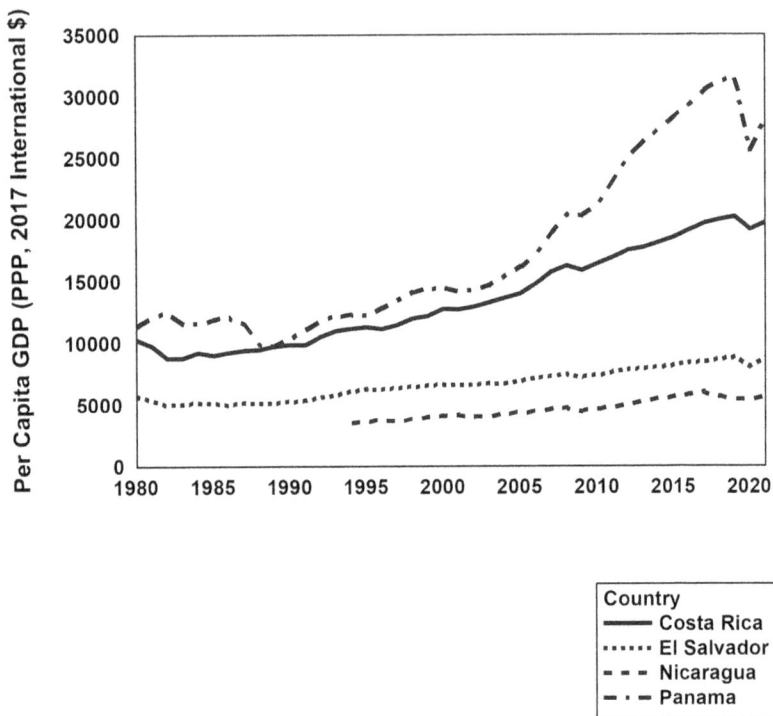

Figure 3.1 Per Capita Income Growth in Central America, 1980–2021
Source: International Monetary Fund, World Economic Outlook Database: October 2021.

Panama

Since the 1990s Panama's economy has been one of the most dynamic in Latin America, with GDP growth rates averaging 6.2% in the 1990s and 5.6% in the 2000s. However, after averaging 7.4% from 2010–15, growth slowed to 1.9% from 2016–21. While some of this slowdown stemmed from the coronavirus COVID-19 pandemic, the falloff in construction activity following an expansion of the Panama Canal was a major contributing factor.[2]

In June 2017 the administration of President Juan Carlos Varela announced that it was severing relations with Taiwan in favour of a closer relationship with China.[3] The Panamanian government's decision to sever ties with Taiwan and pursue a 'one China' policy aimed to bolster trade and investment.

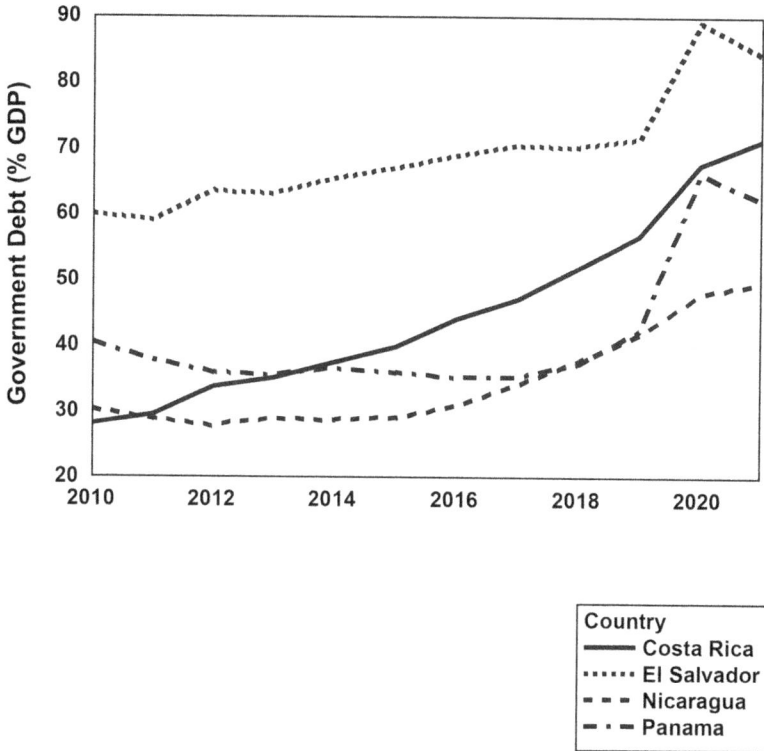

Figure 3.2 Government Debt as a % of GDP in Central America, 2010–21
Source: International Monetary Fund, World Economic Outlook Database:
October 2021.

Panama's BRI membership appears to be paying high dividends. Of the Central American countries signing BRI agreements, Panama has received by far the most projects with seven BRI-type projects totalling US $2,390m., four of which, after June 2017, totalled $1,860m.[4]

From China's perspective, the cementing of ties with Panama has helped to increase its geopolitical presence in Central America, where many states had solid relationships with Taiwan. Also, investment in infrastructure assets provides a stimulus to Chinese companies. Finally, it could further expand the market for Chinese goods in Panama, which has a high per capita GDP by Latin American standards.

Given that Panama seeks to bolster its status as a transport and logistics hub in the Americas, BRI projects into these sectors could further this goal.[5] Cooperation agreements signed between China

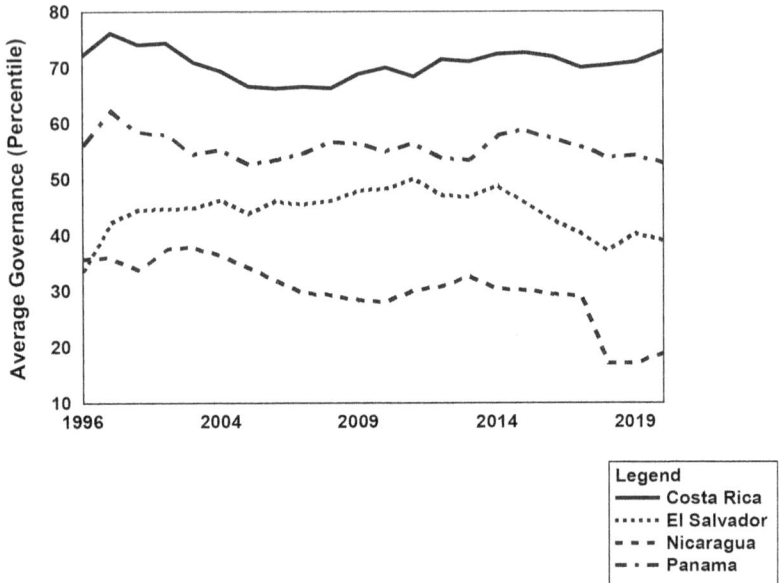

Figure 3.3 Governance Levels in Central America, 1996–2020
Note: Governance is the average of its components: voice and accountability, political stability and absence of violence/terrorism, government effectiveness, regulatory quality, rule of law and control of corruption.
Source: World Bank, Worldwide Governance Indicators Database.

and Panama in November 2017 include many measures that will encourage Chinese investment in infrastructure development.[6] Several projects facilitate Panama Canal operations and involve terminals, container ports, a bridge over the canal, electricity transmission rail lines and telecommunications.

One project that highlights the potential involvement of China in Panama's development was a much-discussed rail line between Panama City and the city of David in the Chiriquí province, near the border with Costa Rica.[7] In March 2019 China Railway Design Corporation delivered a feasibility study to the Panamanian government to construct the railway project. According to the study, the line was to be 391.3 km long and cover the provinces of Panama, Coclé, Herrera Veraguas and Chiriquí. The $4,100m. line should enable travel speeds of up to 80 km/h for freight trains. Depending on the number of stops, it would reduce the journey time between the two cities to 2.5 hours. However, given its costs, the government eventually cancelled the project because it deemed the project unnecessary.[8]

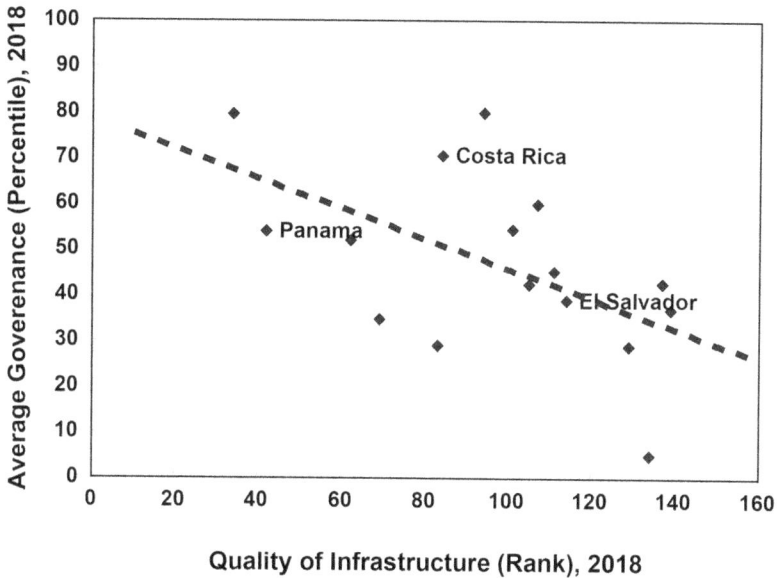

Figure 3.4 Governance/Transport Infrastructure Quality Relationship, Central
America, 2018

Source: Governance: World Bank, Worldwide Governance Indicators
Database; Infrastructure: World Bank, Logistics Performance Index Database.

Perhaps the rail project would have gone through in a country with
lower governance rates and checks and balances. However, Panama
has one of the higher levels of governance in Latin America, with
rankings averaging around the 55th percentile since 1996 (Figure 3.3).
Still, there has been a decline in recent years, with overall governance
falling from the 59th percentile in 2015 to the 53rd percentile by 2020.
Corruption is an increasing problem, with the country declining from
the 44th percentile in 2005 to the 33rd percentile in 2020. Government
effectiveness also declined, falling from the 65th percentile in 2015 to
the 57th percentile in 2020.

In 2018 Panama ranked 44th in infrastructure quality, one of the
highest levels in Latin America. Its overall level of governance that
year was in the 54th percentile. This pattern places the country in the
overachiever group (Figure 3.4) since that level of governance usually
comes with an infrastructure quality ranking in the high seventies. In
part, this infrastructure quality/governance gap stems from the very
high investment rates (much of it in infrastructure) during the

widening of the Panama Canal during 2011–16). Before the widening (2000–10), investment in Panama averaged 27.7% of GDP. During the widening years (2011–16), investment increased to 42.3% of GDP.[9] Subsequently, investment, although declining, remained high at 36.7% of GDP during the period 2017–21.

Can Panama keep improving its infrastructure under the BRI? This strategy would seem to be a highly inefficient way of proceeding. The recent expansion in infrastructure outran its governance foundations. Given that China will place no pressure on the country for improvements in governance, it is easy to see expanded BRI programmes resulting in tremendous waste and inefficiency.

El Salvador

El Salvador's economy is not dynamic, with average annual GDP growth rates of 1.5% in the 2000s and 2.2% from 2010–21. The economy suffers from several significant weaknesses. There is a high crime rate and insecurity linked to criminal gang activity and widespread drug trafficking. The country also lacks natural resources, especially energy.

El Salvador's ageing infrastructure cannot sustain high economic growth rates. Investment and savings rates, averaging 17.0% and 13.6%, respectively, from 2010–21, are too low to undertake a significant upgrade in supporting capital investments. Undoubtedly, the country's dire infrastructure shortfall was due in part to a prolonged civil war from October 1979 to January 1992. This led to between $1,000m. and $1,500m. in infrastructure damage.[10] No doubt the need for finance played a role in the country's decision to establish diplomatic relations with China in August 2018.[11]

On coming to office in June 2019, President Nayib Bukele initially attempted to improve relations with the United States by considering restoring ties with Taiwan. However, Bukele eventually retained the country's relationship with China. The payoff involved $500m. in new deals with China for various projects such as a national library, a new sports stadium and an expansion in tourist facilities along the country's Pacific coast.[12] El Salvador is also moving ahead with China's assistance to construct a new port in the Gulf of Fonseca. When completed, the port will serve as a logistics hub and service a special economic zone (SEZ) composed mainly of Chinese businesses. Despite US objections, the country is also planning to introduce Huawei 5G technology.[13] However, little has transpired owing to the COVID-19 pandemic, which led to the shutdown of the economy for months.[14]

There were no BRI projects listed for El Salvador in the mid-2021 American Enterprise Institute (AEI) Global Investment Tracker.[15]

However, offsetting this to some extent, it is likely that the potential gain in Chinese investment would result in a decrease in US assistance. The Trump Administration, several US senators and the Biden Administration signalled their frustration with China's rising stature in the country. Given substantial US aid for infrastructure development in El Salvador via the Fomilenio II programme, a $365m. infrastructure programme funded mainly by the US government, the potential for a decline in US aid to the country over the coming years will pose a substantial risk to the country's infrastructure sector. It could also limit the overall benefit of China's BRI programme.

Deteriorating governance and rising debt levels will also limit the government's attempt to upgrade the country's infrastructure. The country's overall governance, as measured by the World Bank, declined from the 50th percentile in 2011 to the 39th percentile by 2020. During this period the country's level of corruption deteriorated from the 51st percentile to the 29th percentile. Similarly, government effectiveness fell from the 52nd percentile to the 38th percentile.

In 2018 the quality of El Salvador's transport infrastructure ranked 114th worldwide and was close (Figure 3.4) to the expected value, given its overall level of governance. However, unless reversed, the recent declines in governance suggest that even stepped-up Chinese BRI projects may not be that effective in improving the country's infrastructure.

On the finance side, government debt has increased rapidly in recent years, increasing from 60.1% of GDP in 2010 to 71.3% in 2019. However, following the outbreak of the COVID-19 pandemic in 2020, general government debt rose to 89.2% (Figure 3.2). The International Monetary Fund (IMF) does expect to see a dramatic decline in the debt level, forecasting instead a further increase to 90.3% in 2024 and to 98.6% by 2026. Proposals for reducing the ratio are so far lacking. Still, for political reasons, upcoming fiscal reforms are likely to rely on expenditure-side adjustments that will force the country to abandon its infrastructure plans.

In 2021, given the country's poor fiscal dynamics, the government began to seek a $1,300m. loan agreement from the IMF. The loan is critical for the country's post-pandemic recovery. However, as of mid-2022 an agreement had not materialized after over a year of negotiations. The IMF is concerned about rising budget deficits and financial concerns stemming from Bukele's decision to adopt bitcoin, a cryptocurrency, as legal tender.

Bukele has charted out a hazardous strategy given the importance of the United States to El Salvador's economy, a position that China is unlikely to usurp altogether. Bearing this in mind, he will face a tricky balancing act in his dealings with the United States and China.

Costa Rica

For years Costa Rica was a Latin American success story.[16] The country's democratic institutions and attention to good governance have enabled its resource-poor economy to thrive in a still-dangerous part of the world. The country scores well in various measures of prosperity with its ranking on indices such as economic quality, business environment, governance, education, health, personal freedom, social capital and the natural environment above and often considerably higher than the norm for countries at a similar level of development and wealth.[17] In terms of overall economic growth, the economy expanded at a steady rate of 4.3% in the 2000s and 4.1% between 2010 and 2015. Inflation, which had increased at an annual rate of 10.9% in the 2000s, fell to 4.3% between 2010–15.

During the past few decades much of the country's success has stemmed from a development model focused on foreign direct investment and high-tech exports.[18] The starting point was the mid-1990s when Intel invested in a $300m. in a chip testing plant in the country's capital, San José. With this strategy, Costa Rica is attempting to transition to a post-industrial economy focused on services, but without first developing a traditional strong manufacturing sector. With Intel as the centrepiece, the strategy, based on the theory of clusters devised by Michael Porter of Harvard University which called for the creation of a 'Silicon Valley' technology hub to attract further waves of foreign-owned, high-tech, export-oriented firms.[19] Porter's theory proved correct, and the high-tech component of the export sector took off, with high-tech exports soon averaging over 40% of total manufactured exports.[20]

A rude awakening came in 2014 when Intel relocated its operations to Asia. The decision was entirely out of Costa Rica's hands, but not necessarily a reflection of any shortcoming on the country's part. Intel's adaptation to a rapidly changing global environment called for cost reductions in several areas and countries.

Following Intel's departure from Costa Rica, growth dropped to 2.2% from 2015–21. The government appeared to have been unprepared for the extent to which the Intel decision would affect its economy. Government debt as a share of GDP, which had risen from

28.1% of GDP in 2010 to 39.8% by 2015, rose to 56.7% in 2019, the year before the outbreak of the COVID-19 pandemic. By 2021 it had risen even further to 71.2% of GDP.

Further increases in the government debt are unlikely. At mid-2022 Costa Rica's bonds were at 'junk' levels, which significantly increases the cost of future borrowing.[21] Earlier, perhaps as a sign of desperation, the country approached China in 2016 on the sale of a $1,000m. bond but was eventually turned down.[22]

Costa Rica's current plight provides another reminder of the difficulties that small economies face in today's rapidly changing global environment. Gone are the days when small, open countries such as Singapore, Hong Kong or even Mauritius could count on buoyant international trade and revenues sufficient to sustain domestic growth rates of between 7% and 8% per annum.

Can China help to shift the economy towards a new growth model? In 2007, when Costa Rica became the first Central American nation to break away from Taiwan and recognize China, the economic payoff of this shift was immediate in terms of increased trade and investment with China. A new national sports stadium was soon forthcoming as were several significant development and infrastructure projects.[23] One early project (January 2009) involved a $240m. deal between Costa Rican Electricity and Huawei Technologies.[24]

Costa Rica joined the BRI in September 2018, hoping for the same result.[25] The signing held out the hope for a series of projects ranging from telecommunications, highways and energy to creating SEZs and distribution centres. However, since joining the BRI, Chinese involvement in the country has been minimal because of lengthy bureaucratic processes that cause significant delays.

The slow pace of expropriations, for example, is reportedly holding up progress on the Río Frío-Limón Ruta 32 highway project, under contract to Chinese firm China Harbour Engineering Company and financed by a $395m. loan from the Export-Import Bank of China. This highway project was the only BRI venture as of mid-2022.[26]

Costa Rica has one of the highest levels of governance in Latin America, placing it in the 73rd percentile in 2020, up from the 66th percentile in 2008. Unfortunately, this governance has not lived up to its potential to support a high level of infrastructure quality. In 2018 the country's infrastructure quality ranked 84th, whereas based on the typical infrastructure governance pattern the country should rank around the 40th percentile.

Costa Rica should be an ideal BRI candidate for BRI financing with its existing governance structures. However, given its severe debt constraints, it is unlikely that the government will take on significant amounts of additional BRI borrowing for infrastructure any time soon.

Nicaragua

Nicaragua has become a testing ground for many revolutionary and often contradictory economic and political trends sweeping Latin America. Economically, Nicaragua's unique two-track approach attempts to implement a neoliberal, market-driven development strategy within the confines of a leftist, state-centred, populist agenda.[27] Following Daniel Ortega's election as President in 2006 and the international financial crisis of 2008–09, the economy expanded at one of the highest rates in Latin America, at 5.3% per year between 2010 and 2015. The re-election of Ortega in 2016 appeared to validate the country's unique approach to economic management. As late as 2017 these two potentially conflicting economic approaches were able to generate sustained growth and rising standards of living.

However, the political crisis that began in April 2018 amid a public uprising against the perceived undemocratic rule of Ortega and his wife and Vice-President, Rosario Murillo, cast doubt on the sustainability of the government's economic agenda.[28] Given the ongoing instability and uncertainty, Ortega's unwillingness to negotiate seriously with the opposition, and the outbreak of the COVID-19 pandemic, growth declined to 0.9% from 2016–21. Depending on the severity of the pandemic, it may take several years for the economy to return to favourable economic expansion rates.

Although Taiwan furnished it with help for thirty years, on 9 December 2021 the Nicaraguan government announced that it was breaking official ties with that country and shifting diplomatic recognition to China,[29] despite receiving over $200m. in assistance from that country over the years.[30] In January 2022 Nicaragua joined the BRI. Nicaragua's new relationship with China could result in Chinese infrastructure investment in sectors ranging from energy to transport. The Nicaraguan government is also looking at the agreement as facilitating expanded trade ties with China by opening new export markets for domestic industries, including agriculture and light manufacturing.[31]

Despite its new relationship with China, Nicaragua urgently needs alternative sources of external finance. However, the country's chances of receiving significant financial backing from the Inter-American Development Bank and other multilateral organizations such as the World Bank and the IMF are subject to US pressure, particularly under the newly approved Renacer Act, and therefore are slim.[32]

There is no 2018 figure for the quality of Nicaraguan infrastructure in the World Bank's Transport Infrastructure Quality data set. However, in 2016 the country ranked 83rd. Given the country's governance was in the 29th percentile that year, the typical infrastructure-governance pattern would have predicted it to rank around 140th. The country was a significant overachiever in terms of what its governance could support. By 2020 the country had dropped to the 19th percentile in terms of governance. Without a solid governance foundation, it is unlikely that BRI programmes will play a leading role in reviving the economy.

Assessment

If China hopes to expand its influence in the region, it will probably be confronted by several constraints that were not present when its initial efforts began. Growth rates within the region are declining, and rising debt levels will restrict the number of new loans that these countries want to book. China will also have to face greater opposition and competition from the United States as that country wakes up to its waning influence. China is hardly about to displace the United States as the most consequential external actor in Central America despite its recent efforts.

Notes

1 Luis G. Solís, 'What's behind China's Growing Push into Central America?' *Americas Quarterly*, 10 September 2021. www.americasquarterly.org/article/whats-behind-chinas-growing-push-into-central-america/.
2 Carrie Kahn, 'The $5 Billion Panama Canal Expansion Opens Sunday, amidst Shipping Concerns', *NPR*, 25 June 2016. www.npr.org/2016/06/25/483523910/the-5-billion-panama-canal-expansion-opens-sunday-amidst-shipping-concerns.
3 Benjamin Haas, 'Panama Cuts Formal Ties with Taiwan in Favour of China', *The Guardian*, 13 June 2017. www.theguardian.com/world/2017/jun/13/panama-cuts-diplomatic-ties-with-taiwan-in-favour-of-china.
4 American Enterprise Institute, 'China Global Investment Tracker - American Enterprise Institute'. www.aei.org/china-global-investment-tracker/ (accessed 12 May 2022).
5 Caf.com, 'The Four Challenges of Panama to Consolidate as Logistics and Global Services Hub'. www.caf.com/en/currently/news/2016/06/the-four-challenges-of-panama-to-consolidate-as-logistics-and-global-services-hub/ (accessed 12 May 2022).
6 Álvaro Méndez, 'Panama Could Soon Become China's Gateway to Latin America Thanks to an Imminent Free Trade Agreement', LSE Latin America and Caribbean blog, London School of Economics, 27 September 2019. https://blogs.lse.ac.uk/latamcaribbean/2018/12/05/panama

-could-soon-become-chinas-gateway-to-latin-america-thanks-to-an-immine
nt-free-trade-agreement/.

7 *Global Construction Review*, 'China Gives Panama Its Plan for a $4bn
High-Speed Rail Line to Costa Rica', 21 March 2019. www.globalcon
structionreview.com/china-gives-panama-its-plan-4bn-high-speed-rail-li/.

8 Evan Ellis. 'China's Advance in Panama: An Update', *Global Americans*, 14
April 2021. https://theglobalamericans.org/2021/04/chinas-advance-in-panama
-an-update/.

9 International Monetary Fund, World Economic Outlook Database, October 2021. www.imf.org/en/Publications/WEO/weo-database/2021/October
(accessed 12 May 2022).

10 Refworld, 'El Salvador: FMLN Guerrilla Attacks on Infrastructure and
Commerce in San Miguel and the Response of the El Salvadoran Armed
Forces Third Brigade', United States Bureau of Citizenship and Immigration
Services. www.refworld.org/docid/3dee02f74.html (accessed 12 May 2022).

11 Chris Horton, 'El Salvador Recognizes China in Blow to Taiwan', *New
York Times*, 21 August 2018. www.nytimes.com/2018/08/21/world/asia/ta
iwan-el-salvador-diplomatic-ties.html.

12 Evan Ellis, 'China and El Salvador: An Update', Center for Strategic and
International Studies, 27 April 2022. www.csis.org/analysis/china-and-el-sa
lvador-update.

13 Ernesto Luis Muyshondt, García-Prieto, '5G in Latin America: An Interview
with San Salvador's Mayor', *The Dialogue*, 5 February 2020. www.thedia
logue.org/analysis/5g-in-latin-america-an-interview-with-san-salvadors-mayor/.

14 Carrie Kahn, 'What the Coronavirus Lockdown Looks like in El Salvador', NPR, 18 June 2020. www.npr.org/2020/06/18/880513781/what-the-
coronavirus-lockdown-looks-like-in-el-salvador.

15 American Enterprise Institute, 'China Global Investment Tracker'. www.
aei.org/china-global-investment-tracker/ (accessed 12 May 2022).

16 The paragraphs that follow draw heavily on Robert Looney, 'How Global
Shifts Are Putting Costa Rica's Economic Model Under Stress', *World Politics Review*, 7 December 2016. www.worldpoliticsreview.com/articles/20633/
how-global-shifts-are-putting-costa-rica-s-economic-model-under-stress

17 Legatum Prosperity Index 2021, 10 November 2020. www.prosperity.com/
rankings?pinned=&rankOrScore=1&filter=&v=gap.

18 B. J. Siekierski, 'Costa Rica a Model for Developing Countries, President
Tells WTO', *iPolitics*, 19 September 2011. http://ipolitics.ca/2011/09/19/
costa-rica-a-model-for-developing-countries-president-tells-wto/.

19 *Harvard Business Review*, 'Clusters and the New Economics of Competition', 1 August 2014. https://hbr.org/1998/11/clusters-and-the-new-econom
ics-of-competition.

20 *Trading Economics*, 'Costa Rica: High-Technology Exports (% of Manufactured Exports)'. www.tradingeconomics.com/costa-rica/high-technology-exp
orts-percent-of-manufactured-exports-wb-data.html (accessed 13 May 2022).

21 *Tico Times*, 'Fitch Maintains Costa Rica's "B" Rating with Negative
Outlook', 17 March 2021. https://ticotimes.net/2021/03/17/fitch-maintains-
costa-ricas-b-rating-with-negative-outlook.

22 CentralAmericaData, 'China Says No to Costa Rican Bonds', 12 January
2016. http://en.centralamericadata.com/en/article/home/China_Says_No_
to_Costa_Rican_Bonds.

23 *Tico Times*, '$10 Million Donation from China to Fund National Stadium Improvements', 17 February 2020. https://ticotimes.net/2020/02/17/10-m illion-donation-from-china-to-fund-national-stadium-improvements.
24 BNamericas.com, 'Costa Rica Investigates Alleged Irregularities in Huawei Contract', 14 April 2020. www.bnamericas.com/en/news/costa-rica -investigates-irregularities-in-huawei-contract.
25 BNamericas, 'Costa Rica Presents 2021 Highway Agenda', 30 December 2020. www.bnamericas.com/en/news/costa-rica-presents-2021-highway-agenda.
26 American Enterprise Institute, China Global Investment Tracker'.
27 Robert Looney, 'Authoritarian Populism Loses Its Glow in Nicaragua', *Milken Institute Review*, 26 July 2018. www.milkenreview.org/articles/a uthoritarian-populism-loses-its-glow-in-nicaragua.
28 Ibid.
29 Reuters, 'Nicaragua Breaks Ties with Taiwan, Switches Allegiance to Beijing', 10 December 2021. www.reuters.com/world/china/nicaragua-brea ks-ties-with-taiwan-switches-allegiance-beijing-2021-12-09/.
30 Economist Intelligence Unit, 'Understanding Nicaragua's Adoption of Its One-China Policy', 15 December 2021. www.eiu.com/n/understanding-nica raguas-adoption-of-its-one-china-policy/.
31 Evan Ellis, 'Nicaragua's Flip to China: What Does It Mean for the Region?' Global Americans, 10 December 2021. https://theglobalamerica ns.org/2021/12/nicaraguas-flip-to-china/.
32 US Congress, 'S.1064 - Renacer Act 117th Congress (2021–2022)', 117th Congress, 11 October 2021. www.congress.gov/bill/117th-congress/sena te-bill/1064?s=1&r=5.

4 The BRI in South America

Introduction

The People's Republic of China's Belt and Road Initiative (BRI) loans and projects in South America cover a much broader spectrum of activities and occur in more significant amounts than in the Caribbean or Central America. In addition to traditional mining and agricultural projects, there is an increased focus on power, transport and other infrastructure projects. Recent deals also incorporate high-value activities such as 5G infrastructure, cloud computing, smartphones, electricity transmission and renewable energy surveillance technology.[1]

The rise of China's economic influence in South America dates back to at least 2005, with Sinohydro's US $370m. hydropower project in Ecuador.[2] By the end of 2020 Venezuela, Brazil, Ecuador, Argentina and Bolivia had received $130,800m. from China's top lenders – the Export-Import Bank of China and the China Development Bank. At $62,200m., Venezuela received the greatest amount of Chinese finance, followed by Brazil ($29,700m.), Ecuador ($18,400m.) and Bolivia ($3,400m.).[3]

Brazil is not officially a BRI member. Therefore, the discussion below will focus on the region's member countries, Bolivia, Ecuador, Chile, Peru, Venezuela, Uruguay and the most recent member, Argentina, which joined in February 2022.

The BRI countries fall into three different income categories (Figure 4.1). The high per capita income countries are Argentina, Uruguay and Chile, while the low-income countries are Bolivia, Peru and Ecuador. Venezuela forms a separate category because of its disastrous policymaking and lack of governance.

Debt levels have been rising since 2010 (Figure 4.1), with Argentina's government debt to gross domestic product (GDP) ratio reaching dangerous levels, so much so that the International Monetary Fund

DOI: 10.4324/b23227-4

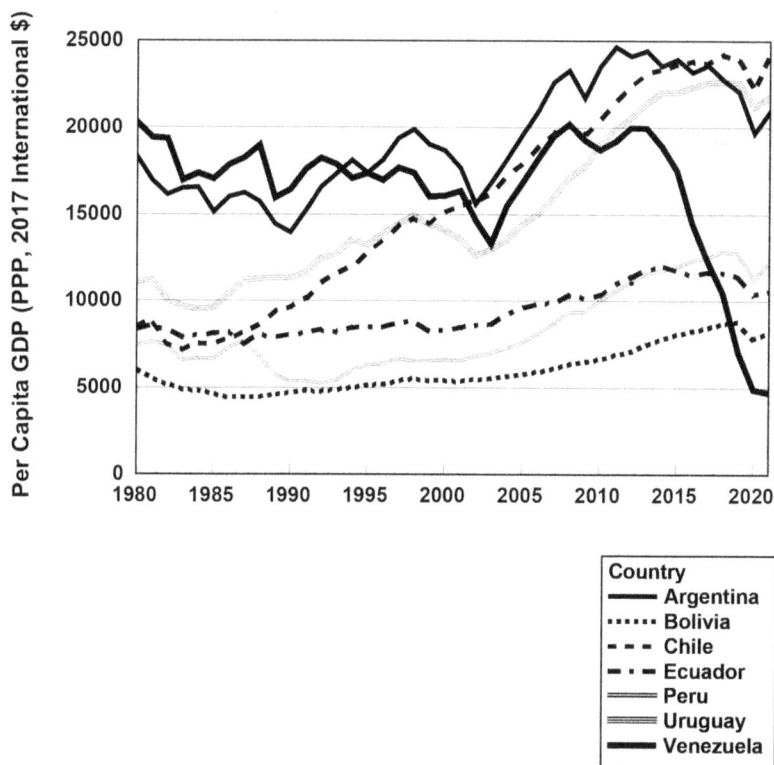

Figure 4.1 Per Capita Income Growth in South America, 1980–2021
Source: International Monetary Fund, World Economic Outlook Database:
October 2021.

(IMF) is reluctant to predict its future status. Bolivia and Uruguay
have also experienced rapid rises, but the IMF is projecting a levelling
off by 2026. While Ecuador's debt also increased during the period
2010–21, the Fund predicts that levels will fall. Meanwhile, although
Peru and Chile's debt levels are not at severe, they are on an upward
trend that may lead to problems in the medium term.

With the exception of Chile and Uruguay, governance levels (Figure
4.3) are low, with a slight improvement over time experienced by
Argentina and Peru. Governance levels in Bolivia fell during most of
the period after 1996, while those of Ecuador have been on a slight
upward trend since 2009.

The quality of transport infrastructure for this group of countries
roughly follows the same governance/infrastructure pattern for the

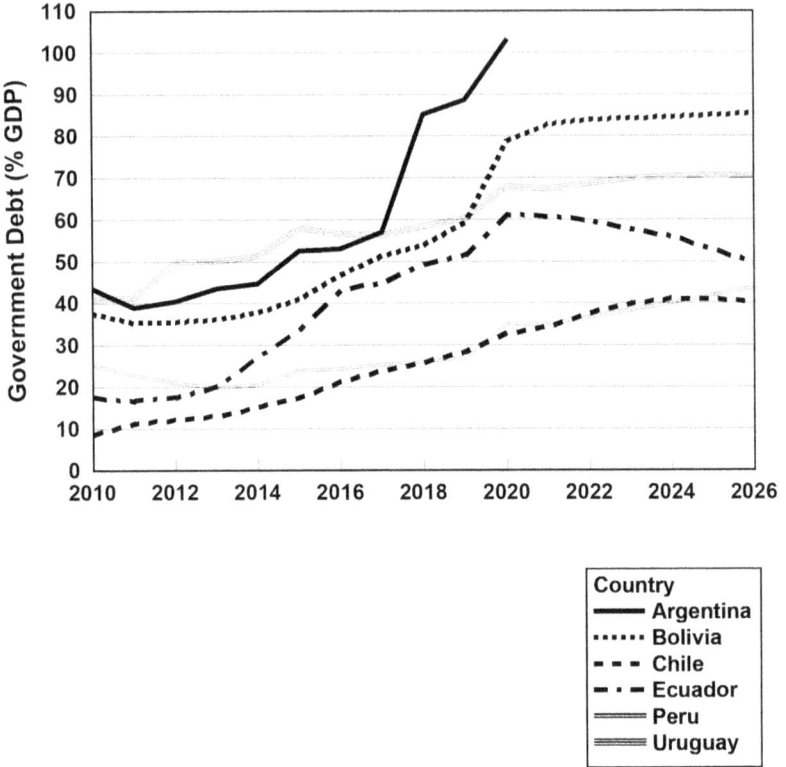

Figure 4.2 Government Debt as a % of GDP in South America, 2010–21
Source: International Monetary Fund, World Economic Outlook Database: October 2021.

Latin America and the Caribbean region (Figure 4.4). Given their governance levels, the quality of transport infrastructure in Chile and Uruguay is considerably lower than that predicted. Argentina, Ecuador and Bolivia are overachievers in that corresponding levels of governance do not support the quality of their transport infrastructures. Peru's level of transport infrastructure is in line with its level of governance.

Bolivia

Historically, the Bolivian economy has performed below its potential. The country possesses abundant mineral resources, including silver, lithium, tin and gold, and it is a significant exporter of natural gas. It

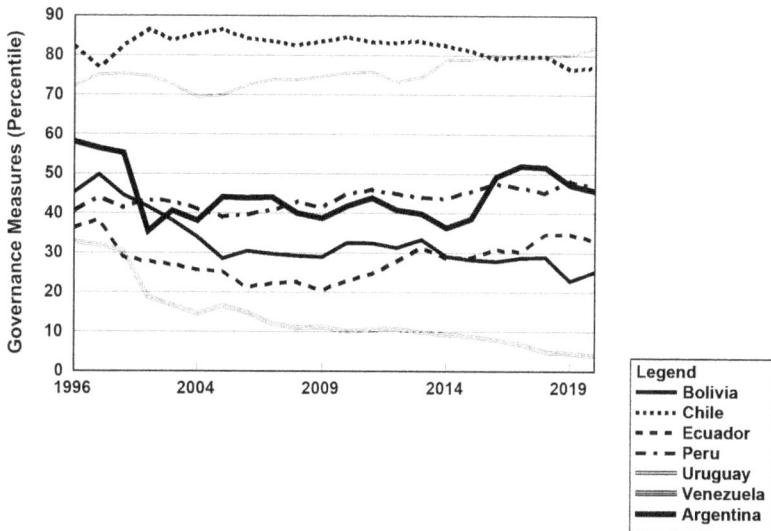

Figure 4.3 Governance Levels in South America, 1996–2020
Note: Governance is the average of its components: voice and accountability, political stability and absence of violence/terrorism, government effectiveness, regulatory quality, rule of law and control of corruption.
Source: World Bank, Worldwide Governance Indicators Database.

has vast hydropower potential. It also has excellent opportunities for tourism and agricultural products, such as quinoa.

However, offsetting these advantages is a series of weaknesses. The economy lacks diversification and remains dependent on hydrocarbons and minerals. The private sector is underdeveloped, leaving the country highly dependent on the public sector. A vast informal sector exists, and there is considerable insecurity with high rates of drug trafficking and corruption. The country is landlocked, placing it at a cost disadvantage, and there are risks to economic stability from social unrest in a highly polarized population.[4] Recently, growth slowed. After averaging 5.3% GDP growth annually from 2010–15, it fell to 1.8% from 2016–21.[5]

Bolivia joined the BRI in June 2018, but the country was a major destination for Chinese project funding and investment long before that.[6] As of mid-2021 China's BRI projects in Bolivia numbered sixteen, totalling $4,890m. China's first BRI-type project began in 2013 and involved the financing and construction of Bolivia's first telecommunications satellite, Túpac Katari 1.[7] The project provided a significant transfer of technology to Bolivia and enabled Bolivian

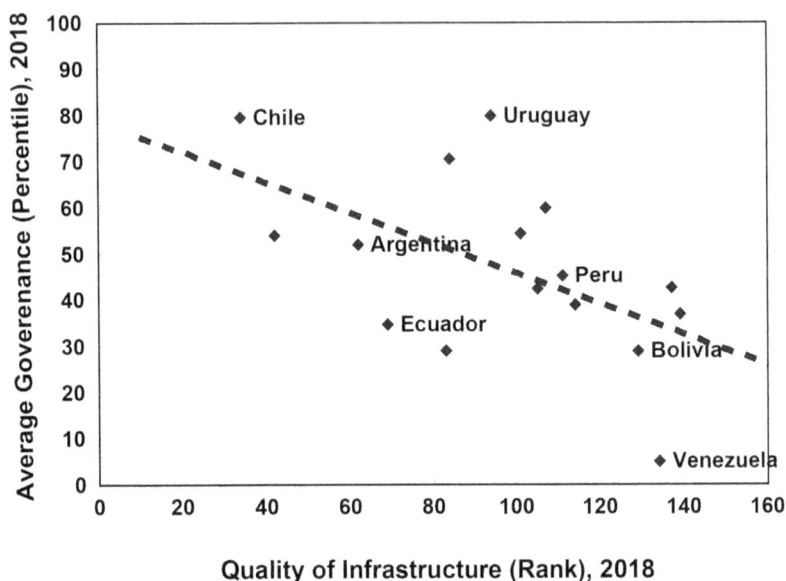

Quality of Infrastructure (Rank), 2018

Figure 4.4 Governance/Transport Infrastructure Quality Relationship, South
America, 2018
Source: Governance: World Bank, Worldwide Governance Indicators Data-
base; Infrastructure: World Bank, Logistics Performance Index Database.

engineers to gain valuable experience in managing satellite communications. Still, the project encountered stiff criticism over its costs and
that it was of greater benefit to China than to Bolivia. Complaints
have dogged Chinese investment in Bolivia ever since. A common criticism of Chinese BRI projects in Bolivia is the lack of transparency
and consultation with affected groups, particularly the country's large
indigenous population.[8]

A sampling of BRI projects currently underway in Bolivia shows a
concentration in the construction of roads extending from Rurrena-
baque to Riberalta in the Amazon. Other roads include a section of
the El Sillar highway from Santa Cruz to Cochabamba, and the
highway from El Espino to Boyuibe in the Chaco.[9] As noted above,
China has also facilitated Bolivia's space programme. Other significant
projects are lithium exploration and the Mutún steel facility.[10], While
China has had some successes, there have also been disappointments.
The controversial Rositas hydroelectric dam faces mounting resistance,
and the extension of the Santa Cruz airport has been cancelled.[11] A
study by Fundación Milenio, a think tank based in the country's

administrative capital, La Paz, shows that Chinese companies have already taken control of over 50% of major public investment contracts in infrastructure (road and rail) and in mining (lithium and iron ore).[12]

Despite China's many infrastructure projects in Bolivia, the quality of the country's transport infrastructure ranked 129th in 2018, down from 100th in 2010.[13] However, perhaps because of this Chinese investment, the country's ranking in 2018 was higher than expected based on the typical infrastructure governance pattern (Figure 4.3).

Bolivia's overall governance has declined considerably in recent decades, falling from the 45th percentile in 2000 to the 33rd percentile in 2010 and to the 25th percentile by 2020.[14] In recent years, corruption has been a problem, with the country slipping from the 39th percentile in 2010 to the 25th percentile in 2020. The Bolivian government wants to attract foreign direct investment (FDI) in order better to exploit its resources. Still, with the rule of law declining from the 40th percentile in 2000 to the 15th percentile in 2010 and to the 12th percentile by 2020, US and European firms will be hesitant to make long-term commitments in the country. Reinforcing the adverse effects of governance on investment is the long-term decline in the country's economic freedom from 'moderately free' in 2000 to 'mostly unfree in 2004 and 'repressed' in 2010.[15]

Flows of FDI to Bolivia fell from 1.9% of GDP in 2017 to 0.8% in 2018.[16] However, 2019 and 2020 witnessed negative flows of 0.6% of GDP and 2.8%, respectively, before turning positive, to just 0.7%, in 2021. Barring the reversal of the country's governance and economic freedom trends, the government will probably become more dependent on Chinese financing.

The country also faces increasingly severe financial constraints with the ending of the commodity super-cycle around 2015. After averaging a surplus of 0.3% of GDP from 2010–14, the government's fiscal accounts averaged a deficit of 8.5% of GDP from 2015–21. Similarly, the central government's external debt increased from a manageable 37.6% of GDP in 2010 to 40.9% of GDP in 2015. However, by 2021 the debt level had reached the dangerous level of 82.7% of GDP. In part, this increase reflected the economy's contraction of 8.8% during the pandemic year of 2021. However, the IMF predicts that government debt will rise to 85.0% by 2025.[17]

Bolivia faces challenging fiscal and external imbalances. The country's lack of diversification away from a commodity-dependent export base, declining levels of governance and inadequate business environment are significant structural constraints on growth. Baring improvements in governance or the business environment, China's BRI programme can still be a positive element in the country's future. Still, its effectiveness will continue dampened in this environment.

Ecuador

Ecuador and China have a long history of projects, starting with a significant road programme in February 2005. China has undertaken twenty-six projects totalling $14,000m.[18] Although Ecuador did not officially join the BRI until 2018, BRI-type projects had been ongoing since February 2014, when China's PowerChina began a $240m. hydro project. The most recent project involved a $420m. transport project undertaken in December 2019 by the China Railway Construction company. During this period twelve BRI projects totalled $5,690. Ecuador is currently the third largest recipient of Chinese finance in the region, just behind Venezuela and Brazil.

External funding from China accelerated under President Rafael Correa (2007–17) as he ramped up public spending and increased the size of the state.[19] With Correa adopting populist economic policies, his administration sought Chinese loans rather than accepting the orthodox conditions associated with IMF financing. During Correa's decade of corrupt authoritarian rule government debt as a share of GDP rose from 28.5% in 2007 to 44.6% in 2017.[20]

In the final three years of the Correa administration alone, wasteful government spending increased the government deficit as a share of GDP from 4.4% in 2013 to 8.2% in 2016. Ecuador's default on $3,200m. in foreign debt in 2008 and 2009 effectively locked the country out of international financial markets.[21]

Chinese FDI in Ecuador also increased under Correa. Chinese firms now operate some of Ecuador's largest mines, including the BRI-financed Mirador copper mine in the southern highland province of Zamora Chinchipe.[22] The Coca Codo Sinclair hydroelectric plant was one of several massive infrastructure projects undertaken by Chinese firms. Investments in the oil sector reflect Beijing's strategic interest in securing control of hydrocarbons to support that country's energy security.

Much of the Correa government's accumulated debt became tied to the future sale of oil. The question of oil-linked debt with China remains controversial, as it has been since it began in 2010 under Correa, who refused to make the contracts public.[23] Just two months after being appointed, Ricardo Merino, the CEO of Petroecuador (the state-owned oil firm), resigned on 1 November 2020. Merino cited fears that the government might agree to deals that were neither in the country's nor the company's best interests and which would not meet terms ordered by Ecuador's Comptroller-General.[24] As of early 2022 Ecuador's debt with China stood at about $5,000m.[25] Of this, approximately $2,000m. was linked to the sale of oil.

Ecuador's current President, Guillermo Lasso (2021–), is attempting to improve that country's ties with multilateral institutions and renegotiate Ecuador's debt with China.[26] This action follows a deal with the US Development Finance Corporation to buy back a large amount of Ecuador's Chinese debt.[27]

In 2018 Ecuador's transport infrastructure ranked 69th, considerably better than that usually associated with its overall level of governance in the 33rd percentile.[28] This pattern suggests that the country does not have the institutional foundation to support its current level of infrastructure quality. Hopefully, the current administration will move ahead with reforms, particularly in corruption, the rule of law and government effectiveness.

Since Correa left office, the government has progressed in this area, with regulatory quality (business environment) improving from the 12th percentile in 2017 to the 17th percentile by 2020. Control of corruption has also improved, moving from the 30th percentile in 2017 to the 32nd percentile during this period, while the rule of law improved from the 22nd percentile to the 32nd percentile. Overall governance improved from the 30th percentile to the 33rd percentile, as mentioned above. With improved governance, Ecuador's transport infrastructure ranking rose from 88th in 2016 (data are not available for 2017) to 69th in 2018.

Chile

The Chilean economy is a Latin American success story. Owing to past high growth rates, the country has the highest per capita income in Latin America. Its economy is a relatively free market. However, the country's economic freedom is on a slight downward trend, and so also is business confidence. Growth is also on the decline, with GDP averaging 6.1% per annum in the 1990s, falling to 4.2% in the 2000s, and to 3.2% from 2010–21. Chile is also the world's largest producer and exporter of copper. Its lithium reserves are vast and undeveloped. However, politics has become more polarized with increasing concerns over growing inequality, poor public education and broken pension systems.

Although Chile did not join China's BRI until 2018, China's first BRI type-project was a $210m. metals project undertaken in September 2016 by Chengdu Tianqi with Sociedad Quimica y Minera. By

April 2021 China had started eleven BRI projects totalling $13,110m. The Export-Import Bank of China began operations in Chile in July 2021.[29] Two other Chinese banks also do business in the country.[30] In July 2021 Chile joined China's Asian Infrastructure Investment Bank (AIIB). From China's perspective, Chile represents an entry market for that country in Latin America.

Several recent BRI projects include the Punta Sierra wind farm.[31] Punta Sierra has been in operation since February 2018. The project represents the first hydro-wind farm in Chile. It is expected to generate about 282 GWh/year, meeting electricity demands for 130,000 households and reducing carbon emissions by 157,000 metric tons per year. Towards the end of 2019, China's State Grid bought Chile's third largest electricity distributor, Compania General de Electricidad CGE. SN, for $3,000m.[32] However, China faces increased resistance to expanding in Chile's high-tech sectors.[33]

In 2018 the quality of Chile's transport infrastructure ranked 34th, the highest for BRI countries in the Latin America and Caribbean region. However, given the country's position on the 80th percentile in terms of governance, the country is a significant underachiever whose ranking in the quality of transport infrastructure should be in the teens. As Chilean debt levels are low by Latin America standards, the country should be an ideal location for BRI programmes.

Lithium mining is one area in which Chinese investment and infrastructure would be highly beneficial. Over the past decade, Chile has lost ground in the lithium market, a trend that is likely to persist and perhaps even to worsen.[34] To reverse this trend, on 12 January 2022 the outgoing centre-right government of President Sebastián Piñera announced the awarding of two lithium exploration and extraction concession contracts. Each involves the production of up to 80,000 metric tons of lithium for up to twenty-nine years. One contract went to Chinese electric vehicle manufacturer BYD; the other to a company belonging to the Chilean Errazuriz group.[35]

However, Chinese resource firms in Chile are facing rising resource nationalism.[36] In January 2022 BYD's $61m. lithium mining deal with Chile was suspended by a local court two days after it won extraction rights.[37] President-elect Gabriel Boric, who assumed office on 11 March, strongly criticized the contracts as being at odds with the country's best interests and his intention to establish a state lithium company. Ironically, creating a state lithium company is unlikely to be in the country's best interests. It would significantly increase government borrowing at a time of tight fiscal resources with the possibility of crowding out badly needed education and health programmes.

Peru

Peru is a major export-oriented economy and a significant supplier of raw materials such as copper, which is critical for alternative energy systems. Over the years, Chinese investment and BRI projects have focused on energy, transport and raw materials to develop the country's resource base. Chinese projects in Peru are more commercially oriented than those typically found along the original Belt and Road routes connecting China with Europe.

As of 2021 China's twenty-seven investments in Peru totalled $27,270m. Although Peru did not officially join the BRI until 2019, the country is home to fourteen BRI-type ventures totalling $21,480m., beginning with the China National Petroleum Corporation's $2,890m. November 2013 energy venture. The last venture took place in February 2021 and was a $560m. China Three Gorges energy investment.

However, much of China's involvement in Peru involves private Chinese companies expanding their operations in its mining sector. Chinese companies such as Aluminium Corporation of China Limited (Chinalco) are leading the way in developing new mines.[38] As of mid-2022 China was Peru's second largest foreign investor in the mining sector, with Chinese firms owning the Marcona iron ore mine and the Las Bambas copper mine.[39] Both mines are a source of disputes with local populations.

The Las Bambas mine, which produces 2% of the global copper supply, has been a source of ongoing difficulties for the Chinese firm MMG. Repeated disputes between communities and the company since production started in 2016 have resulted in the road to the mine being closed for at least 400 days. In the latest clash with local opponents, on 18 December 2021 MMG suspended all production following more than a month of roadblocks at various points along the highway linking the mine with its port facilities.[40] The lesson from Las Bambas is that mining companies thinking of investing in Peru need to be conscious of the social implications of their actions and be aware that restoring good community relations can be highly problematic once a conflict arises.

In recent years, Peru has witnessed a shift in competition for international projects from Latin American firms to European and Chinese firms. Before the Lava Jato corruption scandal, Brazilian firms played a central role in Peruvian infrastructure development, with Odebrecht, in particular, leading the way. [41] [42] With Odebrecht's demise, Chinese firms will probably see the most significant increase in involvement over the coming years.

This development for Chinese firms is playing out because of their relatively high-risk appetite and strong financing support from Chinese institutions. The transport sector is a particular area of focus. Chinese successes include the $390.0m. Oyon-Ambo Highway Improvement Project, awarded to China Gezhouba Group in 2018.[43] The planned $3,000m. Port of Chancay, north of Lima, will be developed by COSCO Shipping Corporation in collaboration with the Peru-based mining firm Volcan Compañía Minera.[44] However, the project is subject to pushback owing to its disruptive effects on the local community.

The $95.0m. Hidrovia Amazónica waterway project is another controversial venture.[45] It is a public-private partnership awarded in 2017 to the COHIDRO consortium, composed of Construcción y Administración and the China-based engineering firm Synohidro Corporation. The project's environmental impact remains unclear, thus causing significant delays in implementation. The China Development Bank is quite active in providing financing for projects such as the San Gaban III Hydro Project undertaken by China's Three Gorges Corporation.[46]

Peruvian infrastructure ranks 111th, which is slightly lower than expected, given the country's overall governance (Figure 4.4). This low ranking suggests that there is some scope for rather significant gains from additional BRI programmes. Also encouraging is that Peru's overall governance has gradually improved from the 39th percentile in 2005 to the 47th percentile in 2020. There are concerns about corruption, with this governance dimension falling from the 47th percentile to the 34th percentile during this period. The government prudently managed Peru's finances with central government debt of only 35.1% of GDP in 2021, up from 25.5% of GDP in 2010. With debt levels in this range, the country is in an excellent position to take on additional Chinese debt in order to expand and upgrade critical infrastructure.

Venezuela

Chinese investments in and loans to Venezuela are the largest in Latin America. According to the Inter-American Dialogue, China has loaned Venezuela more than $67,000m.[47] Venezuela officially joined the BRI in December 2017 and has nine BRI-type projects valued at $8,140m. The terms of many Chinese loans to the country are unclear, although the majority appear to be backed by future oil deliveries.

Progress on many projects ceased because of the chaos that spread through Venezuela under the Maduro administration, as the economy contracted by almost four-fifths from 2014–20. The country's Chinese-constructed power plants, the La Cabrera thermoelectric plant and the El Vigia plant, operate at only a fraction of capacity.[48] Other projects, such as the abandoned rice processing plant in Delta Amacuro, were highly costly failures.[49]

Venezuela's governance has been in free fall since the Hugo Rafael Chávez regime (2002–13), but the decline accelerated under the Nicolas Maduro administration (2013–). In 2000 the country's total governance was at the 31st percentile. By 2013 it had fallen to the 10th percentile and to the 4th percentile by 2020. Similarly, government effectiveness declined from the 25th percentile in 2000 to the 12th percentile by 2013. By 2020 the country's government effectiveness ranked in the 2nd percentile. In 2020 the country's rule of law stood at the 0 percentile. As expected, with the deterioration in governance, there has been a corresponding decline in infrastructure quality. In 2007 the quality of Venezuela's transport infrastructure ranked 59th, declining to 129th in 2012 and to 134th by 2018.

China's most recent BRI loan was for $360m. in September 2018 to Venezuela's state oil company PDVSA. However, because of years of mismanagement by PDVSA, oil production fell from 1,630,000 barrels per day (b/d) in 2018 to 1,021,000 b/d in 2019 and to 640,000 b/d in 2020, although in 2021 it increased to 654,000 b/d.[50] [51]

Venezuela is in technical default. While the government is making repayments, it is in high arrears. The IMF cannot restructure the debt because the Maduro regime is unwilling to adopt an economic programme that is acceptable to its creditors. PDVSA's debt alone in 2021 amounted to $34,900m.[52]

It is hard to see how additional BRI lending, on the slight chance that it might be forthcoming, could significantly improve the country's infrastructure or productive structure so long as Maduro remains in post as President. It will take years for the country to recover from Maduro's mismanagement and the emigration of millions of skilled Venezuelans.[53]

Uruguay

On 19 August 2018 Uruguay became a BRI member.[54] However, the only project of record as of early 2021 is a $180m. energy project undertaken in May of that year.[55] Chinese firms have not had considerable success in advancing BRI projects after losing a bid on the Ferrocarril Central Railway linking Paso de los Toros with the Port of Montevideo.

The most promising areas for BRI cooperation are likely to involve China-Uruguayan trade. Specifically, those involving taking advantage of opportunities opened up by Uruguay's membership of the regional

Southern Common Market (MERCOSUR/MERCOSUL), including Uruguay, Paraguay, Brazil and Argentina. China has been Uruguay's largest export market since 2013, and its market share continues to increase. In 2020 China accounted for 27% of Uruguayan exports, followed by Brazil (15%), the European Union (14%), Argentina (5%) and Mexico (3%).

There is also clearly a need for improved infrastructure in Uruguay. Despite steady improvements in governance, the quality of Uruguay's infrastructure has declined in recent years. World Bank data show that the quality of the country's infrastructure improved from 70th in 2007 to 55th by 2012. However, the country ranked 61st in 2016 and 94th in 2018. Given the country's high level of governance (82nd percentile in 2020), the highest of our sample of six countries, the country has dramatically underachieved. Its infrastructure quality ranking should be in the thirties.

Uruguay should, therefore, be an ideal candidate for Chinese BRI projects. However, the country may not take on large amounts of debt for several years. General government debt as a share of GDP increased from 41% in 2020 to 60.5% in 2019 and to 68.1% in 2020. The IMF predicts that there will be a further increase to 70.7% in 2025.

Argentina

Although Argentina did not officially join the BRI until February 2022, in 2020 loans from China's two policy banks, the China Development Bank and the China Export-Import Bank, amounted to $17,100m.[56] Chinese investments as of early 2021 amounted to $22,810m.[57] Argentina had already joined the AIIB in June 2017. Argentina is by far the largest Latin American country to join the BRI. As of mid-2022 Mexico, Brazil and Colombia were continuing to resist joining the BRI, presumably not wanting to harm their relations with the United States.

The BRI-type programmes amount to around $24,000m. (about 6% of GDP).[58] Recent Chinese lending and investments for BRI-type activities in Argentina include the Portezuelo del Viento hydroelectric dam in Mendoza province (which attracted a single bid of $1,000m.), reconstruction of the San Martín cargo railway (December 2020; $2,600m.), improvement of the Belgrano freight railway (December 2020; $816m.), a rail line linking the Vaca Muerta shale reserves to Bahía Blanca port (September 2020; $1,200m.), and a solar-powered lithium plant in Salta province (June 2021; $580m.).[59]

China-Argentina cooperation has not always gone smoothly. Plans for a Chinese-funded nuclear power plant have been on and off for years.[60] Progress has been slow on two China-funded hydroelectric dams in Patagonia.[61] The Argentina-China relationship also involves cooperation involving a Chinese-run space station in Patagonia.[62] A logistics base in Ushuaia is under consideration.[63] During the coronavirus COVID-19 pandemic China delivered millions of doses of the Sinopharm vaccine.[64] Finally, Chinese firms are eager to develop Argentine lithium.[65]

Realistically, Argentina had little choice but to join the BRI. For several years the country has been in a dire debt situation and locked out of international capital markets. Government budgetary deficits averaged 6.3% of GDP from 2015–20, reaching 8.6% of GDP in 2020. The country's external debt increased from 52.6% in 2015 to 102.8% in 2020.

The country has many fixed payments falling due, and its reserves are running low. To rectify the situation, the administration of Alberto Fernandez has attempted to complete a $44,000m. loan from the IMF but has faced considerable domestic political opposition to the terms of the loan. Even if the loan is completed, the funds received must go towards servicing the country's existing debts.

In 2018 the quality of Argentina's transport infrastructure ranked 62nd, while its overall governance was on the 52nd percentile. Based on the normal governance infrastructure quality relationship, the country's infrastructure quality overachieved by about ten places. Chinese BRI projects may help to improve the country's infrastructure, but unless governance improves, these investments will be much less effective than otherwise. Unfortunately, given the political dynamics currently playing out in Argentina, improved governance is highly unlikely.

Assessment

There are limited prospects for new or expanded BRI programmes in South America as of mid-2022. Venezuela, Ecuador and Argentina are in serious financial difficulties, and taking on new projects or loans is highly unlikely even if China wants to move in that direction. BRI programmes in the lithium sector are logical for Chile and Bolivia, but nationalistic and indigenous opposition may be significant impediments. Both Peru and Uruguay are not over-extended financially and, given their levels of governance, could easily support substantial expansions. Of the existing BRI member countries, these two may be the most promising in South America for high-impact BRI programmes.

Notes

1 Michael Stott, 'US Investment Drive to Take on China in Latin America', *Financial Times*, 18 October 2021. www.ft.com/content/95690221-c623-46a 8-af2f-2d5910f972ba.

2 Matthew Crittenden, Caroline Morin, Remington Fritz, Sophie Pittaluga, Emily Maison, William Weston, Kaitlyn Wilson and Asha Silva, 'China's Bri in Latin America: Case Study – Hydropower in Ecuador', *Tearline.mil*, 15 June 2021. www.tearline.mil/public_page/china-bri-in-ecuador-hydropower/.

3 Jason Yovanoff, 'China-Latin America Finance Databases', *The Dialogue*, 6 May 2021. www.thedialogue.org/map_list/.

4 Robert Looney, 'Bolivia's Populist Experiment', *Milken Institute Review*, 10 August 2021. www.milkenreview.org/articles/bolivias-populist-experiment.

5 International Monetary Fund, World Economic Outlook Database, October 2021. www.imf.org/en/Publications/WEO/weo-database/2021/October (accessed 13 May 2022).

6 Andrés Bermúdez Liévano, 'China's Belt and Road Advances in Latin America's Andean Region', *Dialogo Chino*, 6 March 2020. https://dialogo chino.net/en/infrastructure/27815-chinas-belt-and-road-advances-in-latin-a mericas-andean-region/.

7 Andrew Wight, 'China, Eyeing Bolivia's Lithium Riches, Helps Country into Space', *Sydney Morning Herald*, 20 February 2018. www.smh.com.au/ world/south-america/china-eyeing-bolivia-s-lithium-riches-helps-country-i nto-space-20180220-p4z0yz.html.

8 Crittenden et al., 'China's Bri in Latin America: Case Study – Hydropower in Ecuador'.

9 *El Diario*, 'China Railway Abandonó Obras de Costosa Carretera en Beni'. www.eldiario.net (accessed 13 May 2022). www.eldiario.net/noticias/ 2019/2019_01/nt190130/economia.php?n=10&-china-railway-abandono-ob ras-de-costosa-carretera-en-beni.

10 Daniel Ramos, 'Bolivia Picks Chinese Partner for $2.3 Billion Lithium Projects', Reuters, 6 February 2019. www.reuters.com/article/us-bolivia -lithium-china/bolivia-picks-chinese-partner-for-2-3-billion-lithium-project s-idUSKCN1PV2F7.

11 Miriam Telma Jemio, 'O Polêmico Referendo Para Reativar a Represa Boliviana De Rositas', *Dialogo Chino*, 6 March 2020. https://dialogochino. net/23713-the-controversial-referendum-to-revive-bolivias-rositas-dam/?lan g=es.

12 Fundación Milenio, 'Página Siete: Bolivia Contrató Empresas Chinas por Cerca de 6.000 Millones de Dólares – Economía De Bolivia', 17 May 2021. https://fundacion-milenio.org/pagina-siete-bolivia-contrato-empresa s-chinas-por-cerca-de-6-000-millones-de-dolares/.

13 The World Bank, 'Logistics Performance Index'. https://lpi.worldbank.org/ (accessed 13 May 2022).

14 The World Bank, 'Worldwide Governance Indicators'. http://info.worldba nk.org/governance/wgi/ (accessed 13 May 2022).

15 The Heritage Foundation, 'Bolivia', Bolivia Economy: Population, GDP, Inflation, Business, Trade, FDI, Corruption. www.heritage.org/index/coun try/bolivia (accessed 13 May 2022).

16 UNCTAD, 'World Investment Report 2021'. https://unctad.org/webflyer/world-investment-report-2021 (accessed 13 May 2022).

17 International Monetary Fund, World Economic Outlook Database, October 2021.

18 American Enterprise Institute, 'China Global Investment Tracker'. www.aei.org/china-global-investment-tracker/ (accessed 12 May 2022).

19 Nick Miroff, 'Ecuador's Popular, Powerful President Rafael Correa Is a Study in Contradictions', *Washington Post*, 15 March 2014. www.washingtonpost.com/world/ecuadors-popular-powerful-president-rafael-corre a-is-a-study-in-contradictions/2014/03/15/452111fc-3eaa-401b-b2c8-cc4e85 fccb40_story.html.

20 International Monetary Fund, World Economic Outlook Database October 2019.

21 Financial Times, 'Ecuador Defaults on Sovereign Bonds'. www.ft.com/content/7170e224-c897-11dd-b86f-000077b07658 (accessed 13 May 2022).

22 Paul Moore, 'Ecuacorriente Sa Starts to Ramp up Mirador Copper Mine in Ecuador as XCMG Ships Large Scale Mining Equipment', *International Mining*, 4 November 2021. https://im-mining.com/2021/11/03/ecua corriente-sa-starts-ramp-mirador-copper-mine-ecuador-xcmg-ships-large-s cale-mining-equipment/.

23 Reuters, 'How China Took Control of Ecuador's Oil', *Financial Post*, 26 November 2013. https://financialpost.com/investing/how-china-took-con trol-of-ecuadors-oil-2.

24 Alexandra Valencia and Luc Cohen. 'Executives at Ecuador's State Oil Companies Resign Ahead of Merger', Reuters, 2 November 2020. www.reuters.com/article/us-ecuador-oil/executives-at-ecuadors-state-oil-compani es-resign-ahead-of-merger-idUSKBN27I2FP.

25 Carlos Larrea and Jesús Ramos, 'Debt-for-Nature Swaps with China Could Boost Ecuador's Conservation', *China Dialogue*, 23 February 2022. https://chinadialogue.net/en/business/debt-for-nature-swaps-with-china-cou ld-boost-ecuadors-conservation/.

26 Alberto Araujo, 'China, Ecuador to Renegotiate "Harmful" Loan Terms', *Argus Media*, 9 February 2022. www.argusmedia.com/en/news/2300419-ch ina-ecuador-to-renegotiate-harmful-loan-terms.

27 Demetri Sevastopulo, 'US Development Bank Strikes Deal to Help Ecuador Pay China Loans', *Financial Times*, 14 January 2021. www.ft.com/content/affcc432-03c4-459d-a6b8-922ca8346c14.

28 World Bank, Logistics Performance Index.

29 InvestChile, 'The Export-Import Bank of China to Open Its First Office in Chile', InvestChile Blog, 2 August 2021. https://blog.investchile.gob.cl/the-export-import-bank-of-china-to-open-its-first-office-in-chile.

30 Diego Vera, 'CMF Autorizó Desembarco De Exim Bank, Tercer Operador Bancario Chino Que Funcionará En Chile', BioBioChile, 29 July 2021. www.biobiochile.cl/noticias/nacional/chile/2021/07/28/cmf-autoriza-desembarco-de-exim-bank-tercer-operador-bancario-chino-que-funcionara-en-chile.shtml.

31 Reve, 'Chile Inaugurates Punta Sierra Wind Farm', 26 August 2018. www.evwind.es/2018/08/26/chile-inaugurates-punta-sierra-wind-farm/64326.

32 Reuters, 'Naturgy Sells Chilean Unit to China's State Grid for $3 Billion', 13 November 2020. www.reuters.com/article/us-naturgy-m-a-cge/naturgy-sells-chilean-unit-to-chinas-state-grid-for-3-billion-idUSKBN27T1A6.

33 Bloomberg, 'Chilean Lawmakers Push for Restrictions on Chinese Buying Spree'. www.bloomberg.com/news/articles/2020-12-14/chilean-lawmakers-push-for-restrictions-on-chinese-buying-spree?sref=5LmjrEiv (accessed 13 May 2022).

34 Dave Sherwood, 'Chile, Once the World's Lithium Leader, Loses Ground to Rivals', Reuters, 30 May 2019. www.reuters.com/article/us-chile-lithium-analysis/chile-once-the-worlds-lithium-leader-loses-ground-to-rivals-idUS KCN1T00DM.

35 George Russell (ed.), 'China's BYD Wins Chile Lithium Extraction Contract', *Asia Financial*, 13 January 2022. www.asiafinancial.com/china s-byd-wins-chile-lithium-extraction-contract.

36 Daniel Litvin, 'How to Tackle Resource Nationalism', *Financial Times*, 11 January 2022. www.ft.com/content/7dbf87c0-6524-43dc-a9ca-3c11835c4d4b.

37 Lu Yutong and Manuyn Zou, 'BYD's $61 Million Chile Lithium Deal Hits the Rocks', *Caixin Global*, 17 January 2022. www.caixinglobal.com/2022-01-17/byds-61-million-chile-lithium-deal-hits-the-rocks-101831282.html.

38 Reuters, 'Refinitiv'. www.reuters.com/companies/2600.HK (accessed 13 May 2022).

39 Juan Saldarriaga, 'China Ya No Es El Inversionista Minero Número Uno Del Perú', *El Comercio Perú*, 28 January 2019. https://elcomercio.pe/economia/dia-1/china-inversionista-minero-numero-peru-noticia-601756.

40 Marcelo Rochabrun and Marco Aquino, 'Peru PM Says State of Emergency Would Be "Last Resort" as Las Bambas ...', *US News*, 15 December 2021. www.usnews.com/news/world/articles/2021-12-15/mmg-shuts-copper-production-at-las-bambas-in-peru-as-talks-to-end-blockade-fail.

41 Amelia Cheatham, 'Lava Jato: See How Far Brazil's Corruption Probe Reached', Council on Foreign Relations. www.cfr.org/in-brief/lava-ja to-see-how-far-brazils-corruption-probe-reached.

42 Laura Bunt-MacRury, 'Peru's House of Cards: Odebrecht Scandal Has Engulfed the Country's Political Class', *The Conversation*, 27 February 2022. https://theconversation.com/perus-house-of-cards-odebrecht-scanda l-has-engulfed-the-countrys-political-class-118793.

43 BNamericas.com, 'Oyón-Ambo Highway Improvement: Oyón-Cerro De Pasco (Stretch I)'. www.bnamericas.com/en/project-profile/oyon-ambo-hig hway-improvement-oyon-cerro-de-pasco-stretch-i (accessed 19 May 2022).

44 Leslie Moreno Custodio, 'Peru's New Chancay Mega-Port Shakes a Village to Its Core', *Dialogo Chino*, 21 May 2021. https://dialogochino.net/en/infrastructure/43228-perus-chancay-mega-port-shakes-village-to-core/.

45 Dan Collyns, 'China-Backed Amazon Waterway Mired in Murky Information', *Dialogo Chino*, 13 September 2019. https://dialogochino.net/en/infrastructure/30190-china-backed-amazon-waterway-mired-in-murky-info rmation/.

46 Michael Harris, 'Peru's San Gaban Project Receives Chinese Cash Infusion', *Hydro Review*, 2 September 2019. www.hydroreview.com/business-fi nance/peru-s-san-gaban-project-receives-chinese-cash-infusion/.

47 Yovanoff, 'China-Latin America Finance Databases'.

48 Jeanfreddy Gutiérrez, 'Chinese Investment in Venezuela's Grid Fails to Prevent Blackouts', *Dialogo Chino*, 17 January 2020. https://dialogochino.

net/en/climate-energy/32585-chinese-investment-in-venezuelas-grid-fa
ils-to-prevent-blackouts/.

49 Angus Berwick, 'Intermediarios Lucran Con Proyectos Para Zonas Olvi-
dadas De Venezuela', Reuters, 7 May 2019. www.reuters.com/investigates/
special-report/venezuela-china-food-es/.

50 BP, 'Full Report: Statistical Review of World Energy 2021'. www.bp.com/
content/dam/bp/business-sites/en/global/corporate/pdfs/energy-economics/
statistical-review/bp-stats-review-2021-full-report.pdf (accessed May 19,
2022).

51 Marianna Parraga, 'How Venezuela Pulled Its Oil Production out of a
Tailspin', Reuters, 27 December 2021. www.reuters.com/markets/commodi
ties/how-venezuela-pulled-its-oil-production-out-tailspin-2021-12-27/.

52 Reuters, 'Venezuela's PDVSA Saw Debt Rise to $34.9 Billion in 2021', 19
January 2022. www.reuters.com/business/energy/venezuelas-pdvsa-saw-deb
t-rise-349-billion-2021-2022-01-19/.

53 Rania Abouzeid, 'Millions of Venezuelans Are Fleeing to the South
through South America's "Poetic Heart"', *National Geographic*, 26 January 2022. www.nationalgeographic.com/culture/article/millions-of-vene
zuelans-are-fleeing-to-the-south-through-south-americas-poetic-heart.

54 Xinhua Silk Road Information Service, 'Belt and Road Countries: Uruguay'. https://en.imsilkroad.com/p/316681.html (accessed 19 May 2022).

55 American Enterprise Institute, 'China Global Investment Tracker'. www.
aei.org/china-global-investment-tracker/ (accessed 19 May 2022).

56 Yovanoff, 'China-Latin America Finance Databases'.

57 American Enterprise Institute, 'China Global Investment Tracker'.

58 Economist Intelligence Unit, 'Argentina Looks to China for Finance and
Joins the BRI. http://country.eiu.com/article.aspx?articleid=1701821753&
Country=Argentina&topic=Economy&subtopic_1 (accessed 19 May 2022).

59 *Global Construction Review*, 'Chinese Consortium Enters Sole Bid for
$1bn Argentine Hydro Scheme', 9 July 2020. www.globalconstructionre
view.com/chinese-consortium-enters-sole-bid-1bn-argentine-h/.

60 Fermin Koop, 'Argentina Seeks New China-Backed Nuclear Power Plant',
Dialogo Chino, 20 August 2021. https://dialogochino.net/en/climate-energy/
45420-argentina-seeks-new-china-backed-nuclear-power-plant/.

61 Tais Gadea Lara, 'New Argentina Government Reactivates Controversial
Patagonia Dams', Dialogo Chino, 6 March 2020. https://dialogochino.net/
en/climate-energy/33727-new-argentina-government-reactivates-controvers
ial-patagonia-dams/.

62 Cassandra Garrison, 'China's Military-Run Space Station in Argentina Is
a "Black Box"', Reuters, 31 January 2019. www.reuters.com/article/us-spa
ce-argentina-china-insight/chinas-military-run-space-station-in-argentina-i
s-a-black-box-idUSKCN1PP0I2.

63 *Rio Times*, 'Argentina Moves Forward with Making Ushuaia Strategic
Hub for Entire South Atlantic', www.riotimesonline.com/brazil-news/m
ercosur/argentina/argentina-moves-forward-with-making-ushuaia-a-strateg
ic-location-for-the-entire-south-atlantic/ (accessed 19 May 2022).

64 Government of Argentina, 'Con Un Nuevo Cargamento De Sinopharm,
Argentina Superó Las 47 Millones De Vacunas', 21 August 2021. www.
argentina.gob.ar/noticias/con-un-nuevo-cargamento-de-sinopharm-argenti
na-supero-las-47-millones-de-vacunas.

65 Agustin Geist, 'In Argentina's North, a "White Gold" Rush for EV Metal Lithium Gathers Pace', Reuters, 14 September 2021. www.reuters.com/world/americas/argentinas-north-white-gold-rush-ev-metal-lithium-gathers-pace-2021-09-14/.

5   The BRI in the Pacific Islands

Introduction

The Pacific Islands remained outside the zone of strategic concern in the Asia-Pacific region for much of the Cold War. Divided into four informal 'spheres of influence' led by the United States, Australia, France and New Zealand, they remained afloat economically through donor aid, tourism and income from fishing, their most significant natural resource.[1]

This relative calm encouraged a drift in US and Australian attention, creating a vacuum that the People's Republic of China began to fill. In the early 2000s China began to expand its diplomatic efforts, seeing an opportunity to expand its strategic reach eastward. China's objectives in the region involve extending its security perimeter eastward to create a buffer between the United States and the Chinese mainland.[2] They also include prevailing in the diplomatic contest with the Republic of China (Taiwan) – especially regarding its 'one China' policy, increasing its access to South Pacific natural resources, mainly fish, and selling infrastructure.[3]

In each area, China has made progress. China is the largest trading partner for many of the islands. China is now a significant aid provider, allocating almost US $6,000m. in grants and concessional loans linked to infrastructure and other Belt and Road (BRI) activities.[4]

The United States and other Western allies remain concerned that China's stepped-up lending could cause unsustainable debt levels that force the Pacific Island nations to comply with China's strategic interests. Some fear that China may eventually establish military bases to further its Pacific security objectives. China now demands that the Pacific Islands Forum formally adopt a one China policy, causing a rift.[5]

Given their location and size, the island nations of the Pacific share many similarities. With the exception of Papua New Guinea (PNG),

DOI: 10.4324/b23227-5

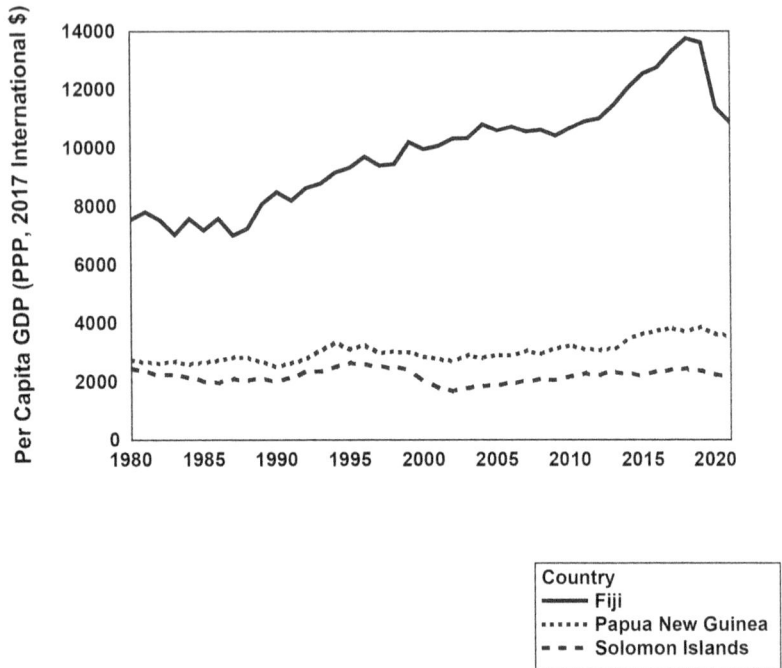

Figure 5.1 Per Capita Income Growth in the Pacific, 1980–2021
Source: International Monetary Fund, World Economic Outlook Database: October 2021.

they have narrow resource bases with limited arable land. Those that possess more diverse resources, including minerals, timber and commercial agriculture, have frequently suffered over-exploitation and depletion of resources. Enormous distances from population centres make tourism expensive and susceptible to economic downturns in the richer countries.

Because they are highly vulnerable to cyclones, droughts and the impact of rising sea levels, sharp economic downturns frequently make high sustained growth rates challenging. In 2021 Fiji had the highest per capita income (on a purchasing-power parity basis at 2017 international dollars) at $10,891 (Figure 5.1), followed by PNG ($3,601) and the Solomon Islands ($2,205). Per capita GDP growth was extremely sluggish after 2010 and even more so after 2015, with declines occurring in all three countries. PNG's economy performed best with an average per capita income growth of 1.3% from 2010–15, dropping to 0.5% from 2016–21. The Solomon Islands were next with

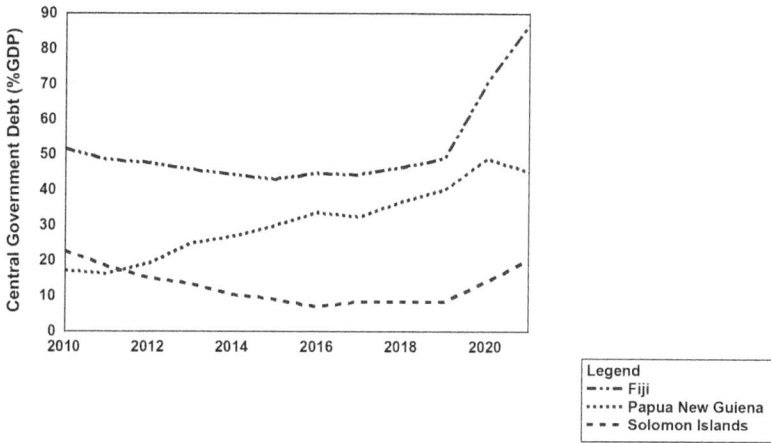

Figure 5.2 Government Debt as a % of GDP in the Pacific, 2010–21
Source: International Monetary Fund, World Economic Outlook Database:
October 2021.

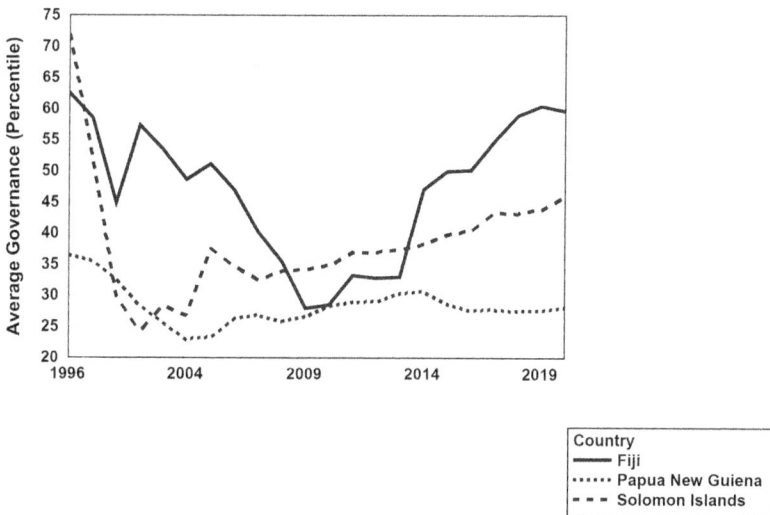

Figure 5.3 Governance Levels in the Pacific, 1996–2020
Note: Governance is the average of its components: voice and accountability,
political stability and absence of violence/terrorism, government effectiveness,
regulatory quality, rule of law and control of corruption.
Source: World Bank, Worldwide Governance Indicators Database.

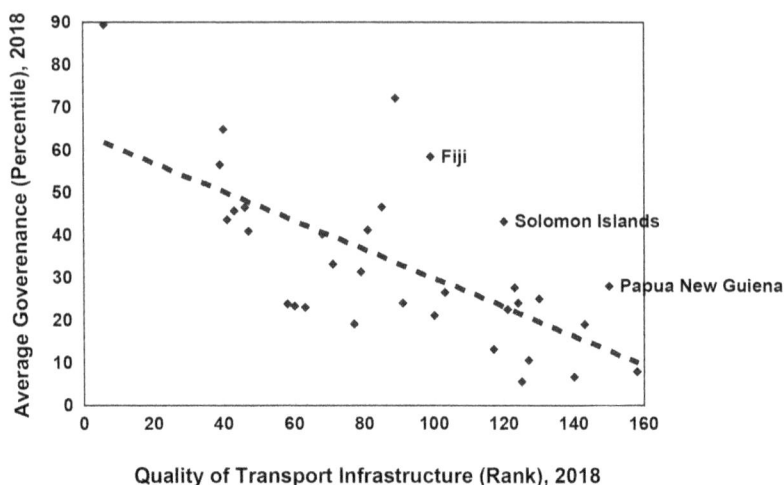

Figure 5.4 Governance/Transport Infrastructure Quality Relationship in the
        Pacific, 2018
Source: Governance: World Bank, Worldwide Governance Indicators Database; Infrastructure: World Bank, Logistics Performance Index Database.

corresponding rates of 0.6% and –0.4%, while Fiji's growth declined from 0.5% per annum in the first period to –0.4% in the second.

BRI programmes play out somewhat differently across the region, given the diverse environments. However, there are some common themes. The coronavirus COVID-19 pandemic, recent natural disasters and resulting expanded government expenditures produced rising debt levels (Figure 5.2), which will constrain government expenditures in all three countries, and perhaps their willingness and ability to take on additional Chinese debt.

Governance levels are low (Figure 5.3), with Fiji at the 60th percentile in 2020 (up from the 28th percentile in 2010, the Solomon Islands at the 46th percentile, and PNG at the 28th with minimal improvement after bottoming out at the 33rd percentile in 2005. The transport quality of all three countries is underachieving in the sense that the quality of their transport infrastructure is considerably below the levels usually associated with their governance levels (Figure 5.4). Under the right fiscal circumstances, they should be ideal candidates for expanded BRI programmes. Unfortunately, all three countries experienced increased fiscal stress following the pandemic.

Papua New Guinea

The PNG economy centres on resource extraction, fishing and agriculture. Its principal exports include liquefied natural gas (LNG) and gold. Politics in PNG is volatile, and social unrest is common. In 2018 PNG became the first Pacific Island nation to join China's BRI formally. The move reflected the country's shifting trade patterns towards China. Although Australia remains PNG's largest bilateral trade partner, China has overtaken that country as the largest source of foreign direct investment in recent years. China's first project in PNG commenced in March 2005. Since then, the government has invested $5,640m. in fifteen projects.

Since October 2013 China has had ten BRI projects totalling $3,350, the most recent in February 2019. Three sectors – metals ($930m.), energy ($880m.) and real estate ($730m.) – have attracted the bulk of Chinese investment.[6] Major projects include a large-scale road construction project involving several Chinese firms. Another BRI project involves an integrated agricultural and industrial park in the Eastern and Western Highlands Provinces.

Several difficulties have arisen from PNG's BRI projects. The $32m. Goroka water supply project has encountered many challenges.[7] In April 2019 protesting landowners cut off the water coming into the treatment plant. The landowners claimed that they had been waiting twenty years for promised lease payments. This incident reflects widespread and growing local resentment towards Chinese projects.

Several factors limit the potential benefits of BRI projects in PNG, especially those expected to generate follow-on investment and business activity. Unfortunately, the country's business climate has deteriorated in recent years, with PNG's ranking falling to 120th (out of 190 countries) in the World Bank's *Ease of Doing Business 2020* report.[8] The World Bank governance indicators for 2020 also give PNG low rankings in several key areas. In 2020 PNG ranked on the 19th percentile for government effectiveness, the 26th percentile for regulatory quality, the 25th percentile for the rule of law, and the 31st percentile for control of corruption.

These deficiencies manifest themselves in several potential projects. The first involves the Chinese-financed Ramu 2 hydropower facility, championed by the Chinese and William Duma, the former PNG Minister for Public Enterprises and State Investments.[9] Preliminary analysis suggests that if Ramu 2 moves ahead, it will become one of the world's most expensive hydropower projects. Its generation costs could be twice the levels in the country's other hydropower plants. The second controversial area involves rural electrification. PNG's parliamentary opposition has claimed that the government has been awarding contracts for power projects to Chinese companies China without calling for open and competitive tendering.[10]

Increased political uncertainty is also likely to affect BRI projects in PNG. Prime Minister James Marape's resource nationalism pledge, 'PNG first', delivered soon after assuming office in May 2019, and to 'take back the economy' from foreigners could see Chinese projects coming under review, influencing future projects and the country's growth and debt servicing capacity.[11]

While the full extent of the conditions with Chinese state-led economic investment is usually unclear, one clause usually entails the use of Chinese labourers. Given reports of locals complaining about job losses to Chinese workers, there is a reasonable likelihood of increased restrictions in this area. There is also an increased anti-Chinese backlash from some segments of the population. In 2009 Asian (primarily Chinese) businesses came under attack in Port Moresby and Lae after shopkeepers protested against new retailers. Furthermore, anti-Chinese riots took place in 2007 in the Western Highlands city of Mount Hagen.[12]

Some of these difficulties involve institutional and cultural factors. A long-time observer, Ian Kemish, a former senior Australian diplomat, notes that 'there is a "top down" assumption by Chinese organizations that successful implementation will follow if agreements occur at the highest level'.[13] This is wrong. 'PNG and other Pacific cultures operate on a consensus-based approach, where individual landowners and other local stakeholders will reject deals framed without consultation at the national level and if there are no clear local benefits'.[14]

Moreover, PNG's relationship with China has not lived up to expectations. PNG officials believed that China would come to the country's aid during periods of high budgetary stress.[15] That has not happened, and the government has had to rely on loans from Australia during these periods.

As for the future, it is likely that there will be ongoing political uncertainty as the Marape government seeks a more active role in the exploitation of natural resources, while environmental groups could also create new legal obstacles to massive projects. A weaker fiscal position following the COVID-19 crisis will restrict the government's ability to drive infrastructure development over the coming years.

The deterioration in the country's fiscal accounts is accelerating. Government revenues averaged 21.5% of gross domestic product (GDP) from 2000–09 but fell to 18.3% from 2010–21. Simultaneously, government expenditures increased from 20.3% of GDP in the first period to 21.9%. While the government experienced an average fiscal surplus of 1.1% of GDP from 2000–09, an average deficit of 3.7% emerged from 2010–21. The deficit has increased significantly in recent years, increasing from 2.0% of GDP in 2018 to 7.3% in 2020 and to 6.6% in 2021. As a result, government debt as a share of GDP increased from 17.3% of GDP in 2010 to 40.0% in 2019, prior to the outbreak of the COVID-19 pandemic. By 2021 the ratio stood at 45.5%.

While the debt ratio of 45.5% is relatively low by developing country standards, it is still higher than its Fiscal Responsibility Act limit of 35%. Debt servicing will soon reach over 10% of government spending, thus exposing the country to adverse external developments. By 2019 the government began to face borrowing difficulties, with delays in securing funds from the Asian Development Bank and the World Bank, and a $300m. (around 1,000m. kina) loan from the China Development Bank.

China has also emerged as PNG's largest bilateral creditor, with 85.8% of the country's bilateral debt together with 23.7% of its external debt.[16] In August 2019 rumours suggested that Prime Minister Marape had asked China to refinance its entire debt stock and to restructure it on more favourable terms.[17]

There are growing concerns that PNG's fiscal troubles will cause the country to be more dependent on Chinese loans and thus increasingly beholden to China's strategic interests in the region. These fears will grow after PNG recently voted to support China's new National Security Law in Hong Kong, a law drawing sharp criticism from Australia and the West. The country is facing a period of increased austerity. Emerging budget constraints are likely to limit the government's capacity for growth-supporting capital spending and its ability to take on many more additional BRI projects.

Fiji

In 1975 Fiji was the first Pacific Island nation to recognize China, and the two countries have maintained close relations over the years. This link was strengthened following sanctions imposed in response to Fiji's 2006 military coup.[18] Fiji joined the BRI in November 2018 with a memorandum of understanding of cooperation within the BRI framework, which ensured that China further expanded its investment in the country.[19] As of early 2021 China had undertaken three significant projects totalling $400m., including construction of the Nabouwalu–

Dreketi road, the Somosomo hydropower station and the Juncao Mushroom Demonstration Center.[20]

Fiji is likely to benefit from BRI membership through structuring it to meet its own specific needs and goals.[21] First, this will garner increased financial assistance to stabilize and expand its economy. Second is the likely increase in aid from traditional allies such as Australia and the United States. The third is the possibility of using the BRI to become a regional hub connecting smaller Pacific economies' trade to China.

Concurrently, Fiji will probably find itself at the centre of a geopolitical struggle between China and Australia in the Pacific region. In this situation, Fiji will probably attempt to strengthen its relations with China and improve its existing ties with Australia. China lacks the same economic leverage over Fiji as do other Pacific nations, such as Tonga and Samoa. As of early 2020 Fiji's debt to China amounted to just 10% of its total public debt – far less than that of its regional peers.[22] Therefore, Fiji will also seek to take advantage of Australia's latest re-engagement within the Pacific.

Since 2016 Fiji has been recovering from a series of cyclones, the most recent of which, Cyclone Cody, struck in January 2022, along with a tsunami from the volcanic eruption near Tonga on 20 December 2021, that has caused widespread damage to its infrastructure. The government hopes to improve its infrastructure's resilience to storms and to structure it to play an essential role in expanding its economic growth rate. However, this effort has strained the country's fiscal resources and resulted in stagnant growth. Per capita incomes declined at an average annual rate of 1.2% from 2015–21. During this period government deficits averaged 6.2% of GDP.

Unfortunately, many of the potential benefits stemming from the BRI will occur further into the future because of the harsh economic impact of the COVID-19 pandemic. According to the International Monetary Fund (IMF), the collapse of tourism caused GDP to contract by 15.7% in 2020 and by 4.0% in 2021. With high budget deficits, government debt increased from 43.0% of GDP in 2015 to 86.8% by 2021. The IMF is forecasting a further increase to 90.1% in 2022 before gradually declining to the still high level of 80.1% in 2026. While low interest rates and concessional loans should contain the immediate risks associated with such a rapid rise in public debt, this debt burden is unsustainable for an economy of Fiji's size and structure. It leaves the country exposed to future economic or fiscal shocks.

In 2018 the World Bank ranked the quality of Fiji's transport infrastructure 99th out of 120 countries. However, given the pattern of infrastructure and governance noted in Appendix A, Fiji's high level of governance would typically result in the country being ranked at around 20th position. Fiji is an infrastructure underachiever and thus a good expansion for BRI programmes where improved governance is not needed to improve the country's infrastructure. Unfortunately, the country's dire fiscal situation will limit its capacity to take on more debt. Instead, the government will have to rely on aid from Australia and the United States for crucial infrastructure upgrades and expansion.

Solomon Islands

Similarly to other Pacific Island countries, growth in the Solomon Islands has been declining in recent years, with per capita incomes contracting at an average rate of 0.4% from 2015–21. The country lacks a dominant industry but is working to diversify its sources of economic growth. Although it does not have a comprehensive development strategy incorporating an expansion in infrastructure, the country is in discussions with China for a series of BRI projects following its decision in September 2019 to switch its diplomatic relations from Taiwan to China.[23]

In October 2021 the country joined China's BRI.[24] In November reports suggested that the China State Railway Group Company would build a port, roads, railways, bridges and a hydropower plant as part of a $825m. programme to revive the Solomon Islands' gold mining industry.[25] China has also shown a willingness to finance the construction of sports facilities, including a new stadium in the capital, Honiara, for the 2023 Pacific Games.[26] However, as of early 2021 the only BRI-type project listed in the American Enterprise Institute database is a $310m. construction and mining project signed by China's Jiangxi Wanguo, AXF, in February 2019.

In sharp contrast to PNG and Fiji, excessive public debt is unlikely to be a constraining factor in influencing the government's decisions on an expanded BRI effort. As of 2021 government debt stood at only 20.4% of GDP, with the IMF projecting a rise to only 30.2% by 2026.

In 2018 the quality of the Solomon Islands' transport infrastructure ranked 120th. Given that the country's governance was on the 42nd percentile, the typical infrastructure pattern would have supported a ranking of around 70th, suggesting that the country was a clear underachiever. Although robust infrastructure-led growth should provide a powerful stimulus to the economy and place the country on a higher growth path, the government's concern with a possible anti-China backlash may limit the BRI's role.

Prime Minister Manasseh Sogavare's decision to switch diplomatic recognition from Taiwan to China in 2009 was highly unpopular and has been a source of ongoing tensions. Riots broke out in the capital, Honiara, in November 2021, and Sogavare survived a vote of no confidence in December of that year.[27] Previously riots had taken place near Chinatown in the capital, prompted by politicians' links with Asian (primarily Chinese) businesses.[28] Similar riots broke out in 2006 over Asian citizens being allowed to buy real estate and other assets.[29]

There is also ongoing concern about China exerting excessive control or influence over the islands. Often cited is the 2019 instance of a Chinese company's attempt to lease the entire island of Tulagi, an action eventually vetoed as unlawful by the Solomon Islands government. In 2021 the Australian government aided the funding of a buyout of telecoms firm Digicel South Pacific to prevent it from falling under Chinese control. However, the country's March 2022 security treaty with China has raised concerns that the Solomon Islands is becoming more and more dependent on China, although it may only be a means of protecting the country's Chinese settlers.[30]

Smaller Countries

Although data on Vanuatu, Tonga and Samoa are not as complete as that on the three countries previously discussed, they all offer interesting BRI insights. Their experiences identify a common set of problems faced by smaller countries when dealing with China.

Vanuatu

When in office, Vanuatu's pro-China Prime Minister, Charlot Salway, agreed that Taiwan was part of China.[31] Under his watch, Vanuatu joined China's BRI in May 2019. Even before then, China's projects in Vanuatu involved various activities, including an airport expansion. However, the project that has attracted the most attention is a massive wharf at Luganville.[32] Potentially, the wharf could dock aircraft carriers, but because the project has not proven profitable, there is widespread suspicion that its real purpose is for future Chinese military use.

Another high-profile project involved the country's $28.5m. national convention centre, completed in 2016 and funded with aid from China. The centre, which is expensive to operate, has failed to attract many events and is often referred to by critics as a 'white elephant', symbolic of the risks of poor planning and the geopolitical struggle for influence in the region.[33] In late 2019 Vanuatu transferred maintenance to a Chinese company and requested auxiliary aid from China for building upgrades.[34] Ralph Regenvanu, the then Minister of Foreign Affairs, International Co-operation and External Trade, conceded that Vanuatu's government had not undertaken a thorough assessment of its needs and was not sufficiently involved in the design process.

It is not clear what 'conditions' China attaches to its loans. In 2016 Vanuatu's government urged maritime claimants in the South China Sea to pursue 'friendly consultation and negotiation' instead of seeking third-party arbitration.[35] In doing so, Vanuatu joined Lesotho and the Palestinian Territories in this position, which China had advanced to challenge the legitimacy of the Philippines' case before a United Nations (UN) Convention on the Law of the Sea tribunal.

Not all Chinese projects in Vanuatu have proved problematic for the country. In Tanna, the island's first tar-sealed road is under construction, with a loan of almost $100m. from the Export-Import Bank of China. However, China's influence in Vanuatu is facing growing competition from developed economies. And there is increasing pushback from citizen groups arguing that there exists a government contracting bias against local companies while favouring large Chinese companies such as China's Civil Engineering Construction Corporation.[36]

According to the IMF, as of 2020 Vanuatu had a government debt-to-GDP ratio of 47.7%, lower than that of Fiji (83.8%) and Samoa (55.6%), but this remained less than ideal, because of the country's vulnerability to natural disasters. The UN Risk Index (in 2017) ranked Vanuatu the world's most vulnerable country for disasters.[37] A prime example was Tropical Cyclone Pam that caused infrastructure damage equivalent to about 60% of GDP in 2015. The reconstruction costs resulted in government debt as a share of GDP increasing to 42.3% in 2016, up from 18.3% in 2014. By the end of 2019 Vanuatu owed China $130m., representing 43% of the country's external debt and 13% of its GDP.[38]

Despite the problems to date, association with China will probably support Vanuatu's growth over the next few years. However, excessive borrowing from China could seriously harm Vanuatu's long-term fiscal outlook, particularly if the Chinese-led projects do not stimulate follow-on private sector investments needed to build up the country's tax base.

Tonga

Tonga's economic growth slowed following the 2008–09 global downturn, dropping from an average annual rate of 4.5% in 1980–2007 to 1.5% in 2008–21. There has also been a significant increase in government expenditure in recent years. As a share of GDP, government expenditure rose from an average of 22% in 1999–2007 to 34.2% in 2008–21. The country's current account also experienced a marked deterioration, with deficits increasing from an average annual rate of 3.7% of GDP from 1980–2007 to 9.6% from 2008–21. External government debt-to-GDP rose from 34.0% in 2008 to 45.6% by 2021.

Reconstruction will dominate economic activity in the next few years, in the wake of the highly destructive Cyclone Gita in February 2018, Cyclone Harold in April 2020, and a devastating tsunami in January 2022.[39] Cyclone Gita alone caused $210m. worth of damage. Furthermore, the country is coping with the economic destruction caused by the precautionary COVID-19 lockdowns. The government imposed strict containment measures for longer than many other states amid fears that it could not cope with a severe local outbreak.

The country effectively received no income from international tourism for most of 2020 and well into 2021 with international travel is unlikely to normalize for several years with the potential for longer-lasting damage to the regional tourism sector given ongoing health concerns, travel restrictions and the financial difficulties facing many airlines. To offset the decline in tourism, the government hopes to attract investment to develop a broader private sector. However, Tonga's far-flung location significantly limits the scope for investment in some sectors (for instance, it cannot expect much in foreign investment in manufacturing for export). Unfortunately, the over-expansion of the public sector, together with weak institutional capacity, has suppressed the private sector's ability to expand and create jobs.

The country has fallen into a vicious circle, whereby slow growth has prompted increased government expenditure to sustain the economy. Unfortunately, the result has been to stifle the private sector, making the country more dependent on government expenditure funded through remittances, foreign assistance, and loans.

China's loans to Tonga started in 2007. Following a period of highly destructive riots in Nuku'alofa, the country's capital, the government contracted for a loan for $160m. to rebuild the central business district, and eventually agreed to borrow the funds from the Export-Import Bank of China.[40] Despite widespread concerns about becoming ensnarled in a Chinese debt trap, extensive borrowing from that country occurred in 2017 to build a series of government offices in the capital.[41] China also lent $33m. for the construction of facilities to enable Tonga to host the 2019 Pacific Games.

In the wake of Cyclone Gita in February 2018, Tonga's government asked China to waive the loan altogether. China denied the request even though King Tupou VI himself delivered the loan waiver plea. By August 2018 Tonga's debt to China amounted to around one-third of its GDP and the government's finances were severely strained from servicing the debt. A new repayment schedule began in September, thereby doubling Tonga's annual bill for servicing external debt. The financial stress of servicing its debt had already led Tonga to withdraw from hosting the 2019 Pacific Games, as China had declined previous requests for debt relief. Tonga appeared to be a classic debt trap case, putting China in a position to demand various government concessions. That picture changed somewhat in November 2018 when Tonga received a five-year moratorium on servicing its debt by joining the BRI.[42]

Samoa

Samoa's economic growth has disappointed, averaging slightly more than 3% per annum from 1990–2007, but falling to 0.7% from 2008–21. Since the closure, in August 2017, of Yazaki EDS Samoa, an automotive parts manufacturer that was the country's largest private sector employer and a major exporter, the government has focused on developing agriculture, tourism and construction projects. Policies to promote these sectors include streamlining the foreign investment process to encourage inward investment, upgrading existing transport and communications infrastructure, and constructing and expanding utility infrastructure.[43]

For growth to return to the 3% range, Samoa is looking to China besides traditional aid partners for infrastructure support. Historically, the country received grants from China and is fortunate in that its funding needs come at a time of increased competition between the West (primarily the United States, Australia, New Zealand and Japan) and China for influence in the Pacific.[44] This geopolitical competition could augur an increase in external grants, as well as loans with more generous conditions. The Pacific's strategic importance to both China and the West means that Samoa will probably reap these benefits without having to choose diplomatic sides.

Samoa developed closer ties with China after becoming the first Pacific island country to join the BRI in October 2018.[45] China has funded critical infrastructure projects, including upgrades to sports and transport facilities in the run-up to the 2019 Pacific Games. China has also provided funds to Samoa for other projects, including two new bridges – one to replace the Vaisigano Bridge next to the Sheraton Samoa Aggie Grey's Hotel on Apia's Beach Road and another across the Mali'oli'o River in Savai'i.

In October 2019 China and Samoa signed seven additional agreements involving Chinese help in infrastructure, agriculture, education and e-commerce.[46] Local media reported that it could help to fund the construction of a new commercial port in Asau or Vaiusu to service larger ships, although the Samoan government scrapped that project in July 2021 owing to the lack of significant benefits to the country.[47]

Despite many grants and assistance, Samoa's debt rose from 28.9% of GDP in 2008 to 47.6% in 2021. Debt levels also increased after damage caused by a tsunami in 2009, and a cyclone in 2012 necessitated spending for reconstruction and stimulus to support economic growth. Samoa, along with Vanuatu and Tonga, now finds itself among the world's most heavily indebted countries to China, leading to a high risk of expanded BRI activity in the country, especially given natural disasters and other external factors that are beyond its control.

Assessment

Given their governance levels, the model in Appendix A suggests that all three countries for which we have transport infrastructure quality data, namely Fiji, PNG and the Solomon Islands, are underachievers with the quality of their infrastructure below that expected. These countries should be ideal candidates for BRI projects with their supporting governance structures in place. However, rising debt levels in PNG and Fiji will limit BRI activity in those countries, while anti-Chinese sentiment remains a factor in the Solomon Islands, thereby significantly constraining infrastructure improvements. Fortunately, increased geopolitical competition between China and the United States, Australia, Japan coalition will probably result in more concessionary funds. Also, to counter China, the United States will probably expand its lending and aid programmes.

Something like the ambitious Blue Pacific Act, proposed by US congressional representative Ed Case, is one viable approach.[48] On paper, it would unlock over $1,000m. in new funding for the Pacific and make the United States the region's largest development partner. Adoption of the act is likely to be partial, however. Renewed US interest in the area promises Pacific Island nations deeper and more diversified funding options in the years to come.

Notes

1 United Nations, '5th United Nations Conference on the Least Developed Countries (LDC5)'. www.un.org/ldc5/about (accessed 20 May 2022).

2 Jonathan Pryke, 'The Risks of China's Ambitions in the South Pacific', Lowy Institute, 23 July 2020. www.lowyinstitute.org/publications/risks-china-s-ambitions-south-pacific.
3 Stephen Dziedzic, 'Beijing Doubles Down on Pacific Nations to Sever Ties with Taiwan and Adopt One China Policy', ABC News, 13 February 2019. www.abc.net.au/news/2019-02-14/beijing-lobbying-pacific-nations-to-recog nise-one-china-policy/10809412.
4 Jamie Smyth, 'Are Chinese White Elephants Drowning the Pacific Islands in Debt?', 21 November 2019. www.ozy.com/around-the-world/are-chine se-white-elephants-drowning-pacific-islands-in-debt/242612/.
5 Dziedzic, 'Beijing Doubles Down on Pacific Nations to Sever Ties with Taiwan and Adopt One China Policy'.
6 Sarah O'Dowd, 'The Belt and Road Initiative in Papua New Guinea', DEVPOLICY Blog. https://devpolicy.org/2019-Australasian-Aid-Confer ence/5FSarahO'Dowd.pdf (accessed 20 May 2022).
7 Mackenzie Smith, 'PNG Govt Pays out Landowners after Water Crisis', RNZ, 11 April 2019. www.rnz.co.nz/international/pacific-news/386830/p ng-govt-pays-out-landowners-after-water-crisis.
8 The World Bank, 'Ease of Doing Business Rank (1=Most Business-Friendly Regulations) - Papua New Guinea'. https://data.worldbank.org/ indicator/IC.BUS.EASE.XQ?locations=PG (accessed 20 May 2022).
9 *Post Courier*, 'US$2B Ramu 2 Hydro Power Project Stalled', 31 July 2019. https://postcourier.com.pg/us2b-ramu-2-hydro-power-project-stalled/.
10 Johnny Blades, 'US and NZ Stand by PNG Electricity Campaign despite Concerns', RNZ, 15 March 2019. www.rnz.co.nz/international/pacific-news/ 384723/us-and-nz-stand-by-png-electricity-campaign-despite-concerns.
11 US Department of State, '2020 Investment Climate Statements: Papua New Guinea'. www.state.gov/reports/2020-investment-climate-statements/ (accessed 20 May 2022).
12 ABC News, 'Nine Dead as PNG Ethnic Clashes Worsen', 5 February 2008. www.abc.net.au/news/2008-02-05/nine-dead-as-png-ethnic-clashes-worsen/1033066.
13 Ian Kemish, 'China Wants to Be a Friend to the Pacific, but so Far, It Has Failed to Match Australia's COVID-19 Response', *The Conversation*, 23 March 2022. https://theconversation.com/china-wants-to-be-a-friend-to-the-p acific-but-so-far-it-has-failed-to-match-australias-covid-19-response-144911.
14 Kinling Lo, 'China, Australia and the Big Questions over a Papua New Guinea Fishing Hub', *South China Morning Post*, 12 December 2020. www.scmp.com/news/china/diplomacy/article/3113690/china-australia-and-big-strategic-questions-over-papua-new.
15 *Belt and Road News*, 'China to Build Fishing Facility in Papua New Guinea', 13 December 2020. www.beltandroad.news/2020/12/13/china -to-build-fishing-facility-in-papua-new-guinea/.
16 Ashlee Betteridge, '2019 Australasian Aid Conference', Devpolicy Blog, 21 February 2019. https://devpolicy.org/events/event/2019-australasian-aid-co nference/.
17 *VOA News*, 'PNG Seeks Chinese Help to Refinance Debt, Boost Trade', 7 August 2019. www.voanews.com/a/economy-business_png-seeks-chinese-help-refinance-debt-boost-trade/6173384.html.

18 Sean McCormack, 'Fiji: U.S. Measures in Response to Military Coup', US Department of State, 19 December 2006. https://2001-2009.state.gov/r/pa/prs/ps/2006/78042.htm.

19 RNZ, 'Fiji Joins China's Belt and Road', 14 November 2018. www.rnz.co.nz/international/pacific-news/375972/fiji-joins-china-s-belt-and-road.

20 *Fiji Sun*, 'Successful Completion of Nabouwalu-Dreketi Highway'. https://fijisun.com.fj/2015/12/31/successful-completion-of-nabouwalu-dreketi-high way/ (accessed 20 May 2022).

21 Silk Road Briefing, 'China's Belt & Road Initiative in the Pacific Islands'. www.silkroadbriefing.com/news/2019/05/23/chinas-belt-road-initiative-paci fic-islands/.

22 Organisation for Economic Co-operation and Development, 'Financing for Sustainable Development', www.oecd.org/dac/financing-sustainable-de velopment/ (accessed 20 May 2022).

23 Kate Lyons, 'China Extends Influence in Pacific as Solomon Islands Break with Taiwan', *The Guardian*, 16 September 2019. www.theguardian.com/world/2019/sep/16/china-extends-influence-in-pacific-as-solomon-islands-b reak-with-taiwan.

24 ABC News, 'Solomon Islands Joins China's Belt and Road, as Leaders Meet in Beijing', 10 October 2019. www.abc.net.au/news/2019-10-10/solom on-islands-joins-chinas-belt-and-road-as-leaders-meet/11590068.

25 Jonathan Barrett, 'China Cites "Early Harvest" Benefits in Guadalcanal Deal', Reuters, 30 October 2019. www.reuters.com/article/us-china-solom onislands/china-cites-early-harvest-benefits-in-guadalcanal-deal-idUSKBN 1X909A.

26 *Saipan Tribune*, 'Preparations for 2023 Pacific Games Moving Forward', 8 October 2020. www.saipantribune.com/index.php/preparations-for-2023-p acific-games-moving-forward-2/.

27 BBC News, 'Solomon Islands PM Survives No-Confidence Vote after Unrest', 6 December 2021. www.bbc.com/news/world-asia-59501054.

28 Michael E. Miller, 'Australia Deploys Forces to Solomon Islands as Protesters Burn Chinatown, Parliament', *Washington Post*, 26 November 2021. www.wa shingtonpost.com/world/asia_pacific/solomon-islands-unrest-protests-china/20 21/11/24/807c68e2-4d18-11ec-a7b8-9ed28bf23929_story.html.

29 *The Economist*, 'Overseas and under Siege', 14 September 2009. www.economist.com/news/2009/08/11/overseas-and-under-siege.

30 *The Economist*, 'China Makes Inroads in the Solomon Islands', 2 April 2022.   www.economist.com/asia/2022/04/02/china-makes-inroads-in-the-so lomon-islands.

31 David Wroe, 'Vanuatu PM Defends China Deals but Vows to Oppose Any New Foreign Military Base', *Sydney Morning Herald*, 12 April 2018. www.smh.com.au/politics/federal/vanuatu-pm-defends-china-deals-but-vows-to-oppose-any-new-foreign-military-base-20180412-p4z96m.html.

32 Ibid.

33 Jamie Smyth, 'China Aid Wins Influence in Pacific despite Rising Concerns', *Financial Times*, 14 November 2019. www.ft.com/content/bf2cfd72 -f6c1-11e9-9ef3-eca8fc8f2d65.

34 Jamie Smyth, 'Are Chinese White Elephants Drowning the Pacific Islands in Debt?' *Ozy*, 21 November 2019. www.ozy.com/around-the-world/a re-chinese-white-elephants-drowning-pacific-islands-in-debt/242612/.

35 *China Daily*, 'China Appreciates Position of Vanuatu, Lesotho, Palestine on S. China Sea Issue'. www.chinadaily.com.cn/world/2016-05/27/content_25490448.htm (accessed 23 May 2022).

36 Smyth, 'Are Chinese White Elephants Drowning the Pacific Islands in Debt?'

37 Duncan Madden, 'The World Risk Report Is out and a Tiny Island Paradise Is the Most Risk Prone Place on Earth', *Forbes Magazine*, 24 April 2018. www.forbes.com/sites/duncanmadden/2018/04/24/the-worldrisk report-is-out-and-a-tiny-island-paradise-is-the-most-risk-prone-place-on-e arth/?sh=5047e4a23da5.

38 The Economist Intelligence Unit, 'Australia and the US Seek Closer Ties with Vanuatu', 3 August 2020. https://country.eiu.com/article.aspx?arti cleid=1629968546&Country=Vanuatu&topic=Politics&subtopic=Forecast &subsubtopic=International%2Brelations.

39 The World Bank, 'Tonga Volcanic Eruption and Tsunami: World Bank Disaster Assessment Report Estimates Damages at US$90m.', 13 February 2022. www.worldbank.org/en/news/press-release/2022/02/14/tonga-v olcanic-eruption-and-tsunami-world-bank-disaster-assessment-report-esti mates-damages-at-us-90m.

40 *Future Directions*, 'Tonga Between an Irresistible Force and an Immovable Object', 30 July 2019. www.futuredirections.org.au/publication/tonga -between-an-irresistible-force-and-an-immovable-object/.

41 *South China Morning Post*, 'Is Chinese Money Creating a Debt Trap in Tonga?' 10 July 2019. www.scmp.com/news/china/diplomacy/article/ 3018029/chinese-money-creating-debt-trap-tonga.

42 ABC News, 'One Belt One Road: China Gives Tonga Five Years' Grace on Loan Repayments', 18 November 2018. www.abc.net.au/news/ 2018-11-19/china-defers-tongas-loan-payments-as-nation-signs-up-to-bri/1 0509140.

43 *Samoa Observer*, 'Economy to Take a Hit as Yazaki Announces Closure'. www.samoaobserver.ws/category/samoa/28432 (accessed 23 May 2022).

44 United Nations Development Programme, 'The Development Needs of Pacific Island Countries'. www.undp.org/content/dam/china/docs/Publica tions/UNDP_CH_SS_Publication_The%20Development%20Needs%20of%20 Pacific%20Island%20Countries%20REPORT.pdf (accessed 23 May 2022).

45 Silk Road Briefing, 'China's Belt & Road Initiative in the Pacific Islands', 13 June 2019. www.silkroadbriefing.com/news/2019/05/23/chinas-belt-roa d-initiative-pacific-islands/.

46 Ibid.

47 Jonathan Barrett, 'Samoa's New Leader Confirms Scrapping of China-Funded Port', Reuters, 30 July 2021. www.reuters.com/world/asia-pacific/ samoas-new-leader-confirms-scrapping-china-funded-port-2021-07-30/.

48 Ed Case, 'Introducing the Blue Pacific Act', 30 July 2020. https://case. house.gov/news/documentsingle.aspx?DocumentID=356.

6 The BRI in South-East Asia

Introduction

While sharing several economic characteristics, the South-East Asia group of sample countries, namely Brunei, Indonesia, Malaysia, the Philippines and Timor-Leste, differ significantly. Brunei is now the richest country (Figure 6.1) in per capita terms reaching US $45,413 (on a purchasing-power parity basis in 2017 international dollars) in 2021. Malaysia ranks next at $26,582, followed by Indonesia ($11,866), the Philippines ($8,145) and Timor-Leste ($2,842).

In recent years, growth in all five countries slowed. While the coronavirus COVID-19 pandemic was a factor, growth was already declining well before 2020. Brunei's per capita income growth declined at an average annual rate of 1.0% from 2010–15 and –0.9% from 2016–21. The corresponding figures for Indonesia were 4.1%, dropping to 2.5%. Malaysia's per capita income declined from 3.8% in the first period to 3.2% in the second, while in the Philippines growth fell from 4.5% to 1.8%. With oil production declining, Timor-Leste's per capita income declined from 0.3% before contracting to 0.2%. With rapidly rising debt levels (Figure 6.2) and slower world trade owing to the disruptive effects of the Russian Federation's invasion of Ukraine, slow growth is likely to continue for some time.

Governance varies considerably throughout the region but generally it has improved (Figure 6.3). Brunei consistently has the highest overall average governance (based on the World Bank's six governance dimensions, see below), followed by Malaysia. Indonesia and the Philippines followed suit after a significant drop-off in governance. However, while Indonesia's governance has shown steady improvement since 2003, governance in the Philippines levelled off in 2014 and has been declining ever since. Historically, Timor-Leste had the lowest level of governance among this group of countries. However, owing to

DOI: 10.4324/b23227-6

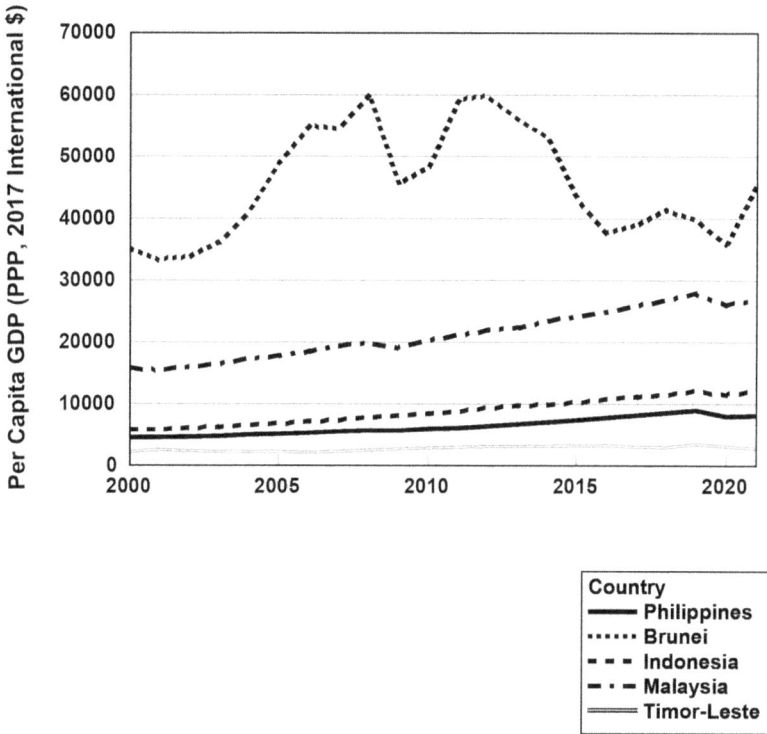

Figure 6.1 Per Capita Income Growth in South-East Asia, 1980–2021
Source: International Monetary Fund, World Economic Outlook Database:
October 2021.

a steady improvement since 2006, the country's governance is on the verge of surpassing that of the Philippines.

The quality of transport infrastructure present in Indonesia and the Philippines is roughly in line with that usually associated with those countries' level of governance (Figure 6.4). However, Malaysia and Brunei are underachievers in that the quality of their transport infrastructure is considerably below that usually supported by their governance structures. On this basis, both countries would seem to be prime candidates for Belt and Road (BRI) programmes.

Among this group of countries, in 2020 Indonesia had by far the most extensive stock of Chinese foreign direct investment (FDI) at $17,939,000m. Malaysia was second with $10,212,000m., followed by the Philippines at $7678m. Timor-Leste had 129.2m., with Brunei last at only $16.58m.

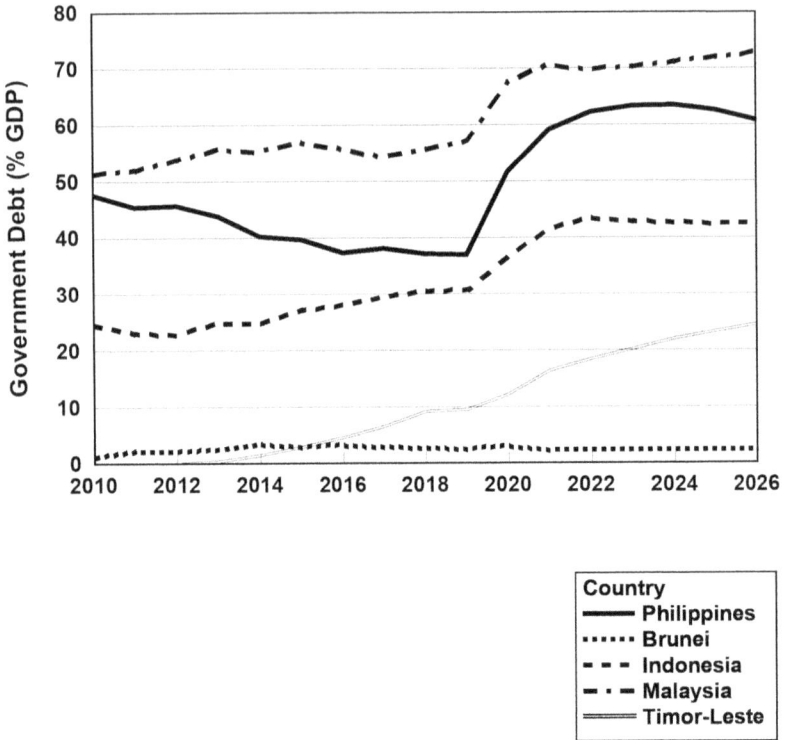

Figure 6.2 Government Debt as a % of GDP in South-East Asia, 2010–21
Source: International Monetary Fund, World Economic Outlook Database:
October 2021.

East Asia is a critical region in the US–China strategic rivalry. The region's states try to avoid being drawn in, individually and under the aegis of the Association of Southeast Asian Nations (ASEAN). If tensions between Washington and the People's Republic of China were to get out of hand, they could come under greater pressure to take sides. Three of our sample countries, the Philippines, Malaysia and Brunei, have territorial and jurisdictional claims that overlap with those of China. Indonesia that says it is not a claimant, even though it has a maritime boundary dispute with China.

While China and the United States compete for influence in South-East Asia, opinion polls repeatedly show that the region has little confidence in either country. In January, Singapore's ISEAS-Yusof Ishak Institute published the results of a survey conducted among

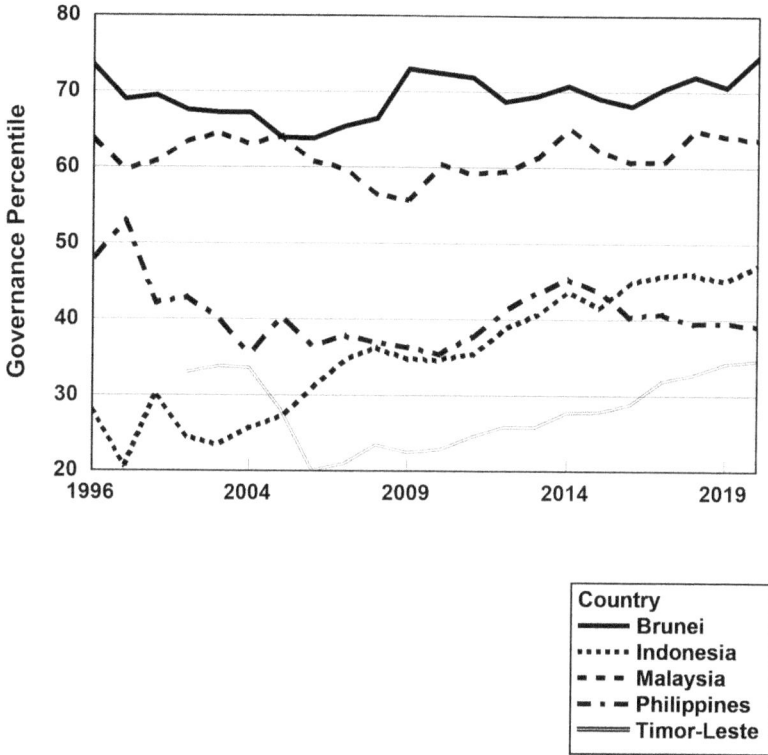

Figure 6.3 Governance Levels in South-East Asia, 1996–2020
Note: Governance is the average of its components: voice and accountability,
political stability and absence of violence/terrorism, government effectiveness,
regulatory quality, rule of law and control of corruption.
Source: World Bank, Worldwide Governance Indicators Database.

select East Asian professionals, which showed that little over 30%
trust the United States, and only approximately 16% trust China.

ASEAN's response to great power rivalry encourages strategic balance through equal engagement. South-East Asia states oppose Beijing's aggression in the South China Sea while maintaining strong
trading relations with China.

Brunei

The Sultanate of Brunei is unique to ASEAN because of its political
system (monarchy) and relatively high level of per capita income of
$65,674 (on purchasing-power parity basis in current prices) in 2021.

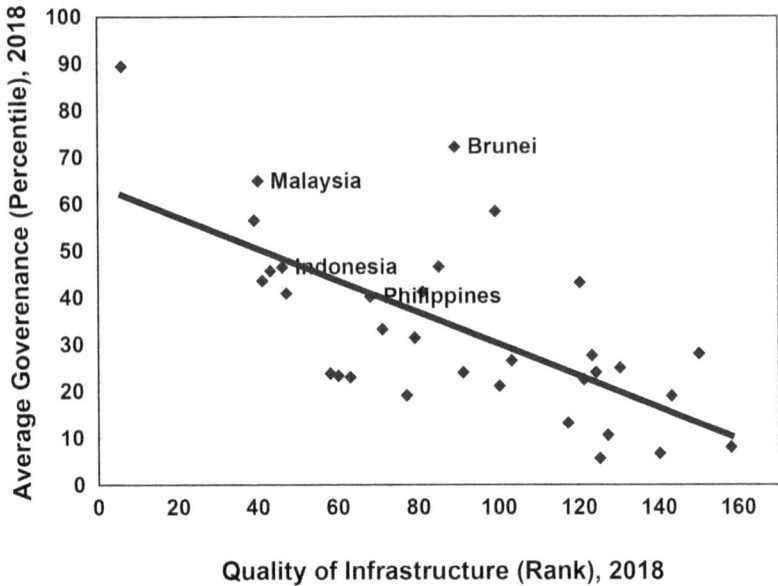

Figure 6.4 Governance/Transport Infrastructure Quality Relationship, South-East Asia, 2018
Note: The solid line represents the governance/infrastructure trend.
Source: Governance: World Bank, Worldwide Governance Indicators Database; Infrastructure: World Bank, Logistics Performance Index Database.

Brunei is Asia's third largest oil producer and fourth largest exporter of liquified natural gas (LNG).[1] Crude oil and natural gas account for nearly all its foreign exchange earnings and over 50% of its gross domestic product (GDP). Brunei joined the BRI in 2018.[2]

Economic growth has declined gradually since the 1980s, with average annual rates of GDP of 2.1% in the 1990s, 0.8% in the 2000s and 0.7% from 2010–21. This decline in growth has occurred despite relatively high investment rates, with investment as a share of GDP averaging 47.8% in the 1990s, 20.7% in the 2000s and 34.0% from 2010–21. Falling output from Brunei's ageing oil- and gasfields, which require regular maintenance, has kept GDP growth at its shallow levels in recent years.[3] However, new discoveries may halt this decline.[4]

As with many oil-producing developing countries, developing activities outside of hydrocarbons has proved difficult.[5] The country has gone through several five-year National Development Plans to promote a broader production base, but progress has been much slower than expected.[6] The government's current efforts appear in Wawasan

Brunei 2035 (The Brunei National Vision 2035).[7] This Plan aims to create a world-class educational system, a skilled workforce, and a dynamic and sustainable economy by 2035.

The government admits that the vision hinges on raising labour productivity. It intends to reduce the country's dependency on foreign labour, close skills mismatches, establish a framework for continuous education and training, and create a talent management and tracking system.

The Plan recognizes the need for greater private sector participation to create additional jobs and broad-based income. However, as of 2020 the private sector remains underdeveloped (3% of GDP), with most small and medium-sized enterprises found in the textiles, furniture and food sectors. The Plan's emphasis is on attracting FDI in the food, pharmaceutical, financial technology and petrochemical sectors. It is also looking to increase tourism.

The government is also undertaking reforms to improve productivity and the functioning of the economy. Among the countries examined in this chapter, Brunei scores relatively high in all the World Bank's governance dimensions, apart from voice and accountability. Improvements are ongoing, with control of corruption improving from the 72nd percentile in 2010 to the 75th percentile by 2020. During this period government effectiveness improved from the 78th percentile to the 90th percentile, and the rule of law rose from the 73rd percentile to the 80th percentile.

However, Brunei lacks the expertise and capacity to manage a substantial restructuring of its economy. Brunei is underachieving based on the normal governance/transport infrastructure quality relationship (Figure 6.4). Given this setting, Chinese investment should be very effective in stimulating growth. The government is turning to Chinese FDI and its engineering companies to expand its infrastructure and reduce its dependence on crude oil exports.[8] While Brunei joined the BRI in 2018, Chinese FDI has played a significant role since 2010 in improving the country's industrial infrastructure and transport network. Chinese construction companies have built highways, a dam and a viaduct. In 2020 China's FDI stock in Brunei was $390m.[9] Unlike in other South-East Asia countries, Chinese activities have attracted little controversy in Brunei.

As of early 2021, Brunei had four BRI-type projects spanning February 2010 to September 2015 and totalling $4,110m. The most significant BRI commitment to Brunei has come from China's Zhejiang Hengyi Group, which has pledged $3,400m. to develop the PMB oil refinery and petrochemical complex.[10] Following the first phase, a

$12,000m. second phase, including a port expansion, was expected to be completed in 2022. The authorities forecast that this project will generate 1,500 jobs. Brunei will refine 175,000 barrels per day (b/d), up from 10,000 b/d currently. The petrochemical facility will produce ethylene and paraxylene. When fully completed, the development could add up to 40% to Brunei's GDP.

Separately, in February 2017 Brunei's Darussalam Assets and China's Guangxi Beibu Gulf International Port Group initiated a joint-venture Muara Port Company to manage Brunei's largest container terminal.[11] A further agreement in September 2017 brought a commitment from Guangxi Beibu Gulf to construct an industrial park near the port.[12] The aim is to quadruple the port's capacity to 1m. 20-ft equivalent units.

While China's importance to Brunei is clear, Brunei's importance to China is more subtle. Some observers contend that China's financial and technical assistance is strategic making it difficult for the region's countries to form a consensus on opposition to Chinese South China Sea claims. Brunei has been reluctant to take a position on the matter.[13]

Indonesia

Indonesia is the largest country in South-East Asia in terms of both geographical size and population. It pursues a non-aligned foreign policy whereby it tries to balance its relations with the major powers. While the government of Indonesia says that it is not a claimant in the South China Sea, effectively it is because its exclusive economic zone (EEZ) around the Natuna Islands overlaps with the 'nine-dash line' that defines China's expansive claims.[14] The Indonesian government has repeatedly protested against Chinese incursions into its EEZ, albeit that the two countries have growing economic ties.

Although Indonesia's economy has maintained steady growth in recent decades, with GDP per capita (on a purchasing-power parity basis in 2017 international dollars) averaging 3.3% in the 1990s), 3.8% in the 2000s and 3.3% from 2010–21, growth is still not sufficient to reduce unemployment in the formal sector below 6.6% (2021). However, many Indonesians work in the informal sector, where under-employment is significant. As in many emerging economies, youth unemployment, which stood at 16.5% in 2020, is considerably higher at around three times the overall rate.[15]

Indonesia's physical infrastructure verges on substandard, although the quality of its transport infrastructure is consistent with its level of governance (Figure 6.4). The geographical reality of the country with its many islands makes it difficult to integrate the different infrastructure components. The World Bank observes that '[a] lack of good roads and transport corridors across the archipelago – a string of over 17,000 islands that would stretch from New York to London – are adding to logistical barriers and driving up costs for business'.[16]

President Joko 'Jokowi' Widodo came to power in 2014 and was subsequently re-elected for a final five-year term in 2019. He has staked his reputation on delivering high rates of economic growth. Jokowi's government set its sights on an infrastructure development-led recovery in 2021 and beyond. Plans for expanded infrastructure investment have faced considerable delays owing to the outbreak of the COVID-19 pandemic. Still, Jokowi delivered on some of his pledges. Indonesia's ranking on the World Bank's Logistic Performance Index (LPI) rose from 53rd position in 2014 to 46th position in 2018.

One of the most important and ambitious projects to be seriously delayed by the COVID-19 pandemic was the $35,000m. relocation of the country's administrative capital from Jakarta to a newly built outpost in East Kalimantan a province in the remote eastern part of the island of Borneo.[17] With this massive capital commitment, Indonesia will need more foreign investment to sustain robust growth, especially in transport infrastructure. Fortunately, the country has the financial freedom to move ahead in this area. During 2010–21 Indonesia's domestic savings, averaging 32.0% of GDP, sufficed to finance an average domestic investment rate of 33.6%. In addition, the country ran an average current account surplus of 0.2% of GDP.

With the government's budget deficits averaging only 2.6% of GDP, government debt levels rose only moderately from 24.5% of GDP in 2010 to 30.5% by 2019. However, owing to the COVID-19 pandemic, debt levels rose to 41.4% of GDP in 2021. There is still considerable flexibility in taking on additional debt to finance the planned step-up in infrastructure spending.

Indonesia's economic ties with China have become stronger during Jokowi's presidency, and the BRI is playing a significant role in expanding Indonesia's infrastructure. The consulting company Baker & McKenzie reported that 'from a geographic perspective, Indonesia stood to be the biggest beneficiary among the ASEAN economies, with more than $87 billion identified in the BRI-related pipeline of infrastructure projects'. As of early 2021, China had started eighty BRI-type projects beginning in October 2013 and running through April 2021, with a value of $39,600m. In Indonesia, infrastructure projects under the BRI scheme range from highways and airports to clean water supply and waste management.

China has had a longstanding interest in investing in the country. In a 2013 address to the Indonesian parliament, Chinese President Xi Jinping first unveiled the initial iterations of the maritime components of the BRI.[18] Indonesia abuts the Straits of Malacca, the busiest shipping route globally, connecting China with much of the Middle East and Europe's lucrative markets. Indonesia also provides China with raw materials such as coal, minerals and paper pulp that fuel Chinese industries. As a result, Indonesia's exports to China have flourished over the past few years, expanding from $15,100m. in 2015 to $27,100m. in 2018 and $31,800m. in 2020.[19] China is now Indonesia's largest export market, and China is Indonesia's largest source of imports.

Chinese FDI to Indonesia has soared in recent years, increasing from $200m. in 2010 to $1,560m. in 2014.[20] After falling to $1,270m. in 2014, FDI flows gradually increased to $2,220m. in 2019. During the pandemic year of 2020 Chinese FDI flows declined slightly to $2,200m. With these inflows, the stock of Chinese FDI in Indonesia increased from $1,150m. in 2010 to $8,130m. in 2015 and $17,940m. in 2020.

In July 2019 Indonesia requested China establish a special fund as part of the BRI to fund projects in Indonesia. The government reportedly offered China around thirty projects worth $91,000m. during the second Belt and Road Forum in April 2019.[21] In Indonesia's case, a critical definition problem has emerged: just what is a BRI project? Ironically, despite its size and scope, there is no official Chinese list of projects classified as BRI. Currently, the Indonesian government considers projects as BRI if they are part of the April 2019 package.[22] By that definition, China's largest project to date, the $6,000m. high-speed railway line connecting Jakarta and Bandung, the capital of West Java province, is not a BRI project. Yet it has many of the features that usually characterize a BRI project. The 140-km high-speed railway is Indonesia's first high-speed railway and will cut the journey time from three hours to 40 minutes.

China outbid Japan in September 2015 for the right to build the railway, mainly because it did not impose a debt guarantee on the Indonesian government.[23] The China Railway Group, which has a 40% share as a consortium member with several Indonesian state-owned companies, is building the railway. A China Development Bank loan provides 75% of the funding. The loan is for forty years with a ten-year grace period. The joint-venture partners will finance the rest of the project. Construction started in 2016, but soon encountered obstacles. It stalled in July 2018 due to three lawsuits seeking compensation for land acquisitions, but by March 2019 almost all the land acquisition had been completed. China suspended work after the onset of the COVID-19 crisis. However, it received a severe blow when the Indonesian government decided to move the administrative capital from Jakarta to East Kalimantan.[24] For the companies involved, the move means that it will be forty years before the project shows a profit.[25] The project also faces a cost overrun of more than $2,000m.

To avoid economic overdependence on China, Indonesia also pursues close ties with Japan. In 2017 Japan won a $4,000m. contract to construct a high-speed railway line between Jakarta and Surabaya, the capital of East Java province.[26] China and Japan have promised to integrate the Jakarta-Bandung and Jakarta-Surabaya links. However, differences in track gauges and train speeds could make it difficult for the systems to function together.

Despite China's involvement in Indonesia's infrastructure expansion, there has been widespread opposition to increased Chinese activity.[27] Complaints chiefly involve undue Chinese influence, losing jobs to Chinese workers and increased indebtedness to China. China must proceed carefully with its BRI programmes, given the history of nationalistic backlashes against its Chinese community. In a December 2019 interview, a deputy chairman of the Corruption Eradication Commission argued that the government should be 'more careful with investment from China' since that country is seeking greater 'economic influence'.[28]

The economic benefits aside, it may not matter to many Indonesians how diversified, or well-thought-out, these investment deals with China are. Indonesians simply judge Chinese money differently. A common , fear is that Chinese workers are stealing Indonesian jobs. Despite solid growth over the past few decades, many Indonesians remain unemployed, with the youth unemployment rate at 16.5% in 2020. The Indonesian media has reported that the influx of Chinese workers has occurred without significant checks and control in some areas. Some of them even arrived without the necessary valid documents.

Indonesia became a battleground during the general election of April 2019 when the opposition contended that the government's pro-China policies were saddling the country with debt. Trailing in the polls by double digits, former General Prabowo Subianto ran on a fiery nationalist ticket and pledged to re-evaluate Chinese investment, particularly the high-speed rail project.[29] Anti-Chinese sentiment is likely to continue to play a significant role in structuring the way in which the BRI evolves in Indonesia. A 2021 poll found that just 30%

of Indonesians would approve of a Chinese firm taking a majority stake in an Indonesian company, while 60% felt that 'Indonesia should join with other countries to limit China's influence'.[30]

Malaysia

Over the past few decades, Malaysia sustained relatively high GDP growth rates of 7.2% in the 1990s, 4.7% in the 2000s and 4.3% from 2020–21. During this time Malaysia evolved from a commodity exporter to a world-class electronics producer. Average governance has improved steadily, raising the country from the 43rd percentile in 2006 to the 52nd percentile by 2020. In 2021 the Heritage House Index of Economic Freedom classified the country as moderately free, up from mostly unfree in 2014.[31] These factors provide a solid foundation for economic growth.

However, Malaysia is very open to world market forces, thus making the country vulnerable to global price shocks and volatile capital flows. Oil-related taxes contribute around 15.0% of government revenues.[32] With other sources of revenue underdeveloped, the country is increasingly encountering budgetary and debt constraints. After running an average budget surplus of 2.0% of GDP in the 1990s, deficits averaged 4.0% per annum in the 2000s and 3.4% from 2010–21. As a result, government debt as a percentage of GDP rose from 51.1% in 2010 to the dangerous level of 70.7% in 2021. By regional standards, wages are relatively high in Malaysia. With government investment constrained by high debt levels, Malaysia needs a steady stream of inward investment to sustain growth and improve living standards. China has been a significant source of such funds.

The two countries have a long history. In 1974 Malaysia became the first country in South-East Asia to normalize relations with China. Since then, Malaysia and China have maintained one of the more positive bilateral relationships in the region. This relationship has become stronger since 1974, with Malaysia undertaking a foreign policy reorientation that saw the country adopting strategic neutrality between the major powers. However, the relationship did not significantly expand until the 1990s when Mahathir Mohamad, who also served as the fourth Prime Minister from 1981–2003, made the strategic decision in the early 1990s that relations with China would have to improve further.[33]

In 2004 Malaysia and China established a 'Strategic Partnership'.[34] In 2013, during the Najib Abdul Razak administration (2009–18), Malaysia-China relations advanced to a 'Comprehensive Strategic

Partnership', which roughly coincided with the launch of the BRI in the same year.

Malaysia's existing transport network is relatively well developed; however, all sectors would benefit from further expansion and modernization, particularly as the country is expanding its role as a regional transit and manufacturing hub. Given the country's relatively high level of governance (65th percentile in 2018), the quality of Malaysia's transport infrastructure should rank in the teens rather than 40th in 2018 (Figure 6.4). Incorporating China's BRI should help to drive investment towards the transport infrastructure segment.

As of early 2021, China had ninety projects in Malaysia, with sixty BRI projects starting in December 2013. The total amount invested came to $43,820m., with $30,610m. in BRI activities. China's BRI involvement in Malaysia has focused on six major projects: Bandar Malaysia terminus, Kuantan Port and Malaysia-China Kuantan Industrial Park, Malacca Gateway port and Jasin Industrial Park, East Coast Rail Link (ECRL), Gemas–Johor Bahru Double Track Railway, and Kuala Lumpur–Singapore High-Speed Rail.[35]

Bandar Malaysia's fate has been uncertain since the termination of an agreement with a Malaysian-Chinese consortium in May 2016 and with the change of government two years later.[36] The ECRL and the High-Speed Rail projects have been suspended at times, with the former project alleged to involve corruption in the Najib government.[37] Several of these projects have been deservedly called 'white elephants', with work suspended or terms renegotiated.[38] Others have come under intense criticism as being too expensive or poorly negotiated on Malaysia's part. The Kuala Lumpur–Singapore High-Speed Rail project was cancelled at great expense in early 2021.

According to the 11th Malaysia Plan (2016–20), formulated under the Najib administration, urban public transport systems such as Mass Rail Transit 1 (MRT 1) and MR2 within the Klang Valley area were built or planned to be built.[39] Highways for regions that have lagged behind the prosperous west coast of Peninsular Malaya, such as the east coast and the Borneo states of Sabah and Sarawak, were also planned to be constructed.

The ECRL was conceived before the Najib administration came to power, but the previous governments shelved it owing to the lack of funding. Given China's willingness to finance the project, the ECRL seemed to be a perfect case to set an example for Malaysia-China cooperation under the BRI: Malaysia needed to develop the east coast through the ECRL and there would be guaranteed local participation in sub-contract works.

Unfortunately, controversy surrounded the project from the outset. The primary concerns involved its cost, direct negotiation instead of open tender, lack of profitability and commercial viability, long-term financial risks to Malaysia in terms of debts, and allegations of corruption.[40] The ECRL, together with several other controversial projects (including the Forest City, a private sector real estate project), typifies the negative perceptions about Chinese companies operating in Malaysia's infrastructure, construction and real estate sectors: being less transparent and corruption-prone; contributing less to in terms corporate social responsibility; employing fewer local workers; sourcing less from local suppliers; having little interest in respecting local culture; and showing scant concern about the possible adversarial effects of such projects on the local ecology in Malaysia's society.[41]

Many of these issues came to a head in May 2018 when Dr Mahathir bin Mohamad came out of retirement at the age of ninety-three to become Prime Minister of Malaysia again.[42] In his election campaign, Mahathir accused his predecessor, Najib Razak, of 'selling out' the country to China.[43] Mahathir pledged a thorough review of Chinese-financed projects and cancelled those that the government could not afford. Mahathir also warned against 'new colonialism'.[44] At the time, Malaysia was the second largest recipient of BRI funding after Pakistan. After his review, Mahathir signalled that several projects were questionable, particularly the $13,000m. ECRL.[45]

Subsequently, the two sides reached a deal, with China reducing the original cost by around one-third.[46] Mahathir expressed his firm support for the BRI. If Malaysia had cancelled the rail contract, it would have been obliged to pay a termination cost of $5,300m. to China. The rail design agreed upon prioritized cultural, heritage and environmental factors. The incident suggests that China is willing and able to work around internal developments in partner nations to reach win-win agreements.

Mahathir also raised questions concerning BRI projects involving the country's two most significant port projects, the Kuantan Port and the Melaka Gateway. Both came under criticism from the former government for being too expensive and not benefiting local workers and businesses. The Melaka Gateway project, valued initially at RM 30,000m., looks unlikely to proceed after the government cancelled key contracts in October 2020. It is debatable whether the uncertainty created by Mahathir affected Chinese FDI, but it has fallen in recent years. In 2016 Chinese FDI reached a high of $1,830m., up from $488.9m. in 2015. Since 2016 Chinese FDI has declined each year, reaching $1,110m. in 2019 before recovering to $1,370m. in 2020.

Shortly after succeeding Mahathir as Malaysian Prime Minister, in mid-March 2020 Muhyiddin Yassin pledged to continue the infrastructure projects included in the 2020 budget. However, the worsening COVID-19 situation in the country forced the government to impose lockdown-like orders. 'Critical works' could proceed; these this included projects that improve the safety of users of infrastructure, such as bridge and pothole repairs. As the pandemic began to wind down in 2022, BRI projects were expected to resume their normal pace. Transport infrastructure development will remain a chief priority, as well as improved connectivity.

In August 2021 the China Communications Construction Company awarded IJM Construction a RM 258.0m. ($60.9m.) contract for the 191.14-km ECRL project in Temerloh, Pahang. The project falls under the BRI. Currently under construction, ECRL should be fully operational in 2027. In the long term, businesses in this region will enjoy lower transport costs and delivery times. The completed rail project will offer companies an efficient alternative to inland shipment of goods.

To many observers, Malaysia's relationship with China provides a model for Asia.[47] It represents a pragmatic approach on both sides, allowing for flexibility to change course or renegotiate when projects are off course or not working to meet originally intended goals.

The Philippines

For many years, observers often referred the Philippine economy to as the 'sick man of Asia'.[48] In sharp contrast to the so-called miracle economies of the Republic of Korea (South Korea), the Republic of China (Taiwan), Hong Kong and Singapore, during the 1960s, 1970s and 1980s, the Philippine economy failed to replicate their annual growth rates of 5%–7% in per capita income. Instead, the Philippine economy experienced a mediocre performance, characterized by 'stop-start' patterns of economic growth, periods of falling incomes and stubbornly persistent poverty. In part, the country's poor economic performance stemmed from its inward-looking, consumption-based development strategy rather than its prosperous neighbours' highly successful export-orientated strategy.[49] During this period the Philippine economy was relatively insensitive to fluctuations in global markets, and internal political instability played a much more significant role in affecting economic growth. Per capita income in the Philippines grew at an average annual rate of 1.8% in the 1960s and 2.9% in the 1970s. However, income growth contracted at an average yearly rate of 0.8% in the 1980s.

Even after the economic miracle, when growth in Asian countries began to slow, the Philippine economy continued to lag behind. While the overall average annual rates of GDP growth in developing and emerging Asia amounted to 5.1% in the 1980s and 4.6% in the 1990s, the Philippines recorded average annual growth of just 2.0% in the 1980s and 2.8% in the 1990s. Then, in the 2000s the situation changed, with growth in the Philippines averaging 4.5% per annum, compared with 4.4% in developing and emerging Asia. This convergence of growth rates continued in 2010–21, when the Philippine economy averaged 4.8% annually, compared with only 4.0% for its Asian counterparts.

Much of the Philippine economy's recent success stems from the reforms started by President Benigno 'Noynoy' Aquino III. Voters elected Aquino President in 2010, and his administration's chief slogan was 'kung walang kurap, walang mahirap' ('if there is no corruption, there will be no poverty').[50] Aquino's principal reforms led to a significant improvement in governance and economic competitiveness. Global investor sentiment regarding the Philippines steadily improved during his administration (2010–16). The country's ranking in the World Bank's regulatory quality dimension of governance indicators improved from the 45th percentile in 2010 to the 54th percentile by 2016, while political stability improved from the 5th percentile to the 10th percentile. During this period the Philippines improved its ranking in the World Bank's control of corruption indicators from the 23rd percentile to the 36th percentile. The country's ranking for the rule of law improved from the 35th percentile to the 39th percentile.

In his election campaign, Aquino's successor, populist Rodrigo Roa Duterte, elected for a six-year term in 2016, pledged to retain Aquino's macroeconomic policies and to increase tax collection. Duterte also proposed spending 5% of GDP on infrastructure development (later raised to 7%) – an Aquino administration target that was not attained.[51]

The Philippines has a problematic geographical terrain, encompassing a series of islands and mountains hindering the connectivity of the overland national transport system. In addition, decades of neglect in maintenance, modernization and expansion have undermined the extent and quality of the country's transport network, particularly roads that are the most used option for internal passenger and freight transportation. The country's road network suffers from excessive congestion and low infrastructure quality. With the absence of an extensive rail network, this condition induces high costs and productivity losses for supply chains.

Early in his administration, Duterte travelled to China to improve relations between the two countries. The Aquino administration had brought a case against China's claims and actions in the South China Sea and obtained a favourable ruling. Duterte was willing to 'set aside' the tribunal ruling in his negotiations.[52] In return, he received $24,000m.worth of pledges for various infrastructure projects.

In May 2017 President Duterte described the BRI as a 'platform for growth in the region'. The BRI arrangement with China appeared ideal since it melded with Duterte's aggressive $158,000m. Build! Build! Build! Infrastructure Plan (BBB).[53] The administration hopes that the programme will initiate a 'Golden Age of Infrastructure'.[54] The overriding aim of the programme is to enable the Philippines to achieve high-income economy status within the space of a generation.

China and the Philippines agreed to a ten-year cooperation arrangement after the visit by Chinese President Xi Jinping to the Philippines in November 2018. This was the first official state visit by a Chinese president in thirteen years. It reflected an improvement in bilateral relations and deepening cooperation. Finally, in October 2019 the Philippine and Chinese governments signed and exchanged six bilateral agreements, two on feasibility studies for big-ticket projects under BBB and four others covering areas of cooperation in trade, customs and communications.

There are mixed perceptions in the Philippines about the BRI. These stem from domestic conditions and external politics. The optimistic view focuses on the benefits and opportunities of participating in the BRI. The BRI's potential to complement the Philippine government's development priorities and its foreign economic and regional engagement policy – for example, its membership of ASEAN. The pessimistic view looks at the problems and challenges confronting the BRI:

1 Path-dependent mentality (previously unsuccessful Chinese projects in the Philippines);
2 Security issues (maritime and territorial disputes);
3 The extensive international narrative on the BRI as a Chinese geopolitical tool;
4 Domestic politics;
5 The government's wariness of falling into a debt trap.

Nevertheless, Chinese investment in the Philippines has not, thus far, had much of an impact. The government's BBB infrastructure programme has got off to a slow start. The $158,000m.) programme involves seventy-five large-scale infrastructure projects primarily in the transport sector, involving road, rail, sea and airports. While several projects have been completed or are well underway, most are still at the study stage, are being re-evaluated or are having trouble securing funding.

Limited follow-up of pledged assistance by China became a significant problem.[55] Firms' reluctance to become involved varied from difficulty in raising funds to their projects receiving unfavourable social and environmental impact assessments.

One note of success, the Estrella-Pantaleon Bridge over the Pasig River, was completed and inaugurated on 29 July 2021. The project was constructed by the China Road and Bridge Corporation and funded by China. It is one of the flagship projects under the BBB programme and the BRI.

Even if many of the BRI and BBB projects are compled, can the momentum of recent years be maintained? The Philippines has a history of nipping progress in the bud. Is the Duterte administration likely to be yet another example of this phenomenon?

Historically, growth has revived in the Philippines following a period of reforms.[56] However, the Duterte administration assumes that the massive infrastructure programme can achieve high growth rates, thus avoiding any significant reform efforts. There has been a considerable slippage in several key institutional indices. Starting in 2010 economic freedom in the Philippines, as defined by the Heritage House Freedom Index, had been on an upward trend, peaking in 2017 in the middle of the 'moderately free' range.[57] Since then, a downward trend brought the country very close in 2022 to the 'mostly unfree' countries threshold. In 2015–16 the Philippines ranked 47th in the World Economic Forum's Global Competitiveness Index. By 2019 the country had fallen to 64th position.

There is also a fundamental contradiction to the BBB strategy: both agriculture and manufacturing, the two sectors that would ordinarily benefit the most from improved infrastructure, are not critical components of Duterte's economic programme. The agriculture sector registered just 1.1% growth in 2018 and 1.2% in 2019 after averaging over 2.0% from 2020–17. However, the administration has shown little interest in reversing this trend. The agriculture department's budget, already low, suffered cuts in 2019.[58] Manufacturing growth declined to 4.9% in 2018, which is the slowest since growth of 4.7% was recorded in 2011. In 2019 manufacturing growth fell further to 3.2%, after averaging 6.2% from 2010–17. Manufacturing also remains concentrated in low value-added activities with limited productivity and growth potential.[59]

China's BRI programme will be most effective if its projects attract large volumes of private investment. However, because Western investors are increasingly holding back because of concerns over human rights and Duterte's inflammatory rhetoric, the Philippines must increasingly rely on new partners such as China as a reliable source of capital. However, China has yet to translate its pledges of capital into a significant number of investments.

In contrast to many other East Asian economies, Chinese flows of FDI to the Philippines, even dating back before the BRI, were highly volatile.[60] From a value of $40.24m. in 2009, Chinese FDI increased to $244.1m. in 2010 and $267.2m. in 2010. Chinese FDI to the country then fell to $74.9m. in 2012 and to $54.4m. in 2013. Chinese FDI then increased to $224.95m. in 2014, only to decline to –$27.6m. in 2015. Volatility continued in 2016 with inflows of $32.2m., increasing to $108.8m. in 2017 before falling to $58.8m. in 2018. In 2019 Chinese FDI was negative again, falling by $4.29m. However, in the pandemic year of 2020, FDI was again positive at $130.43m.

A considerable amount of Chinese FDI flowed into offshore gambling in the Philippines rather than productive investment.[61] The Philippine-China relationship is also tenuous. Further Chinese pressure in the disputed South China Sea may lead to a backlash from voters who largely distrust Beijing. Relations with China could ultimately distract from Duterte's other aims, and given that the economic benefits of close ties with Beijing have yet to be realized, Duterte may eventually cool relations.

It is too early to gauge whether China's BRI combined with Duterte's BBB initiative will be successful, once a recovery from the COVID-19 pandemic has been effected, in helping to sustain the growth rates to which Philippine citizens have become accustomed. It is a high-risk strategy that overly depends on critical components such as Chinese assistance over which the government has limited control.[62] The strategy has been severely tainted by Duterte's human rights actions, which are now limiting international cooperation that may be critical, especially if the global economy continues its slowdown following the Russian invasion of Ukraine.

The government has also shown little inclination to address other areas that are vital for success, such as corruption, economic and governance reforms. These components appear to be moving in the wrong direction. In 2018 the quality of the Philippines' transport infrastructure was roughly in line with that typically occurring in the region, given the country's level of governance (Figure 6.4). However, governance in recent years has been declining or stagnating. Overall governance peaked at the 45th percentile in 2014, and by 2020 it had dropped to the 39th percentile. Control of corruption declined from the 40th percentile in 2014 to the 34th percentile in 2020, while the rule of law fell from the 44th percentile to the 32nd percentile. If the government expects to reap the maximum benefits from upcoming BRI projects, it must reverse this downward trend.

Timor-Leste

In May 2002 Timor-Leste, the former Portuguese colony of East Timor, regained its independence after twenty-four years under Indonesian rule of occupation and almost three years under United Nations (UN) control. The battle for independence from Indonesia left the country with most of its infrastructure destroyed, thousands of people killed, and most public records and property titles lost.[63] The country experienced a significant 'brain drain' during this period, losing most of its professional class. Since independence, Timor-Leste has developed a vibrant democracy, benefiting from a substantial increase in oil revenues, and has achieved strong economic growth rates despite its initial disadvantages. From 2010–15 GDP increased at an average annual rate of 5.1%.

Timor-Leste became a member of the BRI in March 2017.[64] However, China had been active previously through supporting various infrastructure projects. Although no Chinese BRI projects appear in the American Enterprise Institute database, Chinese companies had been involved in several areas, including developing the national power grid, since joining the BRI. A notable project involves the China Railway Group's participation in the initial phases of the country's major thoroughfare, the Suai Highway.[65] China also made a $14m. donation in June 2020 towards the construction of a hospital and a school.[66] One of the government's most notable projects involved the China Harbor Engineering Company in the construction of the port of Tibar Bay.[67] This port will become the major gateway to Timor-Leste.

However, this stepped-up activity did not offset declining oil and gas production rates that are setting in with the depletion of the country's original hydrocarbon deposits and the effects of the COVID-19 pandemic. GDP growth contracted at an average annual rate of 1.0% from 2016–21. Fortunately, on 25 May 2021 an Australian firm began a drilling operation that is likely to extend the emptying of the oil- and gasfields from 2022–23 to 2024–25. The extra time afforded will allow the Timor-Leste authorities to develop new fields in the

Greater Sunrise basin.[68] However, there are significant hurdles to cross before substantial revenues come from this source.

The Tasi Mane project is planned to leverage oil and gas from the Greater Sunrise fields.[69] These energy sources would be piped back to Timor-Leste and linked to a host of facilities along the country's sparsely populated southern coast, including the Suai Supply Base, a refining and petrochemical complex at Betano, and an onshore LNG re-gasification facility at Beaco. Commercial production from the Greater Sunrise fields will probably start in 2030.

However, there are growing doubts about the Tasi Mane's economic and technical feasibility in government ranks, with many calling the venture 'wasteful' expenditure of public funds.[70] In addition, Timor-Leste's Petroleum Fund, a significant source of project financing, is shrinking fast and, at the current rate of depletion, could run out of funds before 2030 as these support crucial social, health and infrastructure programmes.

Many obstacles to the Greater Sunrise development and onshore refining and LNG activities exist. The government's buyout of Conoco and Shell's shares removes two staunch opponents to its onshore plans.[71] However, the departure of Conoco and Shell has created a substantial investment and technological expertise gap. This knowledge shortfall needs to be filled either by the remaining partners or by sourcing for further assistance. Chinese participation in the project remains a possibility.[72] In May 2019 an engineering and construction contract, reportedly worth $943m., went to China Railway Construction to build marine facilities at the port of Beaco to support an onshore LNG plant.

Even if all partners agree on a concerted development plan, constructing a sub-sea pipeline to bring offshore oil and gas onshore and other associated Tasi Mane infrastructures will face myriad risks. Timor-Leste's lack of experience in spearheading, progressing and hosting large infrastructure projects also plays a part in complicating project delivery.

Another significant risk is the complex issue of land rights. Most land in Timor-Leste, including the southern coast, is based on customary, informal social and cultural ties with no legal basis. Confusion and opposition regarding land rights have led to dissent among some facets of local communities.

The government's strategy reflects the poor state of infrastructure throughout the country, caused by many years of conflict, neglect and severe budgetary constraints. It also assumes that by the unbalancing of the economy's structure in favour of infrastructure, the costs of private sector production will fall and thus usher in a period of increased private sector investment.

However, private sector participation is problematic given the country's low governance levels. In 2020 the government efficiency component of the World Bank's governance indices only ranked on the 19th percentile – albeit up from the 9th percentile in 2010. In the all-important area of the rule of law, the country ranked on the 11th percentile.

Given the positive relationship between infrastructure quality and governance, it is possible to make an exemplary case that focusing on improved governance rather than on a period of massive capital formation might be the country's best long-term strategy. Still, there is ample scope for additional infrastructure investment as the government's debt was only 16.5% of GDP in 2021, up from 2.9% in 2015. The International Monetary Fund predicts that debt will increase to 24.6% of GDP by 2026.

Assessment

The South-East Asia countries' experiences with the BRI vary widely. Chinese interest focuses on Malaysia, Indonesia and, to a lesser extent, the Philippines, with Brunei and Timor-Leste very minor participants. Brunei does not desperately need Chinese funding, and there is little Chinese interest in Timor-Leste.

Some trends and patterns identified here are unlikely to continue. The surge in debt will increasingly constrain Malaysia in the near future. It is likely that political change in the Philippines will result in a more pro-US government. Indonesia will probably be able to take advantage of increased competition between China and the West, namely the United States, Australia, the United Kingdom and Japan, all of which are attempting to counter Chinese influence.

Efforts to respond to Beijing's BRI are not new. A range of initiatives has existed for several years. These include, among others, Japan's Partnership for Quality Infrastructure (2015), the European Union (EU)'s Connectivity Strategy (2018), the Australia-Japan-United States Trilateral Infrastructure Partnership (2018), the US Blue Dot Network (2019) and, more recently, the EU's Global Gateway (2022).[73]

Two developments have compelled Western governments to join efforts in countering the BRI. First, China's increasing authoritarianism and coercive diplomacy have worried Western governments, adding political salience and the political will to react accordingly.

Second, the current US Administration strongly values the idea of teaming up with partners to counter China. President Joe Biden has called for a 'democratic alternative to the BRI', proposing a 'Build Back Better World (B3W)' global infrastructure partnership at the G7 summit on 11–13 June 2021.[74]

Third, Chinese entities may find it more difficult to persuade governments to cooperate further with them in infrastructure projects and, at the same time, will face greater competition from contractors from other countries. Key BRI countries in the region, such as the Philippines and Indonesia, are simultaneously embroiled in the South China Sea territorial disputes with China. The US involvement in the area further complicates this situation. These disputes are likely further to strain future collaboration between these BRI countries and China. Such factors could allow Japanese and Australian firms to play a more active role in infrastructure and other productive investments.

Notes

1 Permanent Mission of Brunei Darussalam to the United Nations, *Country Facts*. www.un.int/brunei/brunei/country-facts (accessed 23 May 2022).

2 *CDR Magazine*, 'The Belt and Road Initiative: Brunei', 21 September 2021. https://iclg.com/cdr-essential-intelligence/1100-cdr-the-belt-and-road-initiative-2021/brunei.

3 Rasidah Hj Abu Bakar, 'Over 1,000 Ageing Oil Wells to Close in next 30 Years', *The Scoop*, 6 July 2021. https://thescoop.co/2021/06/28/over-1000-ageing-oil-wells-to-close-in-next-30-years/.

4 Damon Evans, 'Brunei Hopes to Boost Oil and Gas Production after New Discovery: News for the Energy Sector', *Energy Voice*, 14 March 2022. www.energyvoice.com/oilandgas/asia/394964/brunei-hopes-to-boost-oil-and-gas-production-after-new-discovery/.

5 Kieran Cooke, 'Brunei Darussalam: Diversifying Is Hard to Do', *Global*. www.global-briefing.org/2012/07/diversifying-is-hard-to-do/ (accessed 23 May 2022).

6 Centre for Strategic and Policy Studies, 'Strategic Planning in Brunei Darussalam'. www.csps.org.bn/wp-content/uploads/2021/04/StrategicPlanningBrunei.pdf (accessed 23 May 2022).

7 Wawasan Brunei 2035. http://wawasanbrunei.gov.bn/sitepages/Home.aspx (accessed 23 May 2022).

8 *Borneo Bulletin Online*, 'China Remains Increasing Course Brunei's FDI', 17 September 2019. https://borneobulletin.com.bn/china-remains-increasing-source-bruneis-fdi/.

9 Statista, 'China: Outward FDI Stock in ASEAN by Country 2020', 28 October 2021. www.statista.com/statistics/722630/china-outward-fdi-stock-asean-by-country/.

10 NS Energy, 'Hengyi PMB Refinery and Petrochemical Project'. www.nsenergybusiness.com/projects/hengyi-pmb-refinery-and-petrochemical-project/ (accessed 23 May 2022).

11 Ibid.
12 China-ASEAN Panorama, 'Transoceanic Cooperation: Beibu Gulf Port Group Promotes the Development of Brunei Port'. http://en.china-asea n-media.com/show-45-1143-1.html (accessed 23 May 2022).
13 Sofia Tomacruz, 'Brunei, the Quiet Claimant, Breaks Its Silence on the South China Sea', *Rappler*, 22 July 2020. www.rappler.com/world/asia-pa cific/brunei-breaks-silence-south-china-sea/.
14 Beni Sukadis, 'Protecting Indonesia's Sovereignty in the North Natuna Sea', *The Diplomat*, 12 September 2021. https://thediplomat.com/2021/09/p rotecting-indonesias-sovereignty-in-the-north-natuna-sea/.
15 Statista, 'Indonesia: Youth Unemployment Rate 2020', 10 March 2022. www.statista.com/statistics/708301/indonesia-youth-unemployment-rate/.
16 *The Star*, 'Indonesia Still Chasing US$150bil Budget Shortfall', 29 November 2019. www.thestar.com.my/business/business-news/2018/02/01/ indonesia-still-chasing-us150bil-budget-shortfall.
17 Ayman Falak Medina, 'Indonesia Passes Bill to Build New Capital City: Deadline 2024', *ASEAN Business News*, 28 April 2022. www.aseanbriefing. com/news/indonesia-passes-bill-to-build-new-capital-city-deadline-2024/.
18 ASEAN-China Center, 'Speech by Chinese President Xi Jinping to Indo-nesian Parliament'. www.asean-china-center.org/english/2013-10/03/c_1330 62675.htm (accessed 24 May 2022).
19 Statista, 'Indonesia: Export Value China 2020', 30 August 2021. www.sta tista.com/statistics/629207/indonesia-export-value-to-china/.
20 Statista, 'China: Outward FDI Flows to Indonesia', 4 January 2022. www. statista.com/statistics/720273/china-outward-fdi-flows-to-indonesia/.
21 Ko Lyn Cheang, 'How Indonesia Is Trying to Avoid the Pitfalls of Belt and Road Cooperation', *Jakarta Post*, 25 July 2019. www.thejakartapost. com/news/2019/07/25/how-indonesia-is-trying-to-avoid-the-pitfalls-of-belt-and-road-cooperation.html.
22 Wahyudi Soeriaatmadja, 'Indonesia Wants BRI Projects to Be in Line with National Development Plan, No Government Debt', *Straits Times*, 25 April 2019. www.straitstimes.com/asia/se-asia/indonesia-wants-bri-p rojects-to-be-in-line-with-national-development-plan-no-government.
23 Mitsuru Obe, 'Japan Says China Wins Indonesia High-Speed Rail Con-tract', *Wall Street Journal*, 30 September 2015. www.wsj.com/articles/japa n-says-china-wins-indonesia-rail-contract-1443537614.
24 Sebastian Strangio, 'Indonesian Capital Plan Throws China-Backed Rail Link into Disarray', *The Diplomat*, 12 February 2022. https://thediplomat. com/2022/02/indonesian-capital-plan-throws-china-backed-rail-link-into-di sarray/.
25 Reuters, 'China-Backed Indonesian Rail Link Seen Taking 40 Years to Breakeven', 8 February 2022. www.reuters.com/markets/rates-bonds/china -backed-indonesian-rail-link-seen-taking-40-years-breakeven-2022-02-08/.
26 Resty Woro Yuniar, 'Indonesia's Plan to Build Another Railway with China Raises Debt Trap Fears', *South China Morning Post*, 25 September 2021. www.scmp.com/week-asia/politics/article/3150041/indonesias-plan-b uild-mega-railway-china-and-japan-raises-debt.
27 Muhammad Zulfikar Rakhmat and Winanda Aryansyah, 'Rising Anti-Chinese Sentiment in Indonesia', *ASEAN Post*, 4 July 2020. https://thea seanpost.com/article/rising-anti-chinese-sentiment-indonesia.

28 Panos Mourdoukoutas, 'Indonesia Warns about Bad Side of Chinese Investments – and Isn't Alone', *Forbes Magazine*, 13 December 2019. www.forbes.com/sites/panosmourdoukoutas/2019/12/13/indonesia-warns-about-bad-side-of-chinese-investments-and-isnt-alone/?sh=150372ce707e.

29 France 24, 'Indonesia Polls Bring Battle over China's Belt and Road Push', 14 April 2019. www.france24.com/en/20190414-indonesia-polls-bring-battle-over-chinas-belt-road-push.

30 Lowy Institute, 'Indonesia Poll 2021'. https://interactives.lowyinstitute.org/features/indonesia-poll-2021/ (accessed 24 May 2022).

31 The Heritage Foundation, '2022 Index of Economic Freedom'. www.heritage.org/index/ (accessed 24 May 2022).

32 Ministry of Finance, Malaysia, 'Section 2 Federal Government Revenue'. https://belanjawan2021.treasury.gov.my/pdf/revenue/2021/section2.pdf.

33 Ngeow Chow Bing, 'Have Friendly Malaysia-China Relations Gone Awry?' Carnegie Endowment for International Peace, 16 July 2021. https://carnegieendowment.org/2021/07/16/have-friendly-malaysia-china-relations-gone-awry-pub-84981.

34 Ibid.

35 Amanda Lee, 'Terminus Cities Will Reap Rich Rewards: Analysts'. *Today*, 20 July 2016. www.todayonline.com/singapore/terminus-cities-will-reap-rich-rewards-analysts.

36 Trinna Leong and Shannon Teoh, 'Malaysian-Chinese Consortium in Axed Bandar Malaysia Deal Refutes Government Allegation', *Straits Times*, 5 May 2017. www.straitstimes.com/asia/se-asia/malaysian-chinese-consortium-in-axed-bandar-malaysia-deal-challenges-decision.

37 Reuters, 'Malaysia to Cancel $20 Billion China-Backed Rail Project: Minister', 26 January 2019. www.reuters.com/article/us-china-malaysia/malaysia-to-cancel-20-billion-china-backed-rail-project-minister-idUSKCN1PK03P.

38 Wade Shepard, 'Inside the Belt and Road's Premier White Elephant: Melaka Gateway', *Forbes Magazine*, 31 January 2020. www.forbes.com/sites/wadeshepard/2020/01/31/inside-the-belt-and-roads-premier-white-elephant-melaka-gateway/?sh=766e054266ee.

39 Government Printing Office, 'Speech by the Prime Minister in the Dewan Rakyat on 21 May 2015'. www.pmo.gov.my/dokumenattached/speech/files/RMK11_Speech.pdf.

40 Reuters, 'Malaysia to Cancel $20 Billion China-Backed Rail Project: Minister'.

41 Yicong Wang and James Reagan, 'Media Sentiment towards Chinese Investments in Malaysia: An Examination of the Forest City Project', *Asian Journal for Public Opinion Research*, 31 August 2020. www.ajpor.org/article/14481-media-sentiment-towards-chinese-investments-in-malaysia-an-examination-of-the-forest-city-project.

42 BBC News, 'Mahathir Mohamad: The Man Who Dominated Malaysian Politics', 4 March 2020. www.bbc.com/news/world-asia-44028023.

43 Clara Ferreira-Marques, 'Breaking Views: Malaysia Can Push for a Healthy China Rebalance', Reuters, 11 May 2018. www.reuters.com/article/us-malaysia-election-china-breakingviews/breakingviews-malaysia-can-push-for-a-healthy-china-rebalance-idUSKBN1IC08B.

44 Lucy Hornby, 'Mahathir Mohamad Warns against 'New Colonialism' during China Visit', *Financial Times*, 20 August 2018. www.ft.com/content/7566599e-a443-11e8-8ecf-a7ae1beff35b.

45 Reuters, 'Malaysia to Cancel $20 Billion China-Backed Rail Project: Minister'.
46 Channel News Asia, 'East Coast Rail Link Back on after Malaysia, China Agree to Slash Cost'. www.channelnewsasia.com/asia/east-coast-rail-link-p roceed-malaysia-china-slash-costs-885776 (accessed 24 May 2022).
47 Cogitasia CSIS Asia Policy Blog, 'Will China-Malaysia Relations Remain a Model for Asia?'. www.cogitasia.com/will-china-malaysia-relations-rema in-a-model-for-asia/ (accessed 24 May 2022).
48 William Pesek, 'Philippines: "Sick Man of Asia" Risks Relapse', *Nikkei Asia*, 11 November 2018. https://asia.nikkei.com/Opinion/Philippines-sick-man-of-Asia-risks-relapse.
49 Florian Alburo, 'Manufactured Exports and Industrialization: Trade Patterns and Trends of the Philippines', in *Trade and Structural Change in Pacific Asia*, NBER. www.nber.org/system/files/chapters/c6933/c6933.pdf.
50 Kapilermuza, 'Kung Walang Kurap Walang Mahirap Slogan', *kungbloge*, 5 November 2021. https://kungbloge.blogspot.com/2021/11/kung-walang-k urap-walang-mahirap-slogan.html.
51 Ben O. de Vera, 'Duterte Admin to Hike Infrastructure Spending to up to 7% of GDP', *Inquirer.net*, 4 June 2016. https://newsinfo.inquirer.net/ 789048/duterte-admin-to-hike-infrastructure-spending-to-up-to-7-of-gdp.
52 Murray Hiebert, 'The South China Sea Dispute in 2020–2021', Yusof Ishak Institute, 31 August 2020. www.iseas.edu.sg/wp-content/uploads/ 2020/08/ISEAS_Perspective_2020_97.pdf.
53 Ritchel Mendiola, Roger Oriel, Enrique Soriano and Dana Sioson, 'Build, Build, Build: The Duterte Administration's Infrastructure Plans', *Balikbayan Magazine*, 6 April 2018. https://balikbayanmagazine.com/business/the-econom y/build-build-build-the-duterte-administrations-infrastructure-plans/.
54 King Francis Ocampo, 'To Realize Duterte's "Golden Age of Infra-structure" in Philippines, Better Roads a Must', Asia Foundation, 2 October 2018. https://asiafoundation.org/2018/01/31/realize-dutertes-golde n-age-infrastructure-philippines-better-roads-must/.
55 *Worldview*, 'The Philippines Waits for a Chinese Windfall', 2 January 2019. https://worldview.stratfor.com/article/philippines-waits-chinese-windfall (acces-sed 24 May 2022).
56 Panos Mourdoukoutas, 'The Philippines Is Ready to Rise Again', *Forbes Magazine*, 30 September 2018. www.forbes.com/sites/panosmourdoukouta s/2018/09/27/the-philippines-is-ready-to-rise-again/#5f2f1dae55bd.
57 The Heritage Foundation, 'Philippines Economy: Population, GDP, Infla-tion, Business, Trade, FDI, Corruption'. www.heritage.org/index/country/p hilippines (accessed 24 May 2022).
58 Department of Budget and Management, 'Agriculture Budget Not the Culprit for Productivity Woes'. www.dbm.gov.ph/index.php/secretary-s-corner/press-releases/list-of-press-releases/1361-agriculture-budget-not-the-culprit-for-productivity-woes-dbm (accessed 24 May 2022).
59 Rafaelita M. Aldaba, 'The Philippine Manufacturing Industry Roadmap: Agenda for New Industrial Policy, High Productivity Jobs, and Inclusive Growth', Philippine Institute for Development Studies, June 2014. http s://pidswebs.pids.gov.ph/CDN/PUBLICATIONS/pidsdps1432.pdf.
60 Statista, 'China: Outward FDI Flows to the Philippines 2020', 2 November 2021. www.statista.com/statistics/720386/china-outward-fdi-flows-to-the-philip pines/.

61 Alvin Camba, 'Why Is the Philippines the Home for Chinese Offshore Gambling?' *The Diplomat*, 26 November 2018. https://thediplomat.com/2018/11/why-is-the-philippines-the-home-for-chinese-offshore-gambling/.

62 *South China Morning Post*, 'What Happened to the Billions China Pledged the Philippines?' 7 August 2018. www.scmp.com/week-asia/busi ness/article/2158237/what-happened-billions-china-pledged-philippines-not -what-you.

63 Alison Rourke, 'East Timor: Indonesia's Invasion and the Long Road to Independence', *The Guardian*, 29 August 2019. www.theguardian.com/world/2019/aug/30/east-timor-indonesias-invasion-and-the-long-road-to-in dependence.

64 Sebastien Goulard, 'Timor-Leste Confirming Willingness to Develop BRI', OBOReurope, 7 November 2020. www.oboreurope.com/en/east-tim or-bri/.

65 China Railway Group Ltd, 'Suai Highway Phase I, East Timor', 14 March 2019. www.crecg.com/english/10059090/10059186/10059522/index.html.

66 Guilherme Rego, 'China Funds Infrastructures in Timor-Leste with USD 14 Million', Plataforma Media, 1 July 2020. www.plataformamedia.com/en/2020/06/15/china-funds-infrastructures-in-timor-leste-with-usd-14-millio n/?lang=en.

67 CLBrief, 'Chec Starts Work on Timorese Port', 2 January 2020. www.clbrief.com/chec-starts-work-on-timorese-port/.

68 Helen Davidson, 'Australia and Timor-Leste Sign Historic Maritime Border Treaty', *The Guardian*, 6 March 2018. www.theguardian.com/world/2018/mar/07/australia-and-timor-leste-sign-historic-maritime-border -treaty.

69 Bernardo da Costa Maia, 'Voices: Tasi Mane Petroleum Project Brings Concern, Optimism to Timor-Leste's Southern Coast', Earth Journalism Network, 30 September 2020. https://earthjournalism.net/stories/voices-ta si-mane-petroleum-project-brings-concern-optimism-to-timor-lestes-southe rn-coast.

70 Mong Palatino, 'Timor-Leste's Tasi Mane Project', *The Diplomat*, 17 October 2011. https://thediplomat.com/2011/10/timor-lestes-tasi-mane-project/.

71 Niel Ford, 'Dili to Go It Alone in High Stakes Gamble [LNG Con-densed]', *Natural Gas World*, 21 January 2020. www.naturalgasworld.com/dili-to-go-it-alone-in-high-stakes-gamble-lng-condensed-75762.

72 James Massola, 'Big-Spending China Inc Waits Patiently in East Timor, on Australia's Doorstep', *Sydney Morning Herald*, 1 September 2019. www.smh.com.au/world/asia/big-spending-china-inc-waits-patiently-in-east -timor-on-australia-s-doorstep-20190901-p52msq.html.

73 Ministry of Foreign Affairs, Japan, 'Partnership for Quality Infra-structure'. www.mofa.go.jp/files/000117998.pdf (accessed 24 May 2022).

74 Andre Wheeler, 'Commentary: Did the World Just Get a Second Belt and Road Initiative?' CNA, 17 June 2021. www.channelnewsasia.com/commenta ry/build-back-better-world-belt-road-china-g7-how-compares-1961986.

7 The BRI in the Mekong Countries

Introduction: the Mekong Countries

The Mekong River is the world's twelfth longest river.[1] As a source of trade, transport and sustenance for sixty million people, the Mekong countries – the Lao People's Democratic Republic, Cambodia, Myanmar, Viet Nam and Thailand – form a logical grouping, as developments along the river often affect them all. The expanding influence of the People's Republic of China also affects each country's economic and political situation.

China has several regional interests, including expanding infrastructure investment and trade, supporting Chinese businesses' commercial activities, and getting political support from international organizations. With few exceptions, the Mekong countries welcome Chinese investment, trade and lending, which help to support their economies. However, Viet Nam is concerned about excessive dependence on China and the latter's infringements on its South China Sea claims.[2]

These countries have sustained significant increases in per capita incomes since 2000 (Figure 7.1). By 2021 Cambodia's per capita income (on a purchasing-power parity basis in 2017 international dollars) reached US $4,511 with Laos at $7,727, Myanmar at $4,900 Thailand at $17,413 and Viet Nam at $10, 622. However, a significant slowdown has occurred in the past few years in the region since 2015. From 2010–15, Cambodia's gross domestic product (GDP) expanded at an average annual rate of 7.0%, falling to 4.5% from 2016–21. The corresponding figures for Laos were 7.8% and 6.3%, while in Myanmar growth declined from 6.8% in the first period to 1.8% in the second period. Viet Nam maintained high growth in both periods, with GDP expanding by 6.2% in the first period, but dropping to 5.8% in the second period. However, Thailand's growth dropped from 3.7% in the first period to 1.5% in the second period.

DOI: 10.4324/b23227-7

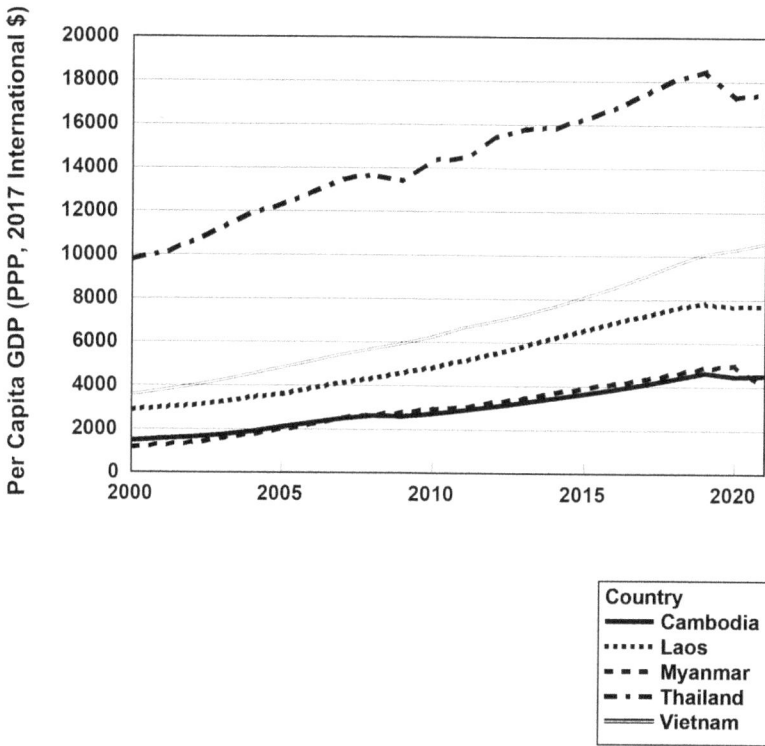

Figure 7.1 Per Capita Income Growth in the Mekong Countries, 1980–2021
Source: International Monetary Fund, World Economic Outlook Database: October 2021.

Recent declines in growth reflect in part the effects of the coronavirus COVID-19 pandemic, with sharp increases in government debt as a share of GDP. The sharpest increases occurred in Myanmar and Thailand, while those in Laos reached dangerously high levels (Figure 7.2). With the exception of Cambodia, these countries may find fiscal constraints a significant factor limiting additional Belt and Road (BRI) programmes.

In recent years, improvement in governance levels has also levelled off (Figure 7.3). Thailand has the highest overall average governance (based on the World Bank's six governance dimensions, see below). However, a slight improvement occurred after 2006. Viet Nam follows with improvements in governance starting in 2006 and running through 2016, and then levelling off until 2020, when it increased from the 40th percentile to the 43rd percentile. Cambodia's governance

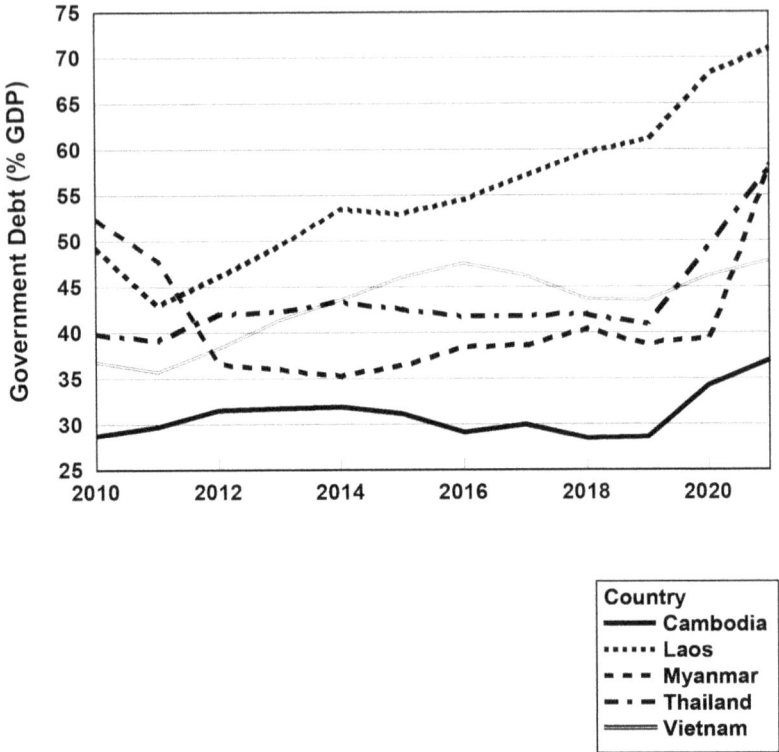

Figure 7.2 Government Debt as a % of GDP in the Mekong Countries, 2010–21
Source: International Monetary Fund, World Economic Outlook Database:
October 2021.

levelled off at the 25th percentile in 2021, where it remained through
2020. Laotian governance improved from the 9th percentile in 2003 to
the 29th percentile by 2014. Subsequently, it declined to the 25th percentile in 2020. Finally, governance levels in Myanmar rose from the
3rd percentile in 2010 to the 21st percentile in 2016, only to decline to
the 19th percentile in 2020. Undoubtedly, this decline has accelerated
following the military coup in February 2021.

The governance/quality of transport infrastructure relationship is
strong throughout the region. In 2018 Thailand, Viet Nam and Laos
were overachieving, while Cambodia and Myanmar were underachievers (Figure 7.4). These patterns suggest that Chinese BRI programmes are likely to be most effective in Cambodia and Myanmar.

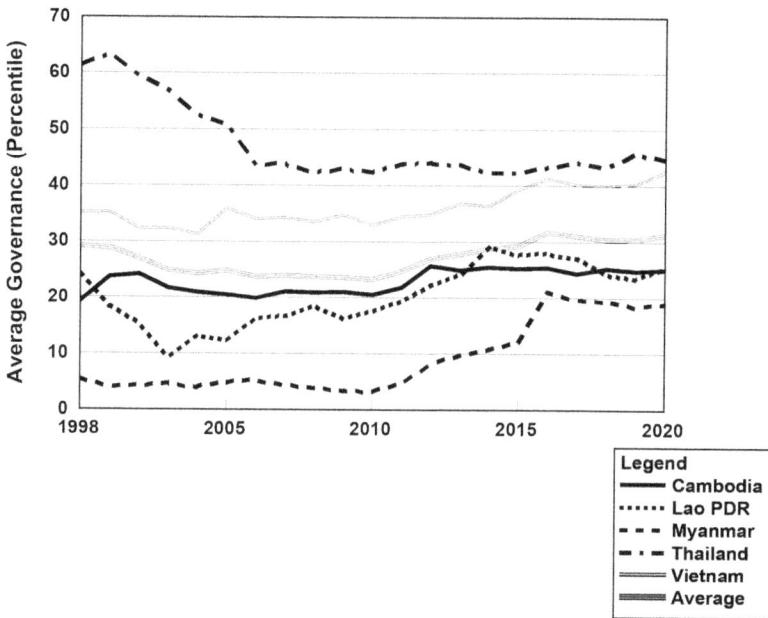

Figure 7.3 Governance Levels in the Mekong Countries, 1996–2020
Note: Governance is the average of its components: voice and accountability, political stability and absence of violence/terrorism, government effectiveness, regulatory quality, rule of law and control of corruption.
Source: World Bank, Worldwide Governance Indicators Database.

In contrast, Laos, Thailand and Viet Nam may find improvements in governance are the best way to develop their infrastructure.

The Mekong basin is an increasingly significant area of rivalry between the United States and China.[3] US–China competition appears in the dynamics of the rival organizations dedicated to the Mekong's management. The United States supports the Mekong River Commission (MRC), which comprises Thailand, Cambodia, Laos and Viet Nam.[4] The China-led Lancang-Mekong Cooperation Initiative (LMC) has greater economic resources involving dam and development projects, special economic zones, and trade.[5] It integrates the region into the BRI and has largely eclipsed the MRC.

China has built eleven dams on the upstream section of the river. They have a combined capacity of roughly 47,000m. cu m.[6] Since the mid-1990s China's dam building has resulted in water volatility and

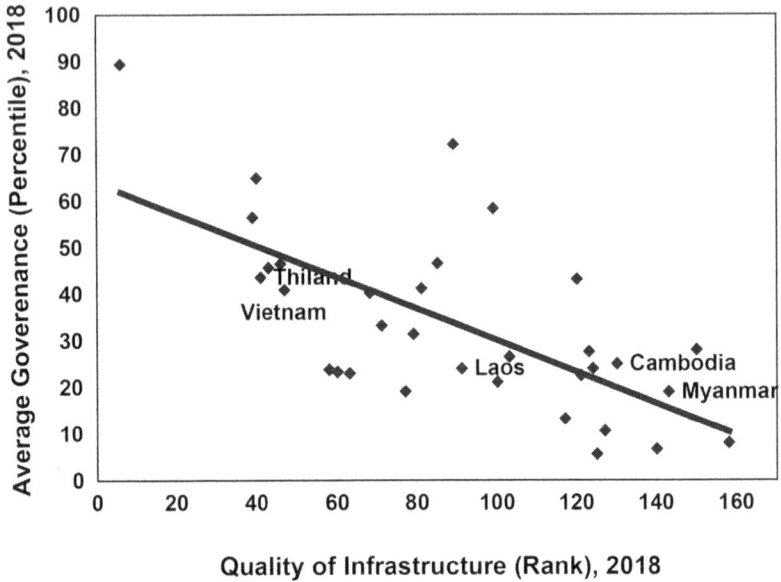

Figure 7.4 Governance/Transport Infrastructure Quality Relationship in the Mekong Countries, 2018
Note: The solid line represents the governance/infrastructure trend.
Source: Governance: World Bank, Worldwide Governance Indicators Database; Infrastructure: World Bank, Logistics Performance Index Database.

periodic droughts in the lower Mekong. This situation has directly affected all aspects that are vital to the region's principal crops and food security.

Lao PDR

The Lao People's Democratic Republic (Lao PDR, also known as Laos) is the only landlocked country in South-East Asia. The absence of direct access to the sea has affected all aspects of the country's development, setting it apart from other economies in the region. Lao PDR was established as a communist state in December 1975, replacing the former Kingdom of Laos. The creation of the Lao PDR was the culmination of decades of war between the Royal Lao Government and the communist Pathet Lao ('Land Laos'). The economy incurred severe damage in the period up to 1975, leaving the new government with the massive task of post-conflict reconstruction and establishing an entirely new economic system and institutional structures.[7]

Although Laos is a communist country, since 1980 the government has adopted pragmatic economic policies. Market-orientated economic reforms were implemented in 1986, and private enterprises were allowed to form.[8] The government's innovative New Economic Mechanism (NEM), which commenced in that year, began to transform the economy from one characterized by top-down, centralized planning to a liberalized, market-orientated open economic system.[9] The NEM ushered in a period of reduced trade restrictions and created an environment conducive to foreign direct investment (FDI). Trade patterns also began to shift, with a significant reduction in the country's economic dependence on Viet Nam. Laos started looking more to Thailand for private investment, technology transfer and trade in its economic transformation.[10]

By the mid-1990s Laos started to attract significant foreign investment in critical sectors such as hydroelectric power. Other areas favoured by foreign investment were tourism, mining and clothing manufacturing. China is by far the largest investor in Laos. As of early 2021, China had undertaken fifty-two projects in Laos between November 2005 and December 2020 totalling $29,810m.[11] Of these, thirty-five were BRI-type projects starting in October 2013, with the last recorded in December 2020. The value of these projects comes to $22,110m. Critical Chinese investments in Laos include the Lao-China Railway and the country's many hydropower dams along the Lower Mekong Delta.[12] In this sense, the BRI has facilitated the Laotian development strategy.

Laos's government has long pursued two major strategic development initiatives. One is to brand landlocked Laos as 'land-linked'.[13] The Lao government believes that with the proper transport infrastructure, the country can serve as a bridge between its mainland South-East Asia neighbours and China, which lies to the north. The key to this vision is building a 400-km railway linking China's Yunnan province to the Lao capital, Vientiane.

The government's other major initiative is to make Laos the 'battery of Asia'.[14] Laos exports electricity from dozens of hydropower plants on the Mekong River and its tributaries. Laos's first hydroelectric dam, built with Japanese assistance, came online in 1971. For the next two decades, the single plant not only fuelled the country's energy needs but provided surplus electricity for export to Thailand. Then, in 1993, spurred by Thailand's increased need for electricity, the Laotian government opened the hydropower sector to foreign investment and embarked on a foreign-financed dam-building spree.[15]

As new projects came online, Laos also began supplying electricity to Viet Nam and Cambodia. By mid-2022 Laos had over fifty dams with more in the pipeline.[16] At first glance, the Laotian hydropower push appears to have paid high dividends. The International Monetary Fund (IMF) reports that the country's average annual growth rose from 6.1% in the 1990s, 7.0% in the 2000s and 6.1% from 2010–21.[17] In 1990 the country's per capita income (on a purchasing-power parity basis in 2017 international dollars) was $2,006, and by 2021 it reached $7,727. However, the current account deficit also rose from an average of 4.0% in the 1990s, to 11.5% in the 2000s and to an unprecedented 15.0% in 2010–21. In addition, the fiscal deficit increased from 1.5% of GDP in 2010 to 4.4% in 2019, suggesting that government debt has been the primary driver of recent growth. The deficit increased further to 5.5% in 2020 and 2021 owing to the COVID-19 pandemic. Debt as a share of GDP in Laos increased from 49.3% in 2010 to 61.2% in 2019. With the increased expenditures associated with the pandemic, debt increased to the unsustainable level of 70.9% by 2021.

In addition to rising debt, the World Bank's Worldwide Governance Indicators show that corruption is a persistent problem.[18] Laos's ranking for control of corruption dropped from the 32nd percentile in 1996 to the 21.2nd percentile in 2014. However, the level has fallen every year since reaching the 15.4th percentile in 2018, suggesting that considerable corruption occurred in the contracting process as the rate of dam construction sped up.[19]

Laos's ruling party has devoted less attention to improving the business environment to help to support private enterprise or raise standards of economic governance. It is wary of initiating economic reform, which could prompt calls for political reform. The country's economic freedom has dropped rapidly in the past few years, and now the country's economy is 'repressed'.[20] Following a visit to Lao PDR in March 2019, United Nations (UN) Special Rapporteur on extreme poverty and human rights Philip Alston warned that the government favours large projects while ignoring the needs of its people.

Furthermore, during this period the country's ranking in the World Economic Forum's Global Competitiveness Report (an indicator of growth potential and manufacturing productivity) dropped from 83rd out of 140 countries in 2015–16 to 113rd in 2019.[21] Laos appears to have fallen victim to a variant of the resource curse common to hydropower-producing countries.[22] Growing debt, corruption, lack of diversification and environmental degradation increasingly act as a drag on growth.

While observers often associate much of the increase in government debt with dam expansion, Laos borrows heavily to finance massive infrastructure initiatives.[23] One BRI project alone, construction of a China–Laos railway, has an estimated cost of $6,000m.[24] Laos is responsible for $1,800m. – a heavy burden for a country of seven million inhabitants whose 2019 GDP was only $19,100m. The government no doubt assumes that future revenues will easily cover the cost of servicing the debt. In principle, the project should make Lao PDR more accessible, but not without many additional investments in better roads and other supporting infrastructure to take full advantage of the railroad. Moreover, net returns on infrastructure projects are notoriously difficult to calculate and will not even accrue until far into the future. Many observers feel the project is of much more value to China than to Laos.[25]

Work on the project fell behind schedule because of the COVID-19 pandemic, as it required Chinese construction workers and personnel. Lao PDR has poor public health infrastructure and limited policy resources to mitigate the effects of the COVID-19 crisis on its economy. The formal opening of the project took place in December 2021.[26]

In addition to questions over the railroad project, Laos's dam building is coming under mounting criticism. Hydroelectric dams also flood valuable agricultural land. In mountainous Laos, only about 4% of the country's total acreage is arable, the lowest percentage of any country in South-East Asia.[27] More and more of this land is ending up at the bottom of reservoirs.

In the short term, dam-building companies are offering resettlement and dry season irrigation programmes to aid displaced farmers, although the quality of these programmes varies.[28] In the longer term, a 97% reduction in the amount of sediment flowing downstream of the dams will dramatically lower the fertility of the remaining farmland, thereby heightening food insecurity.[29]

Even more devastating are the hydropower dams' projected effects on the fisheries of the Mekong River and its tributaries, whose fish stocks were traditionally among the most diverse in the world.[30] The dams not only change the river flows, but often prevent fish from migrating to their spawning pools.

While the trapped fish produce a temporary bonanza for fishermen, how many species will adapt to the changed river system is unclear. Fish stocks could decline by as much as 50%, pushing many fishing families into poverty.

Laos's neighbours will also feel the bite of its hydropower projects. Sedimentation, decreased river flows and declining fish populations downstream from the dams will negatively affect Cambodia, Thailand

and Viet Nam fisheries and farming.[31] Full-scale dam development in the Lower Mekong River basin would cause an estimated $43,000m. loss in native fish stocks. The hydropower projects will also derail Cambodia's growing ecotourism sector by threatening the biodiversity of Mekong River ecosystems and further endangering rare species such as the Irrawaddy river dolphin.[32]

The three countries have been working to persuade Laos to reconsider the cross-border effects of its dam-building projects but to little effect.[33] As a result, Thai activists have pressured the government to table an agreement to import additional Laotian hydro-generated electricity, while Viet Nam and Cambodia are already actively considering cutting their electricity purchases.[34] Given that these countries buy 70%–80% of the energy that Laos exports, the cuts would be economically disastrous.[35]

Then there is the problem of climate change. It is far from clear that the dam-builders considered future weather patterns in their designs. Long-term forecasts suggest that the rainy season will become shorter but more intense – similar to that which occurred just before the Xe Pian Xe Namnoy dam collapsed.[36] The dry season in Laos will also last longer, calling into question the future reliability of the hydroelectric projects.

Unfortunately, dam collapses may be a recurring problem. The Xe Pian Xe Namnoy dam collapse suggested that the government has little capacity to determine if hydropower infrastructure projects adhere to existing regulations or follow best practices. Many recent large-scale infrastructure projects were awarded without an open tender process. In March 2019 the Ministry of Public Works and Transport stated that it was handling over 1,000 corruption cases related to infrastructure projects.

A recent study found that full-scale dam development will cost Laos $9,000m. in GDP growth – a finding that a Laotian government representative dismissed as 'just an estimate', making it unlikely that dam construction will soon slow.[37] Given that Laos is already exhibiting symptoms of the hydropower curse, a grim future lies ahead. With an uncompetitive manufacturing sector and agriculture, fishing, and the potential for ecotourism in steep decline, nothing will cushion the blow when the bottom inevitably falls out of the debt-driven boom.

One UN observer noted that '[t]he government's single-minded focus on large infrastructure projects (such as dams and railways), land acquisition, resource extraction, and foreign investment has created too few jobs for Lao people, generated very large debt repayment obligations, and disproportionately benefited wealthy elites'.[38] He added, [t]hose living in poverty, ethnic minorities, and people in rural areas have seen very few benefits of the economic boom'.

By early 2021 Laos was struggling to meet its debt obligations, exacerbated by the economic fallout of the COVID-19 pandemic. The debt crisis is pushing it deeper into China's sphere of influence. Having been unable to meet its debt obligations, Laos recently gave a Chinese state-owned firm a majority stake in its electricity distribution grid.[39]

The possibility exists that Chinese firms have been granted access to investment projects and natural resources in Laos by the government in exchange for China delaying the country's debt-service payments and issuing further financing.

Cambodia

In 2021 Cambodia, one of the World Bank's lower-middle-income countries had a GDP of $1,647 per head (or $4,930 per head on an international purchasing-power parity basis). The notable achievement of graduating to lower-middle-income status in 2015 was the culmination of the country's recovery from over twenty years of armed conflict, civil strife, genocide and war. During this unstable period Cambodia experienced air bombings, a radical programme of social deconstruction with city dwellers evacuated to work in rural areas, mass killings by the Khmer Rouge regime, invasions by neighbouring countries, and protracted struggles among political factions vying for power.

Destruction of infrastructure was widespread, while disruption occurred in every aspect of the country's economic and social life. Since this tumultuous period, the country has been recovering and developing its potential to participate in regional and global trade.

In recent years, Cambodia's growth has been one of the highest globally, averaging annual GDP growth rates of 6.1% in the 1990s, 8.5% in the 2000s and 5.8% from 2010–21. However, Cambodia's transport and communications systems require a considerable amount of upgrading and expansion if high growth and development rates are to continue. In 2018 the World Bank's Logistic Performance Index ranked Cambodia's transport infrastructure 130th out of 160 countries.[40]

Cambodia is arguably China's closest ally in South-East Asia, and relations between the two countries gained momentum after a comprehensive strategic partnership was established in 2010.[41] In 2016 the Government signed thirty-one agreements with China to expand that country's BRI programme.[42] China also cancelled approximately $89m. of Cambodia's debt. In May 2017 Prime Minister Hun Sen attended the first Belt and Road Forum for International Cooperation in Beijing, where Cambodia and China agreed to an Outline Co-operation Plan.[43] As part of the BRI, China pledged to grant Cambodia $600m. per year for three years.

As of early 2021 there were forty-six Chinese investments in Cambodia, beginning with a hydro project in 2006. Thirty-one of these projects involved BRI-type activities, beginning with another hydro project in December 2013. Total Chinese investment amounts to $18,220m., with $12,530m. in BRI projects. Being part of China's BRI has also garnered Cambodia significant Chinese FDI. In 2020 Cambodia received the seventh largest flow ($956.42m.) of FDI in ASEAN member countries behind Singapore ($5,923m., Indonesia ($2,198m.), Thailand ($1,882m.), Viet Nam ($1,875m.), Laos ($1,454m.) and Malaysia $1,374m.).[44]

Prime Minister Hun Sen's visit to Beijing in January 2019 and again in April 2019 as part of the Second Belt and Road Forum suggests that Chinese investments will probably remain firm with significant funds channelled to infrastructure projects.[45] Construction activity in the residential and non-residential buildings sector will probably focus on special economic zones (SEZ) designated by the government, such as the Phnom Penh SEZ and the Neang Kok Koh Kong SEZ, and key tourism areas such as Sihanoukville and Siem Riep.[46] Transport infrastructure projects include rehabilitating the existing Cambodian rail network and upgrading several national roads.

The two major BRI projects are the Phnom Penh–Sihanoukville Expressway and the Sihanoukville SEZ.[47] The China Road and Bridge Corporation will construct the expressway on a build-operate-transfer basis. The project, believed to be the first expressway in the country, will require around $2,000m. in funding. The expressway will be over 190 km long and will have four lanes for most of its length. However, as with other countries, the COVID-19 pandemic has caused significant delays in BRI construction activity due to travel restrictions, which have affected the import of Chinese labour. The project was scheduled for completion in late 2022. Some Sihanoukville SEZ activities faced significant delays stemming from the pandemic.

Often, BRI activity in Cambodia has not been well received by the local population. Compared to those funded by multilateral organizations and independent donors, the projects have little transparency and quality. Common complaints, along with environmental issues, include the handling of resettlement and compensation. Land grabbing has been a significant issue.

While Chinese investments in Sihanoukville may generate more tourism, there is a question of whether Chinese investments are genuinely beneficial to the city's residents.[48] Casino development and swarms of Chinese tourists benefit a small group of Cambodian business executives. However, many Cambodians are being forced to leave the area due to skyrocketing increases in the cost of housing and living expenses. Furthermore, most of the jobs available to Cambodians are for low-skilled activities rather than management and skilled positions.

The Kamchay dam, China's first significant project in Cambodia, is also controversial.[49] Estimates are that the dam, constructed with little input from residents, destroyed 2,000 ha of forest, lowered water quality and eliminated many local activities. Little or no compensation was forthcoming. Most Chinese investment in the country's real estate market is aimed at upper-income groups, Chinese business executives and tourists. The subsequent increase in housing costs has forced many lower-income Cambodians to move into inferior housing.

However, the biggest problem is the country's growing dependency on China. Cambodia's debt is already equivalent to about one-third of its GDP, with China the largest creditor. Given its debt situation, Cambodia may face coercive pressure from China, forcing it to take the creditor country's position in international discussions. For example, Cambodia has consistently voted for the Chinese position and against its ASEAN counterparts concerning the South China Sea issue. In 2018, after Cambodia supported China's position on maritime claims, China dispersed an aid package of $600m. to Cambodia.[50]

No doubt, BRI projects and high inflows of Chinese FDI, particularly in infrastructure, can help the country to sustain high economic growth rates. However, it is unlikely that it will realize this potential unless investments in infrastructure can stimulate a robust private sector response with follow-on investment and expanded economic activity. Unfortunately, there is reason to believe that the private sector response will dwindle. Increasingly, there is a perception among international investors that Cambodia will support Chinese firms over their own if disagreements or clashes of interest occur. As one observer noted, Cambodia's relationship with China is a 'marriage made in heaven for autocrats ... the win-win is really between China and Cambodia's elites. Infrastructure is a smokescreen for a money delivery mechanism for the elites'.[51]

The deterioration in the business climate is another factor that is likely to dampen private investment. Between 2013 and 2020 Cambodia's regulatory quality (the ability of the government to plan and implement sound policies and regulations that permit and promote private sector development) declined from the 40th percentile to the 30th percentile. As for corruption, Cambodia ranked in the 11th percentile in 2020.

Given the ease of securing Chinese aid and BRI investments, Cambodia is taking on some characteristics of oil-producing developing countries – the so-called resource curse, although in this case, the aid curse is more appropriate. With seemingly endless financial support from China, Cambodian politicians are under little pressure to reform the economy to sustain growth. A weak business environment will continue to hamper Cambodia's ability to diversify its foreign direct investment from China and will perpetuate its ongoing economic over-reliance on that country.

Myanmar

Because China's involvement with Myanmar (formerly Burma) is complex and has shifted over time, an overview of the country's development is key to understanding their relationship. Myanmar is a country of vast natural and human resources. However, the country did not experience an economic boom after independence from the United Kingdom in 1948. Instead, the economy suffered from a malaise brought on by a series of military dictatorships and a prolonged civil war. In 1962 the military staged a *coup d'état*, purportedly to save the country from collapse. Along with the Democratic Republic of Korea (North Korea), the country quickly became one of Asia's 'pariah states'.[52]

As Myanmar's most prominent neighbour and special patron, China has played a unique role both positively and negatively in the country's political and economic development.[53] Following the military takeover, China was the country's primary source of support, as international sanctions and condemnation over the government's human rights violations and authoritarian repression became the norm. The Myanmar-China relationship varied over the years as interests shifted. Primarily, China sees Myanmar's geographic location and abundant natural resources as strategic economic opportunities. For often isolated Myanmar, China serves as a patron and lender of last resort.

In its early years of independence and despite Chinese help, disappointing growth and persistent poverty stemmed from limited state capacity, corruption, excessive state intervention and economic mismanagement. After nearly thirty years in office (1962–89), military governments oversaw average annual per capita income growth rates of 0.9%, leaving Myanmar the poorest country in South-East Asia.[54]

In the early 1990s the military, faced with increasing dissent, started political and economic reform to transform from the 'Burmese Way to Socialism' to the start of a market-based economy.[55] Growth revived with per capita incomes increasing at an annual rate of 4.8% in the 1990s and a spectacular rate of 11.5% in the 2000s.

Reforms continued in 2011 during the quasi-democratic government of Gen. (retd) Thein Sein.[56] Nobel Prize winner Aung San Suu Kyi rose to prominence by promoting reform deepening private sector development, and measures to attract FDI.[57] The economy's expansion at an average rate of 6.3% per annum from 2010–20 remained one of the highest in Asia. High growth continued at an average rate of 6.3% from 2010–20, with the country becoming Asia's last frontier in the view of many investors.[58]

Optimism in Myanmar's future strengthened with the 2015 landslide election victory by the National League for Democracy (NLD), headed by Aung San Suu Kyi.[59] The NLD became the country's first civilian-led government in nearly fifty years. With improved political freedom, economic reforms, and the release of political prisoners came the ending of most sanctions imposed in the early 2000s by the United States, the European Union, Australia and Canada.[60]

In reality, however, the military continued to play a significant role in the country's politics, economy and foreign policy, with its role preserved in the 2008 Constitution, which serves as the basis of a 'military-state' – the co-existence of military and civilian authorities.[61] The country's Constitution grants the military broad autonomy from civilian governments. It also gives the military sweeping emergency powers and immunity from prosecution for actions committed under the junta. The military, largely unchecked, wielded its power to fight various domestic ethnic groups and to enrich itself through military industries and investments, often displacing local populations without consultation or proper compensation.[62]

Despite the first signs of a democratic awakening, the military's influence behind the scenes may have also slowed the pace of reforms and caused some backsliding in governance structures.[63] Control of corruption improved from the abysmal 0.5th percentile in 2011 to the 32nd percentile in 2016, only to plateau in 2017 and then to decline to the 28th percentile in 2020. A similar pattern occurred with the rule of law, increasing from the 4.7th percentile in 2011 to the 17.8th percentile in 2016 before falling to the 10.6th percentile in 2020. Finally, government effectiveness increased from the 3.8th percentile in 2011 to the 16.4th percentile in 2016 and then declined to the 14.42nd percentile in 2020.

Prior to the military coup on 1 February 2021, Myanmar's government staked its legitimacy on maintaining strong economic growth rates. Because of stalled reforms and declining governance structures, an efficiency-led approach to growth was not likely to sustain growth, as it had in the past. The government, therefore, opted for an investment-led strategy. The need for expanded infrastructure investment was obvious. Myanmar's infrastructure stock was among the most underdeveloped in Asia. The Asian Development Bank has estimated that if growth is to continue at a high pace, Myanmar must address a potential $120,000m. infrastructure shortfall by 2030.[64]

China's BRI represented a logical source of infrastructure funding, with the American Enterprise Institute database listing fifteen BRI-type projects beginning in October 2013 and ending in June 2020. These projects totalled $5,700m., with China viewing Myanmar as a geographic 'keystone' with the potential to become a transport and logistics corridor directly linking south-west China with the Indian Ocean. The China-Myanmar Economic Corridor (CMEC) corridor would allow goods to bypass existing chokepoints in the Straits of Malacca and the South China Sea.[65]

However, while the project benefits China, the gains for Myanmar are more problematic. Concerns about high debt emerged and led to the Myanmar government scaling back the size of the project from $7,300m. to $1,300m. – roughly equal to the cost of Sri Lanka's Hambantota port.[66] Myanmar is one of many countries, including Malaysia, Nepal and Pakistan, that have forced the renegotiation or cancellation of Chinese projects. In 2011 the government cancelled the construction of the $3,600m. Myitsone Dam in northern Myanmar following nationwide protests over the potential displacement of thousands of residents and concerns regarding cost and debt repayment.

The government was also looking for countries other than China as sources of financing. Given the initial enthusiasm in East Asia and the West for building new ties with the Aung San Suu Kyi administration, the stage appeared to be set in 2016 for diversification in sources of infrastructure funding. However, in August 2017 the military launched attacks on the Muslim population, the Rohingya, in Rakhine.[67] With thousands killed and over 600,000 fleeing to Bangladesh, where they remain today, international condemnation quickly followed. Economic motives were at work, with forty-five companies and organizations in Myanmar donating $6.5m. to the military to gain access to deserted parts of Rakhine, where they began seizing land and resources in the region for economic gain and profit.[68]

The unresolved conflict in Rakhine State continues to damage the country's image. FDI dropped sharply from $4342m. in 2017 to $3,554m. in 2018 during the Rohingya crisis and fell further to $2,766m. in 2019 and to $1,834m. in 2020.[69] At around 2% of GDP, the country's FDI lags considerably behind that found in Viet Nam (14.1%), the Philippines (9.4%) and Thailand (8.0%). The United States reintroduced select sanctions on Myanmar in December 2017.

China appeared to be back in the dominant position it had assumed during the military junta years with the leverage it needed to advance its agenda. With partial sanctions and falling Western investment, the Rohingya crisis created a trilemma for Myanmar's civilian policy-makers. They faced three policy goals, only two of which were attainable simultaneously. The first goal was to sustain economic growth. The second goal involved increased domestic support, and the third increased Chinese investment. Suppose that they chose increased growth and Chinese BRI activity. In that case, they are likely to alienate large segments of the population already concerned about increased Chinese involvement in the country and associated environmental damage and debt burdens. If they chose growth and public support, Chinese investment would decline. However, the government would need to undertake difficult reforms and improved governance to sustain growth without Western funding.

Suppose they chose increased public support and increased Chinese investment. In that case, growth might slow, provided that China shifted some of its investments from massive infrastructure programmes towards smaller-scale activities designed to improve conditions at the local level. It is likely that China's willingness to do this was contingent on that country getting its way with the CMEC programme. To get the CMEC process started again, Chinese President Xi Jinping visited Myanmar in January 2020 – the first visit by a Chinese leader in almost two decades. The two leaders signed thirty-three deals for future projects. However, little progress followed.[70]

On 2 September 2020 China's top diplomat, Yang Jiechi, visited Myanmar to push for progress on Chinese-backed infrastructure projects in the country.[71] These included the long-touted CMEC Kyaukphyu port and SEZ, a new city project near Yangon, and a high-speed railway line from Mandalay to the Chinese border. However, following the military coup and the subsequent bloody crackdown, most countries again view Myanmar as an international pariah.[72]

China has refused to criticize the junta for the coup and its fallout. It has helped to shield Myanmar from UN Security Council pressure. Meanwhile, several Western powers, led by the United States, have imposed sanctions targeting Myanmar's military and military-linked businesses. Given the instability in Myanmar and ongoing fighting, there is every reason to believe that BRI projects will fall further and further behind schedule, if not cancelled outright.

Thailand

The Thai economy has slowed gradually since 1990, with GDP growth rates of 5.4% in the 1990s, 4.3% in the 2000s and 2.6% from 2010–21. Growth has slackened significantly in the last decade, with rates of 3.7% from 2010–15 declining to 2.6% from 2016–21. The economy contracted by 6.1% in 2020 owing to the COVID-19 pandemic. In 2021 it suffered a weak recovery of just 1.0% thanks to a slow recovery in tourism.

Budget deficits have increased in recent years. After averaging 0.3% of GDP from 2010–16, they increased to 2.0% from 2016–21. As a result, government debt as a share of GDP increased from 39.8% in 2010 to 58.0% in 2021. The IMF projects a further rise to 61.2% by 2024. Despite chronic budget deficits, the country ran current account surpluses averaging 2.1% from 2010–15, increasing to 6.0% from 2016–21. The current account surpluses stem from a general surplus of savings over investment. From 2010–16, savings averaged 27.7% of GDP compared to 25.7% for investment. This gap widened with savings averaging 30.0% in 2021 with investment at 23.6%, making Thailand a rare emerging economy experiencing an outflow of capital.

Several factors underlie the economy's poor performance in recent years. Governance has gradually stagnated and declined. In 2000 the country's average governance placed it on the 63rd percentile, but by 2020 it had declined to the 45th percentile. Increased corruption is also a problem, with the country declining from the 51st percentile in 2000 to the 38th percentile in 2020. During this period the rule of law declined from the 68th percentile to the 58th percentile. Political stability has been a significant problem, declining from the 65th percentile to the 24th. Voice and accountability dropped from the 63rd percentile to the 26th percentile.

Thailand's political scene remains highly volatile owing to the entrenched political divide between the rural poor and the urban middle class.[73] The army plays an influential role in Thai politics, with key former military figures dominating the nominally civilian government.[74] Since 2006 overall governance levels in Thailand have continued to hover around the 44th percentile, although the critical dimension of control of corruption declined from the 62nd percentile in 1998 to the 38th percentile in 2020. With increasing corruption and a relatively small skilled labour force, Thailand risks being stuck in the middle-income trap, forcing workers to take lower wages in order to remain internationally competitive.[75]

China's BRI offers the possibility of invigorating the economy through increasing overall investment rates while better integrating the country's various regions. FDI flows to the country have declined dramatically in recent years, falling from $3,554m. in 2018 to $2,766m. in 2019 and to $1,834m. in 2020.[76] In sharp contrast, during this period FDI flows to Viet Nam amounted to $15,500m., $16,120m. and $15,800m, respectively.

As of early 2021 China had thirty-six projects in Thailand, twenty-eight of which are BRI-type investments with a value of $8,260m. Several projects stand out. On 29 October 2020 Thailand and China signed a contract to construct a 253-km high-speed rail link between the capital, Bangkok, and the north-eastern province of Nakhon Ratchasima. The 50,500m. baht project is part of China's BRI and forms the first section of a much-delayed railway project to link Bangkok with the city of Nong Khai on the border between Thailand and Laos.[77]

The Thai government will pay for the project and handle public works; Chinese companies will provide know-how and technology. They will also manage procurement. The firms involved are the State Railway of Thailand and two state-owned enterprises, China Railway and China Railway Design. However, Thailand has been reluctant to proceed with the project due to 'deteriorating ties and both countries' diverging priorities'.[78]

The rail project delays are a significant setback for the BRI. The high-speed railway is the missing link in China's BRI to connect China with Singapore via Laos, Thailand and Malaysia – a symbol of Chinese-Thai relations and a test of the Thai government's willingness to foster regional economic integration.

Viet Nam

Viet Nam's economy has been a major Asian success story, with average annual rates of GDP of 7.4% in the 1990s, 6.9% in the 2000s and 6.0% from 2010–21. In contrast to most countries, growth did not contract during the pandemic year of 2020 but expanded at 2.9%, increasing to 3.8% in 2021. Investment rates are high, averaging 37.6% of GDP in the 2000s and 32.0% from 2020–21. While government deficits increased from an average of 1.6% of GDP in the 2000s to

3.6% from 2010–21, the government debt-to-GDP ratio only increased from 36.8% in 2010 to 47.9% in 2021. The IMF expects that debt will remain in a safe range, declining to 45.3% by 2026.[79]

Overall governance steadily improved from the 33rd percentile in 2010 to the 43rd percentile by 2020. The corresponding rates for control of corruption saw the country improve from the 31st percentile to the 42nd percentile, and the rule of law from the 33rd percentile to the 49th percentile. The all-important government effectiveness improved from the 46th percentile to the 67th percentile, while regulatory quality (a proxy for the business environment) improved from the 29th percentile to the 47th percentile.

Viet Nam's approach towards the BRI differs considerably from the other countries examined here. It officially supports the initiative but has been reluctant to engage actively, being cautious about its potential effects. This caution is understandable, stemming from the prolonged suspicion between the two countries in the South China Sea dispute.[80] Instead of receiving funds under the BRI, Viet Nam has relied on other sources to finance its infrastructure projects. Official development assistance partners such as Japan and South Korea and international financial organizations such as the Asian Development Bank the World Bank offer more relaxed conditions and lower interest rates than loans from the BRI.[81]

As noted above, the country receives a large and steadily expanding amount of FDI, which increased from $9,200m. in 2014 to $11,800m. in 2015, $12,600m. in 2016, $14,100m. in 2017, $15,500m. 2018, $16,120m. in 2019 and to $15,800m. in 2020.[82] However, FDI from China is much lower, with flows of $333m. in 2014, $560m. in 2015, $1,279m. in 2016, $764m. in 2017, $1,151m. in 2018, $1,649m. in 2019 and $1,876m. in 2020.[83]

The Vietnamese have misgivings about BRI projects. First, there is concern that an increasing number of Chinese workers could enter Viet Nam's labour market, posing a threat to Vietnamese labourers' employment opportunities and Vietnamese security, culture and social order. Second, China often requires Chinese companies to be the bid winner on loans provided for infrastructure projects. The Chinese companies could use Chinese workers at the expense of Vietnamese workers, again causing social tensions. Third, Chinese contractors often use outdated technology, produce low-quality structures and incur increased costs.

The fourth concern centres on the lack of transparency, which increases the chance of Chinese contractors' collusion, corruption, overvaluation and cost increases in infrastructure projects. Fifth, joining the BRI might weaken Viet Nam's assertion of sovereignty over the Paracel and Spratly Islands. In order to obtain loans from the BRI, Viet Nam and other countries in the region are obliged to sign bilateral agreements with China, which is outside of the ASEAN framework. Because the BRI treats each country in ASEAN differently, it would divide the ASEAN countries, causing difficulties for Viet Nam in resolving the East Viet Nam Sea dispute. Viet Nam's concern is that BRI loans and projects in Laos have shifted that country's votes in international organizations away from Viet Nam and towards China. The same problem appears to be occurring due to increased BRI activities in Cambodia.

Most of these concerns stem from the fact that there is a lack of mutual trust between the two countries. Viet Nam has also had an unpleasant experience with a significant BRI project, the 2011 Cat Linh–Ha Dong tramline project.[84] This involved a 12-km elevated sky train in Hanoi. The project ran considerably behind schedule and over budget. It finally launched in November 2021.

Viet Nam also wants to promote its public-private partnership (PPP) model.[85] From 2011–17 Viet Nam mobilized 200,000,000m. new dông ($9,000m.) from private enterprises for PPP investment projects. PPP projects have the advantage of reducing the government's financial burden. The feeling in Hanoi is that BRI from China would increase the possibility of emerging debt issues similar to those that have plagued other BRI countries.

Assessment

The region's countries form a spectrum of BRI experiences. The two countries with improving or stable governance, Viet Nam and Thailand, are not dependent on China for improvements in their infrastructure but can find other funding or undertake projects independently. The three countries with poor and declining governance, Myanmar, Cambodia and Laos, are becoming more dependent on BRI programmes and are falling deeper under China's control.

The United States and Japan will probably increase their development assistance and technical aid to the region. Japan's 'Strategy 2018', aimed at developing infrastructure in the Mekong region, is currently a direct competitor of China's BRI.[86] However, the United States and Japan will probably struggle to match Chinese aid flows. Still, all the Mekong countries will welcome extra-regional efforts to balance China's local influence.

Notes

1 WLE Mekong, 'Mekong River Basin'. https://wle-mekong.cgiar.org/cha nges/where-we-work/mekong-river-basin/ (accessed 25 May 2022).

2 Huong Le Thu, 'Rough Waters Ahead for Vietnam-China Relations', Carnegie Endowment for International Peace, 30 September 2020. https:// carnegieendowment.org/2020/09/30/rough-waters-ahead-for-vietnam-china -relations-pub-82826.

3 Aun Chhengpor, 'Mekong Region Grows More Important to China-US Relations', VOA, 23 June 2019. www.voanews.com/a/east-asia_mekon g-region-grows-more-important-china-us-relations/6170466.html.

4 Mekong River Commission for Sustainable Development. www.mrcm ekong.org/ (accessed 25 May 2022).

5 Sovinda Po and Christopher Primiano, 'Lancang-Mekong Cooperation: China's Institutional Shield', *The China Story*, 8 July 2021. www.thechina story.org/lancang-mekong-cooperation-chinas-institutional-shield/.

6 Kay Johnson, 'Chinese Dams Held Back Mekong Waters during Drought, Study Finds', Reuters, 13 April 2020. www.reuters.com/article/us-mekon g-river/chinese-dams-held-back-mekong-waters-during-drought-study-finds -idUSKCN21V0U7.

7 Bounlonh J. Soukamneuth, 'The Political Economy of Transition in Laos: From Peripheral Socialism to the Margins of Global Capital', PhD dissertation, Cornell University, August 2006. https://ecommons.cornell. edu/bitstream/handle/1813/3430/The Political Economy of Transition in Laos.pdf.

8 Jayant Manion and Peter Warr, ADB Economics Working Paper Series', Asian Development Bank, January 2013. www.adb.org/sites/default/files/p ublication/30138/economics-wp330-lao-economy.pdf.

9 Lao National Chamber of Commerce and Industry, 'Lao Economic Overview'. https://lncci.la/lao-economic-overview/ (accessed 25 May 2022).

10 Pheuiphanh Ngaosyvathn, 'Lao-Thai Trade: An Aggiornamento', *Southeast Asian Affairs*, 1990. www.jstor.org/stable/pdfplus/27911999.pdf.

11 American Enterprise Institute, China Global Investment Tracker Enterprise Institute. www.aei.org/china-global-investment-tracker/ (accessed 25 May 2022).

12 Poramet Tangsathaporn and Aye Kein KhamKham, 'All Aboard the Laos-China Railway', *Bangkok Post*, 19 December 2021. www.bangkokp ost.com/thailand/general/2234251/all-aboard-the-laos-china-railway.

13 The World Bank, 'Transforming Lao PDR from a Land-Locked to a Land-Linked Economy, 16 September 2020. www.worldbank.org/en/coun try/lao/publication/transforming-lao-pdr-from-a-land-locked-to-a-land-lin ked-economy.

14 The following sections on hydropower draw heavily on Robert Looney, 'Laos and the Hydropower Curse', *Milken Institute Review*, 8 July 2019. www.milkenreview.org/articles/laos-and-the-hydropower-curse.

15 International Hydropower Association, Laos. www.hydropower.org/coun try-profiles/laos (accessed 25 May 2022).

16 Emmy Sasipornkarn, 'Why Is Laos Building Mekong Dams It Doesn't Need?' DW, 15 January 2021. www.dw.com/en/why-is-laos-building-m ekong-dams-it-doesnt-need/a-56231448 (accessed 25 May 2022).

17 International Monetary Fund, World Economic Outlook Databases. www. imf.org/external/pubs/ft/weo/2019/01/weodata/weoselgr.aspx (accessed 25 May 2022).

18 The World Bank, Worldwide Governance Indicators. https://datacatalog. worldbank.org/dataset/worldwide-governance-indicators (accessed 25 May 2022).

19 Radio Free Asia, 'Lao Officials Slam Corruption', 11 October 2020. www. rfa.org/english/news/laos/laocorruption-02112009175322.html.

20 The Heritage Foundation, 'Laos'. www.heritage.org/index/country/laos (accessed 25 May 2022).

21 World Economic Forum, 'The Global Competitiveness Report 2018'. http://reports.weforum.org/global-competitiveness-report-2018/ (accessed 25 May 2022).

22 Melissa Mittelman, 'The Resource Curse', Bloomberg, 19 May 2017. www.bloomberg.com/quicktake/resource-curse.

23 Marwaan Macan-Makar, 'Chinese Dams Ramp up Lao External Debt', Nikkei Asia, 2 November 2018. https://asia.nikkei.com/Economy/Chinese-dams-ramp-up-Lao-external-debt.

24 Ashley Westerman, 'In Laos, a Chinese-Funded Railway Sparks Hope for Growth - and Fears of Debt', *Houston Public Media*, 26 April 2019. www. houstonpublicmedia.org/npr/2019/04/26/707091267/in-laos-a-chinese-fund ed-railway-sparks-hope-for-growth-and-fears-of-debt/.

25 Joe McDonald, Sam McNeil and Elaine Kurtenbach, 'Laos Will Open $5.9 Billion Railway as Debt to China Mounts', Bloomberg, 2 December 2021. www.bloomberg.com/news/articles/2021-12-02/laos-china-railway-to-launch-as-debt-to-beijing-mounts?sref=NoEVqJH2.

26 Reuters, 'Laos Gives Buddhist Blessings to Its New High-Speed Rail Line', 2 December 2021. www.reuters.com/markets/deals/laos-gives-bud dhist-blessings-its-new-high-speed-rail-line-2021-12-02/.

27 United States Department of Agriculture, 'Crop Explorer for Major Crop Regions', 13 December 2011. https://ipad.fas.usda.gov/highlights/2011/12/ Laos_13Dec2011/.

28 Stephen Sparkes, 'Hydropower Development and Food Security in Laos', *Aquatic Procedia*, 12 July 2013. www.researchgate.net/publication/263319 460_Hydropower_Development_and_Food_Security_in_Laos.

29 Stefan Lovgren, 'Mekong River Dams Threaten Southeast Asia's Fish, Soil, and People', *National Geographic*, 3 May 2021. www.nationalgeograp hic.com/environment/2018/08/news-southeast-asia-building-dams-floods-cli mate-change/.

30 Mekong River Commission, 'The Council Study', 29 December 2017. www. mrcmekong.org/assets/Publications/Council-Study/Council-study-Reports-The matic/Impacts-of-Domestic-and-Industrial-Water-Use-28-Dec-2047.pdf.

31 Stephen Wright, 'Vietnam Warns of Dire Impact from Planned Mekong Dams', Associated Press, 5 April 2016. https://apnews.com/9d406b611a ec43e8bcaa9f2fe1689269.

32 *DW*, 'Laos: Controversial Dams on the Mekong', 25 December 2014. www.dw.com/en/laos-controversial-dams-on-the-mekong/a-18129126.

33 Pech Sotheary, 'Laos Urged to Address Dam Project Impacts', *Khmer Times*, 7 April 2019. www.khmertimeskh.com/594355/laos-urged-to-a ddress-dam-project-impacts/.

34 Johanna Son, 'Looking for Space in the Lao Dam Debate', Heinrich Böll Foundation, 31 January 2019. https://th.boell.org/en/2019/01/31/looking-space-lao-dam-debate.

35 Economic Research Institute for ASEAN and East Asia, 'Lao PDR Energy Statistics 2018'. www.eria.org/uploads/media/0_Lao_PDR_Energy_Statistics_2018_complete_book.pdf.

36 Alex Kirby, 'Climate Change Will Harm Mekong Basin Harvests', Climate Central, 31 March 2013. www.climatecentral.org/news/climate-change-will-harm-mekong-basin-harvests-15798.

37 Mekong River Commission, '3rd MRC International Conference: Enhancing Joint Efforts and Partnerships towards Achievement of the Sustainable Development Goals in the Mekong River Basin', 20 November 2018. www.mrcmekong.org/.

38 Murray Hiebert, 'China's Belt and Road: From Malaysia to Philippines, Projects Face Hurdles', *South China Morning Post*, 8 September 2020. www.scmp.com/week-asia/opinion/article/3100628/chinas-belt-and-road-malaysia-philippines-asean-projects-face.

39 Sebastian Strangio, 'Laos Grants 25-Year Power Grid Concession to Chinese', *The Diplomat*, 17 March 2021. https://thediplomat.com/2021/03/laos-grants-25-year-power-grid-concession-to-chinese-majority-firm/.

40 The World Bank, Logistics Performance Index. https://lpi.worldbank.org/ (accessed 25 May 2022).

41 Chris Barrett, 'Cambodia, China's Closest Ally in South-East Asia, Looks to "Reset Ties" with US', *Sydney Morning Herald*, 1 June 2021. www.smh.com.au/world/asia/cambodia-china-s-closest-ally-in-south-east-asia-looks-to-reset-ties-with-us-20210601-p57x2f.html.

42 Qi Lin, 'Money Talks: China's Belt and Road Initiative in Cambodia', *Global Risk Insights*, 7 January 2018. https://globalriskinsights.com/2018/01/money-talks-chinas-belt-road-initiative-cambodia/.

43 East Asia Research Center, 'Outcome Report'. https://cicp.org.kh/wp-content/uploads/2021/02/Outcome-Report-of-Overview-and-Outlook-of-Cooperation-between-China-and-Cambodia-under-Belt-Road-Initiative.pdf (accessed 25 May 2022).

44 C. Textor, 'China: Outward FDI Flows to ASEAN by Country 2020', Statista, 2 November 2021. www.statista.com/statistics/722607/china-outward-fdi-flows-to-asean-by-country/.

45 Ibid.

46 Peter Warr and Jayant Menon, 'Cambodia's Special Economic Zones', Arndt-Corden Department of Economics, Australian National University, September 2015. https://acde.crawford.anu.edu.au/publication/working-papers-trade-and-development/7804/cambodias-special-economic-zones.

47 Road Traffic Technology, 'Phnom Penh-Sihanoukville Expressway'. www.roadtraffic-technology.com/projects/phnom-penh-sihanoukville-expressway/ (accessed 25 May 2022).

48 Hannah Ellis-Petersen, '"No Cambodia Left": How Chinese Money Is Changing Sihanoukville', *The Guardian*, 31 July 2018. www.theguardian.com/cities/2018/jul/31/no-cambodia-left-chinese-money-changing-sihanoukville.

49 Simon Marks, 'Chinese Dam Project in Cambodia Raises Environmental Concerns', *New York Times*, 16 January 2012. www.nytimes.com/2012/01/17/business/global/17iht-rbog-cam17.html.

50 Sok Khemara, 'China Gives Cambodia $600m in Exchange for International Support', VOA, 17 July 2016. www.voanews.com/a/china-gives-cambodia-millions-exchange-international-support/3421648.html.

51 Natalie Song, 'What China's Belt and Road Initiative Means for Cambodia', USC Annenberg, 21 July 2020. https://china.usc.edu/what-china s-belt-and-road-initiative-means-cambodia.

52 McCain Institute, 'The Crisis in Myanmar (Burma)', 9 March 2017. www. mccaininstitute.org/wp-content/uploads/2017/03/burma-paper-3-9-17.pdf.

53 *The Irrawaddy*, 'Timeline: China-Myanmar Relations', 14 January 2020. www.irrawaddy.com/specials/timeline-china-myanmar-relations.html.

54 Paul Vrieze, 'Un Ranks Burma among 3 Least Developed Asian Nations', *The Irrawaddy*, 20 August 2016. www.irrawaddy.com/news/burma/un-ra nks-burma-among-3-least-developed-asian-nations.html.

55 Mark Tallentire, 'The Burma Road to Ruin', *The Guardian*, 28 September 2007. www.theguardian.com/world/2007/sep/28/burma.uk.

56 *The Irrawaddy*, 'U Thein Sein Wins Award for Leadership during Burma's Transition', 9 December 2016. www.irrawaddy.com/news/burma/u-thein-sein-wins-award-for-leadership-during-burmas-transition.html.

57 The Nobel Prize, 'The Nobel Peace Prize 1991'. www.nobelprize.org/p rizes/peace/1991/kyi/facts/ (accessed 25 May 2022).

58 Justin Kent, 'Myanmar, The Last Frontier?' *Forbes Magazine*, 28 November 2012. www.forbes.com/sites/connorconnect/2012/11/09/myanmar-the-la st-frontier/#46909b215dce.

59 BBC News, 'Myanmar's 2015 Landmark Elections Explained', 3 December 2015. www.bbc.com/news/world-asia-33547036.

60 *Myanmar Times*, 'US Officially Terminates Sanctions Order', 10 October 2016. www.mmtimes.com/national-news/22991-us-officially-terminates-san ctions-order.html.

61 Reuters, 'New Myanmar Constitution Gives Military Leading Role', 19 February 2008. www.reuters.com/article/us-myanmar-constitution/new-mya nmar-constitution-gives-military-leading-role-idUSBKK10184120080219.

62 Gary Kleiman, 'Myanmar Military Business Sketch Alerts Investors', *Asia Times*, 18 February 2020. https://asiatimes.com/2019/08/myanmar-milita ry-business-sketch-alerts-investors/.

63 The World Bank, Worldwide Governance Indicators. http://info.worldba nk.org/governance/wgi/ (accessed 25 May 2022).

64 Asian Development Bank, 'Myanmar: Country Partnership Strategy (2017–2021)'. www.adb.org/sites/default/files/institutional-document/23716 1/cps-mya-2017-2021.pdf (accessed 25 May 2022).

65 Nicholas Lo, 'Trouble for Belt and Road in Myanmar', *China Dialogue*, 19 May 2021. www.chinadialogue.net/article/show/single/en/11585-Trouble-fo r-Belt-and-Road-in-Myanmar.

66 Thai PBS World, '"Debt Trap" Alert Arises in Myanmar as More 'Belt and Road' Projects Scrapped', 30 September 2018. www.thaipbsworld.com/debt-trap-alert-arises-in-myanmar-as-more-belt-and-road-projects-scrapped/.

67 BBC News, 'Myanmar Rohingya: What You Need to Know about the Crisis', 23 January 2020. www.bbc.com/news/world-asia-41566561.

68 United Nations Human Rights Council, 'The Economic Interests of the Myanmar Military', 5 August 2019. www.ohchr.org/en/hr-bodies/hrc/ documents.

69 Tridivesh Singh Maini, 'Why US Criticism of the Belt and Road Initiative Is Not Enough?' *IPP Review*, 27 November 2019. https://cn.ippreview.com/index.php/blog/single/id/366.html (accessed 26 May 2022).

70 United States Institute of Peace, 'Xi Jinping's Visit to Myanmar: What Are the Implications?' 17 September 2021. www.usip.org/publications/2020/01/xi-jinpings-visit-myanmar-what-are-implications.

71 Sebastian Strangio, 'China's Top Diplomat Checks in on Myanmar Projects', *The Diplomat*, 16 September 2020. https://thediplomat.com/2020/09/chinas-top-diplomat-checks-in-on-myanmar-projects/.

72 BBC News, 'Myanmar: What Has Happened since the 2021 Coup?', 27 April 2022. www.bbc.com/news/world-asia-55902070.

73 Janjira Sombatpoonsiri, 'Two Thailands: Clashing Political Orders and Entrenched Polarization - Political Polarization in South and Southeast Asia: Old Divisions, New Dangers', Carnegie Endowment for International Peace, 18 August 2020. https://carnegieendowment.org/2020/08/18/two-thailands-clashing-political-orders-and-entrenched-polarization-pub-82438.

74 BBC News, 'Thailand Army's Pivotal Role in Politics', 22 May 2014. www.bbc.com/news/world-asia-27483816.

75 The World Bank, 'Aging and the Labor Market in Thailand', World Bank Blogs. https://blogs.worldbank.org/eastasiapacific/aging-and-labor-market-thailand (accessed 26 May 2022).

76 UNCTAD, 'World Investment Report 2021', 21June 2021. https://unctad.org/webflyer/world-investment-report-2021.

77 Michael Hart, 'From Bangkok to Nong Khai: China's Thai Railway Vision Edges Forward', *Geopolitical Monitor*, 26 April 2021. www.geopoliticalmonitor.com/from-bangkok-to-nong-khai-chinas-thai-railway-vision-edges-forward/.

78 Toru Takahashi, 'China's Pan-Asian Railway Sputters to a Halt in Thailand', Nikkei Asia, 16 January 2022. https://asia.nikkei.com/Economy/China-s-pan-Asian-railway-sputters-to-a-halt-in-Thailand.

79 International Monetary Fund, World Economic Outlook Database, October 2021. www.imf.org/en/Publications/WEO/weo-database/2021/October.

80 Crisis Group, 'Vietnam Tacks between Cooperation and Struggle in the South China Sea', 7 December 2021. www.crisisgroup.org/asia/north-east-asia/china/318-vietnam-tacks-between-cooperation-and-struggle-south-china-sea.

81 John Hurley, Scott Morris and Gailyn Porelance, 'Examining Debt Implications Belt and Road Initiative Policy Perspective', Center for Global Development, March 2018. www.cgdev.org/sites/default/files/examining-debt-implications-belt-and-road-initiative-policy-perspective.pdf.

82 UNCTAD, 'World Investment Report 2021'.

83 Statista, 'China: Outward FDI Flows to Vietnam', 4 January 2022. www.statista.com/statistics/720408/china-outward-fdi-flows-to-vietnam/.

84 Tomoya Onishi, 'Vietnam's China-Built Metro Line Falls 2 Years behind Schedule', Nikkei Asia, 20 July 2020. https://asia.nikkei.com/Business/Transportation/Vietnam-s-China-built-metro-line-falls-2-years-behind-schedule.

85 Alan Rosengarten, 'Vietnam's New Law on Public-Private Partnerships', White & Case LLP, 26 October 2020. www.whitecase.com/publications/alert/vietnams-new-law-public-private-partnerships.

86 Ministry of Foreign Affairs, Japan, 'Tokyo Strategy 2018 for Mekong-Japan Cooperation', 9 October 2018. www.mofa.go.jp/files/000406731.pdf.

8   The BRI in South Asia

Introduction

The South Asian countries, namely the Maldives, Pakistan, Sri Lanka and Bangladesh, all have the potential to play significant roles in the People's Republic of China's Belt and Road Initiative (BRI). However, these roles have been shifting as China's interests refocused, and the countries began to encounter impediments to further expansion in their investment programmes. Per capita incomes are relatively low, and their economies in the post-coronavirus COVID-19 pandemic era are struggling (Figure 8.1). The Maldives achieved the highest per capita income (on a purchasing-power parity basis in 2017 international dollars), increasing from US $11,768 in 2000 to $21,814 in 2021. The corresponding increases were $2,014 to $5,266 for Bangladesh, $5,988 to $12,924 for Sri Lanka and $3,341 to $4,985 for Pakistan.

With the exception of Bangladesh, debt levels were already rising among the four South Asian countries prior to the outbreak of the COVID-19 pandemic in 2020 (Figure 8.2). Thereafter, they accelerated rapidly in the Maldives, rising from 54.9% of gross domestic product (GDP) in 2015 to the precarious level of 137.2% in 2021. During this period Pakistan's debt burden increased from 63.3% of GDP to 83.4%, while in Sri Lanka the corresponding increase was from 78.5% to 109.3%.

Governance levels are low and have remained so since around 2010 (Figure 8.3). The countries fall into two groups, with the Maldives and Sir Lanka having relatively high levels of governance. In contrast, governance levels in Bangladesh and Pakistan remained lodged at around the 20th percentile, with no sign of improvement on the horizon.

The four countries follow the typical pattern of increased transport infrastructure, improving with better levels of governance. In 2018 Sri

DOI: 10.4324/b23227-8

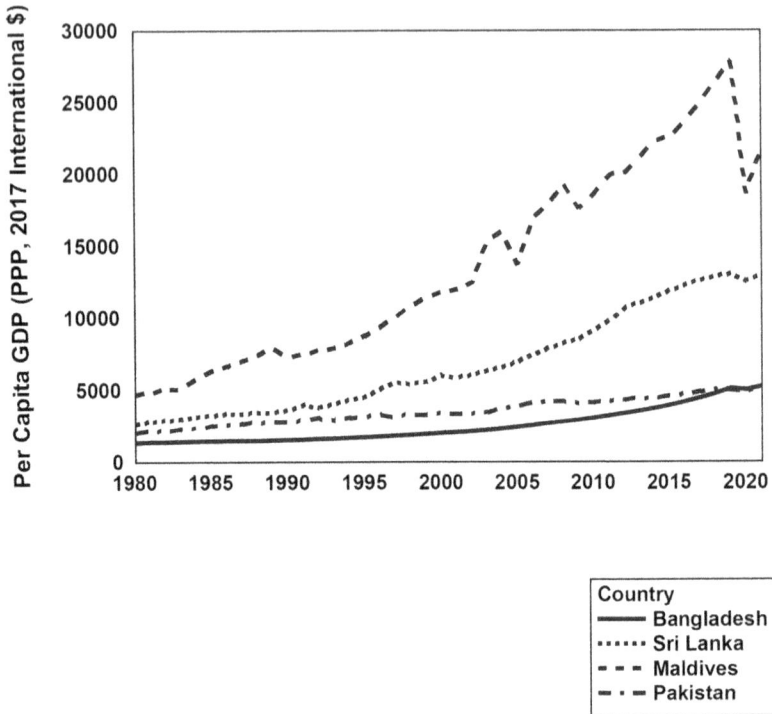

Figure 8.1 Per capita income growth in South Asia, 1980–2021
Source: International Monetary Fund, World Economic Outlook Database:
October 2021.

Lanka significantly underachieved on infrastructure quality, with the country ranked 85th out of 160 countries, considerably below the expected levels in the low fifties. The Maldives and Bangladesh over-achieved, whereas, at 121st position, Pakistan's infrastructure ranking was in line with its level of governance.

The Maldives

The Maldives is a low-lying group of twenty-six atolls comprising 1,192 islands approximately 300 miles south-west of India. In 2021 the country had a small population of approximately 384,000 inhabitants. It is of interest to China mainly because of its location near the central Indian Ocean shipping lanes that act as a vital conduit for oil shipments.[1]

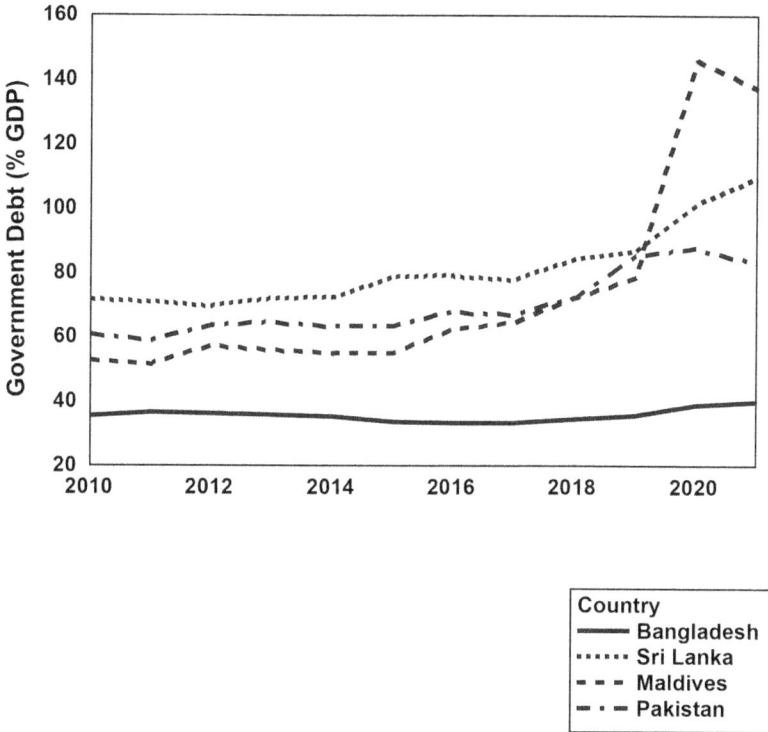

Figure 8.2 Government Debt as a % of GDP in South Asia, 2010–21
Source: International Monetary Fund, World Economic Outlook Database: October 2021.

The country's economy has been one of the region's better performers until recently, with GDP growth rates averaging 10.5% in the 1980s, 6.6% in the 1990s and 6.9% in the 2000s, before declining to 4.3% from 2010–21. In the last decade, growth dropped from 6.0% during 2010–15 to 2.6% during 2016–21.

Unfortunately, past improvements in prosperity are unlikely to be sustained in the next decade. While tourist activity will eventually return following the COVID-19 pandemic, several factors will probably constrain future growth.[2]

The country has one of the world's lowest domestic savings rates, and these have been declining since the 1990s. As a share of GDP, savings fell from 23.8% in the 1990s to 7.5% in the 2000s and further to 4.2% from 2010–21. The decline in savings has resulted in a growing balance of payments deficit, with the current account deficit increasing

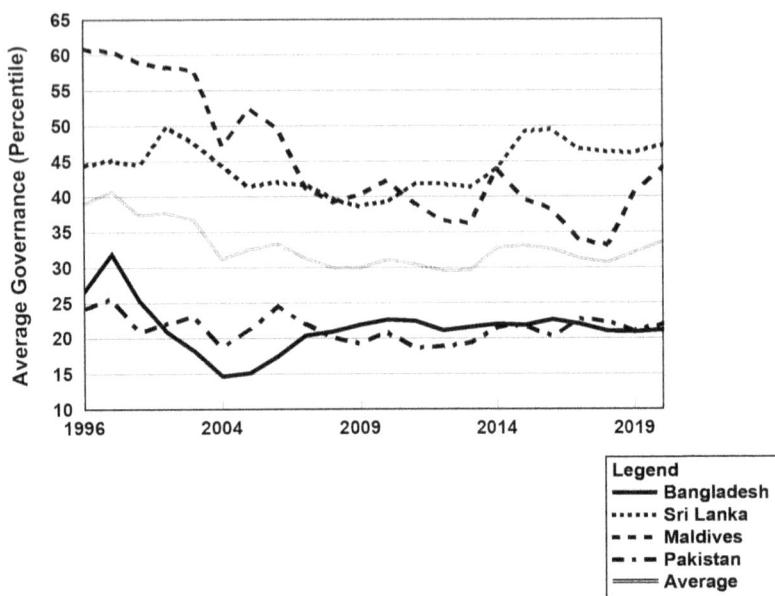

Figure 8.3 Governance Levels in South Asia, 1996–2020
Note: Governance is the average of its components: voice and accountability, political stability and absence of violence/terrorism, government effectiveness, regulatory quality, rule of law and control of corruption.
Source: World Bank, Worldwide Governance Indicators Database.

from 3.5% of GDP in the 1990s to 12.5% in the 2000s and to 15.8% from 2010–21. Much of the current account financing came from external borrowing, with the government's debt increasing from 34.7% in 2004 to the dangerous range of 55.1% in 2014. By 2021 government debt reached the unmanageable level of 137.2% of GDP.

Much of the recent surge in debt coincides with the country's shift away from India and towards China. The Maldives has had an 'India First' policy.[3] Before 2011 China did not even have an embassy in the Maldives. However, things changed rapidly after the 2012 election of Abdulla Yameen, a leader with authoritarian tendencies who changed the diplomatic dynamics of the country by opening up to China.[4]

The Maldives joined the BRI in 2017. By early 2021 the country had received six BRI projects totalling $1,230m. The BRI programme sought to strengthen the Maldivian government's aim of diversifying the economy away from its narrow base of fishing and tourism. President Abdulla Yameen's government also sought funds from the

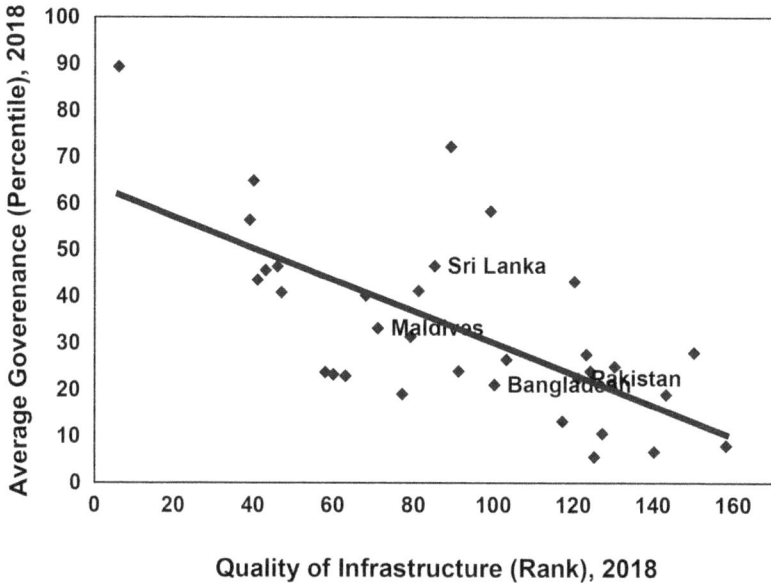

Figure 8.4 Governance/Transport Infrastructure Quality Relationship in South Asia, 2018

Note: The solid line represents the governance/infrastructure trend.

Sources: Governance: World Bank, Worldwide Governance Indicators Database; Infrastructure: World Bank, Logistics Performance Index Database.

programme to improve connectivity between the islands and to prepare defences against rising sea levels.[5]

The first major BRI project was the $200m. China-Maldives Friendship Bridge that links the island's capital Malé with the residential island of Hulhumalé.[6] China also financed the airport's expansion, at a cost of $800m., and the construction of 7,000 apartments on the artificial island of Hulhumalé.[7]

Chinese infrastructure projects in the Maldives have created considerable debt.[8] China not only provided loans at high interest rates but also lent hundreds of millions of dollars through a sovereign guarantee line.[9] If a company goes bankrupt, the Maldivian government has to repay the debt to Chinese banks. Excessive levels of debt have brought about political change. In the election of 2018, Yameen lost to Ibrahim Mohamed Solih, an ally of Indian Prime Minister Narendra Modi. Subsequently, Yameen was sentenced to five years' imprisonment for money laundering.[10] The courts also convicted him of awarding construction contracts to Chinese companies at inflated prices.[11] However, the government wanted to avoid a earning a reputation for evicting investors summarily and allowed existing China-funded projects to proceed.

In mid-2020 the World Bank classified the Maldives as one of nine countries in 'debt distress'.[12] China agreed to cut $25m. from the $100m. due to be repaid in that year.[13] Chinese action was part of an agreement under the Group of 20 Debt Service Suspension Initiative, of which the Maldives is a member, to postpone debt servicing on bilateral loans.[14] In October 2021 the credit rating agency Fitch Ratings upgraded the country's rating from CCC to B– with a stable outlook.[15] The upgrade reflects a more robust tourism recovery than expected, but Fitch still warned that the country's refinancing would remain challenging.

As measured by the World Bank, governance has worsened since the 1990s, but particularly during the presidency of Abdulla Yameen (2013–18). During his administration the country's control of corruption ranking declined from the 28th percentile (2012) to the 17th percentile (2018). Other governance dimensions essential for economic growth and sustained development also declined. Government effectiveness fell from the 45th percentile to the 35th percentile, regulatory quality from the 38th percentile to the 34th percentile, and the rule of law from the 36th percentile to the 31st percentile. Fortunately, a reversal occurred in the past few years, with control of corruption rising to the 45th percentile in 2020, while government effectiveness reached the 49th percentile.

In 2018 the quality of the country's transport infrastructure ranked somewhat above that usually associated with the country's overall governance (Figure 8.4). However, with governance improving in recent years, much of this gap will probably close. Given the country's debt situation, further infrastructure improvements will probably come from non-BRI investments and help from other countries. In essence, BRI projects enabled the country to improve its infrastructure at considerable cost despite an environment of deteriorating governance – a situation that is not sustainable.

The Solih administration has reverted to the country's traditional pro-India policy and raised concerns about debt arising from China-funded BRI programmes.[16] The Maldives has recently received financial help from India in the form of currency swaps and low interest loans for infrastructure projects.[17] India, the United States, Japan and Australia form the 'Quad' security grouping.[18] Each is worried about China's growing power. In September 2020 the Maldives and the United States agreed to work towards closer security and defence cooperation.

Pakistan

The Pakistani economy has achieved relatively strong rates of GDP since the 1980s. However, the trend has been downward, with growth averaging 6.4% in the 1980s, 4.5% in the 1990s, 4.7% in the 2000s and 3.6% from 2010–21. Debt has increasingly financed growth, with government budget deficits averaging 3.5% in the 2000s, before increasing to 6.7% from 2010–21.

During this period the current account deficit of the balance of payments increased from 2.7% of GDP to 6.5% from 2010–21, while debt as a share of GDP increased from 60.7% in 2010 to 83.4% in 2021. Because foreign direct investment (FDI) did not increase significantly, with values of $2,496m. in 2017, $1,737m. in 2018, $2,234m. in 2019 and $2,105m. in 2020, it is safe to say that increased borrowing has financed the current account deficit.[19]

Inadequate infrastructure has long constrained the Pakistani economy with inadequate transport, leaving many areas barely connected to commercial centres. Power shortages are frequent, which has inhibited the emergence of energy-intensive industries.[20] Agriculture and other water-intensive sectors, such as textiles, face challenges owing to Pakistan's worsening water shortages, underscored by weak utility management and climate risk. The result has been a vicious circle of slowing growth, increased instability and restrained inflows of FDI.[21]

With the announcement of the $62,000m. China-Pakistan Economic Corridor (CPEC) in 2013, Prime Minister Nawaz Sharif felt that it would solve all these problems.[22] Comprising a series of energy and infrastructure projects spanning the length of Pakistan, the CPEC formed the centrepiece of Chinese President Xi Jinping's BRI.[23] In return for Pakistan's participation, China would provide expertise, labour and loans, the last of which Pakistan would be required to repay with substantial interest once the profits began to come in.

The CPEC project, which runs through the heart of the Baluchistan region, is of significant interest to China. It will involve a 3,000-km trade route (comprising road, rail and energy pipelines) linking western China to the Arabian Sea. When completed, possibly by 2030, it will offer China an alternative to shipping goods via its eastern and southern ports. Under Chinese operational control, it will also provide China with a strategically located base at the Port of Gwadar. China stands to gain an alternative route for trade rather than the South China Sea, with the shorter distance saving transport costs (the distance will be reduced by almost 9,000 km) and less uncertainty.

However, the project faces threats from the ongoing separatist rebellion in Pakistan's Baluchistan province. The insurgency is disrupting the construction of the project. It will increase security costs for foreign nationals working on the project and those looking to use the corridor's transport links over the long term.

Prime Minister Sharif and other proponents of the CPEC argued that it would improve Pakistan's regional income balance by connecting impoverished areas such as Southern Punjab, rural Sindh and most of Baluchistan with more prosperous urban commercial hubs. One government report estimated that the CPEC would boost Pakistan's economic growth from 5.8% in 2018 to 7% by 2023, thereby providing the government with more income than is required to service its growing Chinese debt.

This forecast assumed that a strategy of infrastructure-led development based on Albert Hirschman's unbalanced growth model was realistic in present-day Pakistan.[24] Theoretically, a rapid expansion in infrastructure would ease bottlenecks and constraints on growth and drastically lower private sector costs for transport, power and other infrastructure-related inputs. The dramatic drop in infrastructure-related expenses would spur follow-on growth in other areas of the economy by allowing even inexperienced entrepreneurs to identify profitable avenues for investment.

Unfortunately, empirical evidence suggests that infrastructure investment in Pakistan has failed to start a private sector investment surge.[25] Instead, Pakistani growth has spurred infrastructure investment. Even if China's efforts could switch the causation to infrastructure causing private sector investment, it would have a limited effect, given Pakistan's poor business environment and macroeconomic instability, combined with the ongoing threat of violence.

Pakistan ranked 153rd out of 180 countries for its business environment in the 2022 Heritage House Index of Economic Freedom.[26] In the past few years, a downward trend in the business environment has resulted in the economy shifting from the 'mostly unfree' category to 'repressed' in the 2022 index. Heritage House attributed the country's recent deterioration in economic freedom to declines in business freedom, fiscal health and the rule of law.

Other contributing factors included regulatory inefficiencies, the government's oppressive involvement in economic activity, and the fact that most Pakistani firms lack access to bank lending. Also cited were Pakistan's prolonged judicial system and corruption-plagued civil service. Lower infrastructure-related costs are unlikely to offset investor concerns in such an environment.

Besides backsliding on critical areas of economic freedom, poor policy decisions continue to plague the country, putting the economy at a disadvantage relative to other emerging Asian markets, such as Bangladesh. Pakistan's debt and fiscal constraints mean that there is little money available to upgrade the country's woefully inadequate educational system, another prerequisite for private sector growth.[27] Without significant reforms in governance and significant upgrading of the country's educational system, Pakistan will have a challenging time absorbing the massive amounts of investment flowing into CPEC projects.

Many of Pakistan's financial problems predate the CPEC, as evidenced by a succession of International Monetary Fund (IMF) balance of payments support programmes, the most recent of which was scheduled to end in October 2022. However, Pakistan's massive borrowing from China exacerbated the problem. It is unclear whether Pakistan limited the borrowing to CPEC projects. In the run-up to the July 2018 elections, Pakistan's foreign exchange reserves increased by over $1,000m., suggesting an influx of Chinese assistance to boost the election chances of the then-ruling pro-CPEC party.[28]

If Pakistan's dismal business environment and high debt were not bad enough, add violent unrest to the mix. Some of the CPEC's highest-value components occur in dangerous places. For example, the CPEC's route takes it through Baluchistan, where there are plans to expand the small fishing village of Gwadar into a thriving port city to rival Dubai (United Arab Emirates) and serve as China's opening to the Arabian Sea.[29] Unfortunately, Baluchistan is home to a violent independence movement, the Baloch Liberation Army.[30] In May 2017 the Baloch killed ten Chinese labourers working on a new road project and warned China 'to vacate Baluchistan and stop plundering its resources'. In response, China proposed deploying its troops to protect the project workers, a suggestion that Pakistan has successfully rebuffed – at least for now. Several other incidents have occurred in recent years. The latest was a bus blast on 14 July 2021 in Khyber Pakhtunkhwa province, that killed nine Chinese workers, two Pakistani paramilitary soldiers and two locals. Pakistani authorities found traces of explosives at the site.

China is nowhere close to withdrawing its commitment to the CPEC but probably is growing more doubtful about Pakistan's ability to mitigate risks to the infrastructure and personnel associated with it. Pakistan will probably continue to provide security to the corridor, but China may assume a more significant role in overseeing related arrangements.

As for the financial impact of the CPEC, a March 2017 IMF report found that CPEC loans accounted for a considerable portion of Pakistan's rising current account deficit and external debt obligations.[31] The report concluded that Pakistan's economic growth would be unable to reach the 7% needed to finance its Chinese loans by 2023 but correctly predicted that growth would drop below 5% for the next few years before flatlining at 5% starting in 2021. By late 2018, Pakistan's finances had deteriorated to the extent to which the government had to request help from the IMF to avoid defaulting on international payments, prompting US Secretary of State Mike Pompeo to warn the IMF against making any loans that would ultimately service the Chinese debt.[32] Pakistan received a $6,000m. IMF programme in July 2019, which subsequently stalled several times. Finally, in early February 2022 the IMF's board approved a $1,000m. disbursement designed to ease the macroeconomic crisis.

In 2018, alarmed by Pakistan's increasing Chinese debt and the lack of transparency surrounding the previous government's financial agreements with China, newly elected Prime Minister Imran Khan ordered an investigation into the terms of the various CPEC projects for which his predecessors had contracted.[33] The inquiry found that contracts for CPEC projects had been so poorly negotiated that they overwhelmingly favoured China.[34] For example, Pakistan reportedly guaranteed Chinese power plants annual returns as high as 17% over the next three decades, with Pakistan obligated to cover shortfalls.[35] The Khan administration also found that many CPEC projects had been approved, showing little evidence of financial viability.[36] The Pakistani government is currently reviewing its options regarding the future of CPEC.

In early February 2022 Pakistan's Prime Minister, Imran Khan, visited China, meeting China's President, Xi Jinping, and China's Premier, Li Keqiang, and signing agreements for continued infrastructure creation by China in Pakistan. Pakistan and China agreed to step up cooperation in fields including energy, infrastructure, technology, agriculture and housing, primarily via the continued investment by Chinese businesses in Pakistan. The two nations are expected to begin the second phase of the CPEC in late 2022, and this will involve work in the Pakistan-administered region of Kashmir, which India claims.

While remaining strategically allied with China, Pakistan faces mounting difficulties in repaying loans from that country and purportedly asked for an additional loan of $3,000m. Although China has already granted about $11,000m. in the form of commercial loans and foreign exchange reserves, it has become increasingly wary about falling into a potential debt trap owing to Pakistan's cash-strapped situation. The Chinese government's lack of direct financial commitment suggests that China will tighten its terms for further financial support to Pakistan.

While it is still too early to pass any final judgement on the CPEC, there is little reason to expect it to provide anywhere near the benefits initially touted by its supporters. At worst, the CPEC could be a horrendously expensive folly that further burdens the already struggling economy. It may eventually play a positive role, but only after a series of painful governance and economic reforms, macroeconomic stabilization programmes and educational improvements, combined with transparency in the country's financial dealings with China.

Sri Lanka

The Sri Lankan economy has sustained moderate, albeit declining, GDP growth rates in recent decades, averaging 5.9% in the 1990s, 5.2% in the 2000s and 4.4% from 2010–21. However, much of this growth has come at the cost of increased indebtedness.

Government fiscal deficits have increased with time, averaging 6.7% of GDP in the 1990s, 7.0% in the 2000s and 7.1% from 2010–21. Budget deficits came about because of falling revenues and expenditures, but revenues fell faster. While government expenditures declined as a share of GDP from 24.1% of GDP in the 1990s to 21.1% in the 2000s and to 19.4% from 2010–21, the corresponding revenue figures were 17.4%, 14.1% and 12.4%.

With growing budgetary deficits, government debt as a share of GDP increased from the already dangerous level of 71.6% in 2010 to 109.3% by 2021, with the IMF expecting a further increase to 111.6% in 2024.[37] Similar increases in the country's current account deficit have also occurred, with the government running deficits of 4.8% of GDP in the 1990s, 3.0% in the 2000s, and 3.1% during 2010–21.

As of mid-2022 Standard & Poor's credit rating for Sri Lanka stood at CCC (junk bond, currently vulnerable to non-payment), with a negative outlook.[38] In late September 2020 Moody's credit rating for Sri Lanka stood at Caa2 (junk bond, poor standing subject to very high credit risk) with a stable outlook. In late December 2021 Fitch Ratings downgraded Sri Lanka's sovereign rating to CC from CCC, citing an 'increased probability of a default event in coming months'.[39] Sri Lanka's foreign exchange reserves fell to $1,600m. at the end of November 2021, enough to finance only about one month's imports.

Owing to its recent downgrades, financial markets shut Sri Lanka out of the international market for private debt. If private creditors hold back from lending to the country, Sri Lanka could struggle to meet its debt servicing requirements, which amount to more than $4,000m. per year for the period 2021–25. The country faces turning to emergency financing from the IMF. That possibility occurred in early 2022 when the country fell into the grip of a foreign exchange crisis, making it difficult to pay for imports, causing inflation to surge, and raising the risk of a sovereign debt default. Given the state of the economy, it is no surprise to find that FDI flows into the country are barely a trickle at $1,373m. (2017), $1,614m. (2018), $758m. (2019) and $434m. (2020).[40]

In the past, the government appeared resistant to approaching the Fund for a bailout, wary of the conditions that would probably accompany a programme. Instead, it has relied on partners, including China and India, for financial support. However, anti-government protests have picked up as more people contend with economic hardship.

Many observers blame China and its BRI programme for this dire situation. As of early 2021 the country had forty-one Chinese projects amounting to $14,820m. Twenty projects between November 2013 and February 2021 totalled $8.86b. China is also among the leading providers of new credit to Sri Lanka. In April 2021 the country received a $500m. loan from the China Development Bank.[41] For some time, the government has counted on currency swaps with China. China already accounts for a sizeable share of Sri Lanka's outstanding debt. China's critics say that it has pushed Sri Lanka into a debt trap, forcing the government to make strategic concessions.[42] An example frequently cited is the 2017 debt-for-equity deal, whereby Sri Lanka handed over the Hambantota port to China on a ninety-nine-year lease.[43] More recently, in February 2021, the government cancelled an agreement for India and Japan – strategic rivals to China – to help to develop the Colombo port's East Container Terminal. It subsequently awarded the contract for the project to the China Harbor Engineering Company.

However, Sri Lanka's debt crisis has been long in the making. The twenty-six-year-long civil war, which ended in 2009, depressed foreign exchange earnings. Since then, exports have remained relatively low owing to the adverse impact of the global financial crisis. The exports-to-GDP ratio was approximately 20% in 2010 and has hovered at around that figure subsequently.[44]

President Mahinda Rajapaksa's government (2005–15), which won the civil war against ethnic insurgents, undertook massive public investment following the end of the conflict.[45] It wanted to project its image as a powerful stabilizing force and undertook several prestige projects, such as a port in Rajapaksa's home city of Hambantota.

Due to low-interest rates and quantitative easing policies adopted by advanced countries during the 2008–09 recession, Rajapaksa's administration found cheap credit readily available. Financial markets considered Sri Lanka a favourable market for investors, especially after an IMF decision in 2009 to support the government with a credit of $2,600m.[46]

Rajapaksa's government borrowed heavily through international sovereign bond issues. The commercial and non-concessional bonds had maturities of between five and ten years and interest rates of 5%–8%. Meanwhile, bilateral loans from China came to around $8,000m. The government used the Export-Import Bank of China loan to finance construction of the Hambantota port.

With exports depressed and debt rising quickly, Sri Lanka became trapped in a vicious circle. It borrowed from abroad to finance investments but did not earn the foreign exchange to service that debt. Many of China's loans to Sri Lanka were for large infrastructure projects that yielded low or negative returns and earned very little foreign exchange, Hambantota being a prime example.

Both Sri Lanka and China have portrayed the Hambantota agreement as a strictly commercial agreement. Both reject speculation that it is a means for China to gain a strategic foothold. China was careful not to enact the deal as a government-to-government exchange, instead preferring to negotiate through commercial entities. Sri Lanka has repeatedly stated that the port's security will be its responsibility, and that it will not allow its use for military purposes. Still, Hambantota has become a lightning rod for critics of the BRI.

A frequent refrain in global discourse is that it exemplifies a Chinese conspiracy to trap developing countries in unsustainable debt to gain control of strategic assets. Sri Lanka is in a debt trap, but not an expressly Chinese debt trap. However, Sri Lanka's debt crisis is because of its economic decision-making and excessive commercial borrowing rather than iniquitous Chinese lending. Chinese loans to Sri Lanka have differed from the commercial loans that Sri Lanka has mobilized through the international market. Roughly 60% of loans from China have been concessional, with a maturity of between fifteen and twenty years and interest rates of 2%–3%.[47] Only 10% of Sri Lanka's foreign debt is from Chinese sources.

Unfortunately, despite the physical expansion in infrastructure and the debt accrued, the country's transport infrastructure quality ranks considerably below that usually associated with its level of governance (Figure 8.4). While the country improved its quality of transport infrastructure ranking from 89th to 85th out of 160 countries between 2012 and 2018, this may have been more associated with the slight improvement in governance (up from 41st percentile to the 47th percentile) that occurred during this period.

Bangladesh

Bangladesh sits at a strategic confluence in South Asia, bordering India, China's principal rival in Asia. In addition, it is strategically located along the route of the Maritime Silk Road. In 2020 the stock of Chinese FDI totalled $1,710.58m., considerably behind Pakistan's $6,218.94m. but well above Sri Lanka's $523m. and the Maldives's $43.98m.[48]

The attractiveness of Bangladesh to Chinese investors stems in part from the country's accelerating rates of growth. GDP expanded at an average annual rate of 3.5% in the 1980s, 4.8% in the 1990s, 5.8% in the 2000s and 6.3% from 2010–21. Owing to sustained growth, per capita incomes increased from $1,358 (on a purchasing-power parity basis in 2017 international dollars) in 1980 to $5,246 in 2021. High and consistent growth over the last decade has been a critical factor in bringing down the government debt-to-GDP ratio; in 2010 it was 35.5%. However, by 2021 the ratio was still only 39.9%, the lowest of the South Asia countries. Bangladesh achieved lower-middle-income country status in 2015.[49]

However, in sharp contrast to most developing economies, growth occurred without an appreciable improvement in governance (Figure 8.3). Average governance (based on the World Bank's six governance dimensions) remains extremely low. It is on a slightly long-term declining trend, falling from the 25th percentile in 2000 to the 14.6th percentile in 2004 before gradually increasing to the 20.1st percentile by 2020. At this level, Bangladesh ranked slightly below Pakistan (22nd) as having the lowest level of governance in South Asia apart from Afghanistan. The country scores particularly low in political stability at the 16th percentile (albeit up from the 9th percentile in 2012).

Governance declines occurred across the spectrum. Corruption has worsened, with the country declining from the 22nd percentile in 2015 to the 16.8th percentile in 2020. Regulatory quality has also recently suffered, falling from the 18.2nd percentile in 2015 to the 16.4th percentile in 2020. Voice and accountability declined steadily from the

47th percentile in 1998 to the 27th percentile by 2020. Government effectiveness fell from the 31st percentile in 2000 to the 20.0th percentile in 2020.

Despite the decline in governance, investment as a percentage of GDP has gradually increased from 17.5% in the 1980s to 19.9% in the 1990s, 25.4% in the 2000s and 29.3% from 2010–19. The country's external accounts have not been under pressure because there has been a corresponding increase in domestic savings (17.5%, 19.9%, 25.4% and 29.4%, respectively).

Chinese investor interest in Bangladesh stems from the fact that, with wages rising in China, Bangladesh offers a way for Chinese companies to move offshore to keep labour costs down. The garment industry is an example of a sector that will struggle to remain competitive at the low end in China; however, Bangladesh is already a major international producer. Opportunities for Chinese investment are being enhanced by a series of BRI projects planned or underway in Bangladesh.

Bangladesh joined China's BRI in 2013. A surge in Chinese investment in 2018 followed the approval of a $24,000m. loan programme by Chinese President Xi Jinping during his visit to Bangladesh in 2016. By early 2021 there were sixty Chinese investments with a total value of $28,850m., forty-five of which were BRI-type totalling $25,260m.

Bangladesh's transport infrastructure sector has significant room for growth. The country's road and rail networks are underdeveloped, while its current lack of a deep-water port limits its export potential. Underdeveloped urban expressways and transit systems have also left the capital, Dhaka, with severe traffic congestion and air pollution. The World Economic Forum's 2019 Global Competitiveness Report ranks Bangladesh's transport infrastructure as among the worst in Asia.[50] The World Bank ranked the quality of the country's transport 138th out of 160 countries in 2014 and 100th in 2018.[51]

Domestic transport in Bangladesh is reliant mainly on inland waterways, rivers and canals, carrying over 50% of arterial freight traffic and 25% of passenger traffic. As a result, the government has emphasized developing road and rail corridors to improve domestic logistics by increasing capacity and travel speeds.

One significant project currently under construction by China's Sichuan Road and Bridge Corporation and the Bangladeshi firms Unique Dream Consultant and Shamim Enterprise is the Padma Multipurpose Bridge, which will become the largest bridge in the country on completion.[52] At an estimated cost of $3,700m., supported by China through loans taken from the Export-Import Bank of China, the bridge will facilitate easier road and rail access from the central Dhaka region to the country's south-west, connecting the two local economies and spurring development in the area. However, progress on the project has lagged owing to various factors, such as poor execution and delays in financing. The COVID-19 pandemic has also led to further delays in the project owing to staffing constraints, particularly among the large number of Chinese nationals working on the project.

Another major project, the $470.2m. Dhaka Bypass Expressway has recently broken ground, and although authorities were expecting it to be completed in 2022, it may also suffer delays.[53] A Chinese company is to tunnel under the Karnaphuli River in Chittagong to improve road connections. China is also backing power generation and power transmission projects.

However, Chinese-backed projects in Bangladesh are not without controversy. Chinese personnel often comprise a large share of the workforce on project sites in Bangladesh.[54] There have been clashes between Bangladeshi and Chinese workers. The latest resulted in the death of a Chinese worker and injuries to dozens of others at the Payra power plant in June 2019.

Bangladesh benefits economically from the geopolitical rivalry between China, Japan and India. This rivalry has been much in evidence in the contest to build Bangladesh's first deep-water seaport. Initially, four sites were under consideration: Chittagong, Sonadia, Payra and Matarbari. China preferred Chittagong, the country's principal port. It almost secured Sonadia, but Bangladesh yielded to US and Indian pressure and security fears regarding the Bay of Bengal. The focus for Japan was on Matarbari. Port expansions need supporting infrastructure, and so it was all or nothing for Chinese companies if they lost out on the main project. Japan has long been a significant aid donor to Bangladesh. In 2016 Japan signed a historic $1,500m. concessionary loan agreement with Bangladesh. Bangladesh will spend the money on power, communications, disaster management and energy conservation. In September 2020 Japan won the Matarbari project.[55]

Challenges facing China's BRI in Bangladesh may increase over the coming years. The country's debt level is well under control. Before the introduction of BRI programmes (and other investments), Bangladesh was an underachiever. Its transport infrastructure quality was much lower than that usually associated with its level of governance at the time (Figure 8.5). However, by 2018 the country's transport infrastructure quality had outrun increases in governance. (Figure 8.4). Future BRI programmes without continued governance improvements might find much less success than that achieved in the past.

Assessment

With the exception of Bangladesh, the South Asia countries examined here have encountered severe debt problems in recent years. While it is tempting to attribute this situation to China's BRI programmes, many other factors, especially poor policymaking, were significant contributors. The debt situation of these countries will severely curtail BRI programmes in the near term.

The case of Bangladesh is instructive. Prudent fiscal policy, with expanded BRI programmes, appears to have contributed to accelerating economic growth rates. However, the country will have to follow up with improved reforms. If not, the government may find that BRI programmes are not nearly as effective as they once were.

Notes

1 International Monetary Fund, World Economic Outlook Database, October 2021. www.imf.org/en/Publications/WEO/weo-database/2021/October (accessed 26 May 2022).
2 Yi (Claire) Li and Valerie Mercer-Blackman, 'The Changing Face of Tourism and Work: How Maldives Is Successfully Adapting to the Pandemic', World Bank Blogs, 26 January 2022. https://blogs.worldbank.org/endpovertyinsouthasia/changing-face-tourism-and-work-how-maldives-successfully-adapting-pandemic.
3 *Hindustan Times*, 'Maldives Committed to "India First" Policy: Male to New Delhi', 11 January 2018. www.hindustantimes.com/india-news/maldives-committed-to-india-first-policy-male-to-new-delhi/story-uvWplzYARSuYTisa5NyyZL.html.
4 Robert A. Manning and Bharath Gopalaswamy, 'Is Abdulla Yameen Handing over the Maldives to China?' *Foreign Policy*, 21 March 2018. https://foreignpolicy.com/2018/03/21/is-abdulla-yameen-handing-over-the-maldives-to-china/.
5 Daniel Manzo, Ginger Zee, Sohel Uddin and Dragana Jovanovic, 'Facing Dire Sea Level Rise Threat, Maldives Turns to Climate Change Solutions to Survive', ABC News, 3 November 2021. https://abcnews.go.com/International/facing-dire-sea-level-rise-threat-maldives-turns/story?id=80929487.
6 Anbarasan Ethirajan, 'China Debt Dogs Maldives' "Bridge to Prosperity"', BBC News, 17 September 2020. www.bbc.com/news/world-asia-52743072.
7 *Xinhua*, 'Chinese-Built Social Housing Complex a Boon for Maldivians'. www.news.cn/english/asiapacific/2021-11/27/c_1310336533.htm (accessed 26 May 2022).
8 Siman Mundy and Hathrin Hille, 'The Maldives Counts the Cost of Its Debts to China', *Financial Times*. www.ft.com/content/c8da1c8a-2a19-11e9-88a4-c32129756dd8 (accessed 26 May 2022).
9 *Nikkei Asia*, 'China Debt Trap Fear Haunts Maldives Government', 15 September 2020. https://asia.nikkei.com/Spotlight/Belt-and-Road/China-debt-trap-fear-haunts-Maldives-government.

10 Mohamed and Junayd, 'Maldives Ex-President Sentenced to Five Years for Money Laundering', Reuters, 28 November 2019. www.reuters.com/article/uk-maldives-yameen-idUKKBN1Y218D.

11 *Global Construction Review*, 'India Builds Bridges in the Maldives with $500M Infrastructure Package', 17 August 2020. www.globalconstructionreview.com/india-builds-bridges-maldives-500m-infrastructure/.

12 The World Bank, 'Overview: The World Bank in Maldives', 8 April 2022. www.worldbank.org/en/country/maldives/overview#1.

13 Marwaan Macan-Markar, 'India and China Compete over Indian Ocean Debt-Relief Diplomacy', *Financial Times*, 6 December 2020. www.ft.com/content/79363b3b-534d-436c-9ede-af713d913570.

14 The World Bank, 'Debt Service Suspension Initiative', 14 March 2022. www.worldbank.org/en/topic/debt/brief/covid-19-debt-service-suspension-initiative.

15 Fitch Ratings, 'Fitch Upgrades the Maldives to "B–"; Outlook Stable', 28 October 2021. www.fitchratings.com/research/sovereigns/fitch-upgrades-maldives-to-b-outlook-stable-28-10-2021.

16 PK Vasudeva, 'Maldives Gets Pro-People and Pro-India Government under Ibrahim Solih', *Indian Defence Review*, 27 November 2018. www.indiandefencereview.com/news/maldives-gets-pro-people-and-pro-india-government-under-ibrahim-solih/.

17 Nayanima Basu, 'Delhi's Financial Aid to Male Exceeds $2 Billion as Maldives Returns to "India First"', *ThePrint*, 13 August 2020. https://theprint.in/diplomacy/delhis-financial-aid-to-male-exceeds-2-billion-as-maldives-returns-to-india-first/481052/.

18 TamilNet, 'Modi Brings Maldives into Quad-Agenda, Announces USD 1.4 Billion in Assistance', 18 December 2018. www.tamilnet.com/art.html?catid=79&artid=39286.

19 UNCTAD, 'World Investment Report 2021'. https://unctad.org/webflyer/world-investment-report-2021 (accessed 26 May 2022).

20 Charles K. Ebinger and Kashif Hasnie, '"Power"-Less Pakistan', Brookings, 28 July 2016. www.brookings.edu/opinions/power-less-pakistan/.

21 Robert M. Hathaway, Bhumika Muchhala and Michael Kugelman (eds), 'Fueling the Future', Woodrow Wilson International Center for Scholars, March 2007. www.wilsoncenter.org/sites/default/files/media/documents/publication/Asia_FuelingtheFuture_rptmain.pdf.

22 Ministry of Planning, Development and Special Initiatives, China-Pakistan Economic Corridor (CPEC) Authority Official Website. http://cpec.gov.pk/ (accessed 26 May 2022).

23 The following sections on Pakistan's CPEC draw heavily on Robert Looney, 'Pakistan's Morning After', *Milken Institute Review*, 5 December 2018. www.milkenreview.org/articles/pakistans-morning-after.

24 The History of Economic Thought, 'Albert O. Hirschman, 1915–2012'. www.hetwebsite.net/het/profiles/hirschman.htm (accessed 26 May 2022).

25 Robert E. Looney, 'Infrastructure and Private Sector Investment in Pakistan', *Journal of Asian Economics*, January 1997. www.relooney.com/REL_Pubs/RelJAE.pdf.

26 The Heritage Foundation, '2018 Index of Economic Freedom', 2 February 2018. www.heritage.org/international-economies/commentary/2018-index-economic-freedom.

27 Riazul Haq, 'Higher Education Body's Budget Slashed by 50%', *Express Tribune*, 25 April 2018. https://tribune.com.pk/story/1695231/1-high er-education-bodys-budget-slashed-50/.

28 Reuters, 'China Lends $1 Billion to Pakistan to Boost Plummeting FX Reserves: Sources', 30 June 2018. www.reuters.com/article/us-pakista n-china-loans/china-lends-1-billion-to-pakistan-to-boost-plummeting-fx-re serves-sources-idUSKBN1JQ0TV.

29 Rina Saeed Khan, 'Thirsty to Thriving? Parched Pakistani Port Aims to Become a New Dubai', Reuters, 24 April 2018. www.reuters.com/article/ us-pakistan-port-water/thirsty-to-thriving-parched-pakistani-port-aims-to-become-a-new-dubai-idUSKBN1HV07K.

30 *Al Jazeera*, 'Gunmen Kill 10 Labourers in Pakistan's Balochistan', 13 May 2017. www.aljazeera.com/news/2017/05/gunmen-kill-10-labourers-balochis tan-gwadar-170513111330168.html.

31 International Monetary Fund, 'Pakistan: First Post-Program Monitoring Discussions – Press Release; Staff Report; and Statement by the Executive Director for Pakistan', 14 March 2018. https://www.imf.org/en/Publica tions/CR/Issues/2018/03/14/Pakistan-First-Post-Program-Monitoring-Disc ussions-Press-Release-Staff-Report-and-Statement-45724.

32 Christine Lagarde, 'Statement by IMF's Managing Director Christine Lagarde on Pakistan', Press Release No. 18/390, International Monetary Fund, 11 October 2018. www.imf.org/en/News/Articles/2018/10/11/pr1839 0-statement-by-imf-managing-director-christine-lagarde-on-pakistan.

33 Drazen Jorgic, 'Fearing Debt Trap, Pakistan Rethinks Chinese "Silk Road" Projects', Reuters, 30 September 2018. www.reuters.com/article/ us-pakistan-silkroad-railway-insight/fearing-debt-trap-pakistan-rethinks-c hinese-silk-road-projects-idUSKCN1MA028.

34 Gerry Shih, 'Pakistan Has Second Thoughts on Chinese Investment: It Probably Won't Be the Last Country to Get Cold Feet', *Washington Post*, 11 September 2018. www.washingtonpost.com/world/2018/09/11/pakista n-has-second-thoughts-chinese-investment-it-probably-wont-be-last-countr y-get-cold-feet/.

35 Jeremy Page and Saeed Shah, 'China's Global Building Spree Runs into Trouble in Pakistan', *Wall Street Journal*, 24 July 2018. www.wsj.com/articles/ chinas-global-building-spree-runs-into-trouble-in-pakistan-1532280460.

36 PTI, 'China Pak Reject Media Report That Imran Khan's Govt Wants to Renegotiate BRI Deals', *The Week*, 31 March 2020. www.theweek.in/ wire-updates/business/2018/09/11/fgn17-china-pak-cpec.html.

37 International Monetary Fund, World Economic Outlook Database, October 2021.

38 Trading Economics, Sri Lanka: Credit Rating. https://tradingeconomics. com/sri-lanka/rating (accessed 26 May 2022).

39 Fitch Ratings, 'Correction: Fitch Downgrades Sri Lanka's Long-Term Foreign-Currency IDR to "CC"', 17 January 2022. www.fitchratings.com/ research/sovereigns/correction-fitch-downgrades-sri-lanka-long-term-foreig n-currency-idr-to-cc-17-01-2022.

40 UNCTAD, 'World Investment Report 2021'.

41 Munza Mushtaq, 'China Offers Sri Lanka a Lifeline as Critics Question Cost', Nikkei Asia, 20 April 2021. https://asia.nikkei.com/Politics/Interna tional-relations/China-offers-Sri-Lanka-a-lifeline-as-critics-question-cost.

42 Lee Jones, 'World Investment Report 2021: Investing in Sustainable Recovery', UNCTAD, 1 October 2020. www.chathamhouse.org/2020/08/debunking-myth-debt-trap-diplomacy/4-sri-lanka-and-bri.
43 Kiran Stacey, 'China Signs 99-Year Lease on Sri Lanka's Hambantota Port." Financial Times, December 11, 2017. https://www.ft.com/content/e150ef0c-de37-11e7-a8a4-0a1e63a52f9c.
44 The World Bank, Exports of Goods and Services (% of GDP) – Sri Lanka. https://data.worldbank.org/indicator/NE.EXP.GNFS.ZS?locations =LK (accessed 26 May 2022).
45 R. M. B. Senanayake, 'The Economy Mahinda Rajapaksa Left to His Successors', *Columbo Telegraph*, 7 April 2015. www.colombotelegraph.com/index.php/the-economy-mahinda-rajapaksa-left-to-his-successors/.
46 International Monetary Fund, 'Press release: IMF Executive Board approves US$2.6 billion Stand-by Arrangement for Sri Lanka', 24 July 2009. www.imf.org/en/News/Articles/2015/09/14/01/49/pr09266.
47 Dushni Weerakoon and Sisira Jayasuriya, 'Sri Lanka's Debt Problem Isn't Made in China', East Asia Forum, 13 November 2019. www.eastasiaforum.org/2019/02/28/sri-lankas-debt-problem-isnt-made-in-china/.
48 Statista, 'China: Outward FDI Stock along the Belt and Road Initiative 2020', 2 November 2021. www.statista.com/statistics/722707/china-outward-fdi-stock-along-the-belt-and-road-initiative-by-country/.
49 The World Bank, 'The World Bank in Bangladesh'. www.worldbank.org/en/country/bangladesh/overview#1 (accessed 26 May 2022).
50 World Economic Forum, 'Global Competitiveness Report 2019'. www.weforum.org/reports/how-to-end-a-decade-of-lost-productivity-growth (accessed 26 May 2022).
51 The World Bank, Logistics Performance Index. https://lpi.worldbank.org/ (accessed 26 May 2022).
52 Prothomalo, 'Padma Bridge Project Included in China's BRI', 24 April 2019. https://en.prothomalo.com/bangladesh/Padma-Bridge-project-included-in-China%E2%80%99s-BRI.
53 Munima Sultana, 'Dhaka Bypass Expressway: China-Led JV Breaks Ground Today', *Financial Express*, 26 December 2019. www.thefinancialexpress.com.bd/national/dhaka-bypass-expressway-china-led-jv-breaks-ground-today-1577339212.
54 BBC News, 'Bangladesh and China Power Plant Workers in Deadly Mass Brawl', 19 June 2019. www.bbc.com/news/world-asia-48689943.
55 Indo-Pacific Defense Forum, 'Bangladesh Partners with Japan on Deep-Sea Port, Dropping PRC-Funded Proposal', 7 November 2020. https://ipdefenseforum.com/2020/11/bangladesh-partners-with-japan-on-deep-sea-port-dropping-prc-funded-proposal/.

9 Future Directions

Now nearly ten years old, previous chapters in this volume found the People's Republic of China's Belt and Road Initiative (BRI) to be an evolving process, with mistakes identified and solutions attempted. It is safe to that assume additional difficulties will emerge with perhaps a shift in emphasis from the heavily debt-burdened Caribbean, parts of Central America and the Pacific towards the Mekong countries, South Asia and finally Central Asia. The focus will be more on resource development and on its supporting infrastructure rather than directly on development projects for the host country. However, the answers to fresh problems will face what analysts might term a 'path dependency' constraint.[1] Institutions in many BRI countries are relatively rigid and will increasingly constrain their economies and the effectiveness of BRI programmes.[2]

The principal area of concern is governance. Infrastructure improvements can occur through more investment, such as that embodied in BRI programmes, improved governance – or some combination of the two. Yet, as the previous chapters suggest, most BRI country policymakers have been unable (or unwilling) to support BRI programmes with improved governance.[3] Governance has often declined in BRI countries, with China making little or no effort to require improvements as a condition for loans or investments. The result is infrastructure levels outrunning their supporting institutional base, rendering BRI programmes less and less effective.

Countries in this position are also often those whose governments have taken on an excessive amount of debt.[4] As a result, the early successes of BRI programmes stemming from excess fiscal space – the ability of governments to mount significant supporting investments and adequate levels of governance in order to take on additional amounts of infrastructure efficiently – are no longer possible.

The solution is logical: the recipient countries will have to undertake governance reforms with Chinese help and support – both financially

DOI: 10.4324/b23227-9

and by including governance stipulations for new projects and loans. This shift in approach would represent a pragmatic continuance of the BRI programmes while increasing their effectiveness.

While it is still too early to speculate, this course of action does not appear to be developing. Instead, perhaps because of slowing growth and internal debt problems in China, deglobalization, the uncertainty surrounding the coronavirus COVID-19 pandemic and now the Russian Federation's invasion of Ukraine, there are troubling signs of China increasingly resorting to economic coercion to bully its critics and impose its political will on smaller economies.[5]

For example, when the Chinese political and human rights activist, Liu Xiaobo, received the Nobel Peace Prize in 2010, China curtailed salmon imports and froze free trade agreement (FTA) talks with Norway.[6] [7] In 2012 China halted tropical fruit imports from the Philippines following a confrontation over the disputed Scarborough Shoal.[8]

One interpretation is that China's growing use of economic coercion follows the country's economic evolution over the past four decades. From the 1980s to the late 2000s China's government broadly pursued a 'hide our capacities and bide our time' strategy, during which it relied on expanding its manufactured exports to developed countries to drive the economy.[9] This so-called middle-income stage required open markets, a stable world trading system and, above all, good relations with its trading partners.[10] With an ongoing process of international deglobalization and China more focused on developing domestic markets as a significant source of growth, this environment is of lesser importance.

The economic pressure is incredibly intense where the Republic of China (Taiwan) is involved. In November 2021, after Taiwan opened a representative office in Vilnius, the capital of Lithuania, China downgraded diplomatic relations, banned Lithuanian imports and exports, and warned that China would no longer do business with international companies continuing to trade with Lithuania.[11] China's attempt to remove Lithuania from global value chains heralded an aggressive tilt away from economic carrots such as debt forgiveness towards a big economic stick.[12]

Of course, China is not alone in engaging in coercive economic diplomacy. The United States has regularly employed economic coercion. Trump's trade war with China is a notable example, as are decades of US sanctions against Cuba, Iran, Myanmar (formerly Burma), Venezuela and Afghanistan under the Taliban.[13] But China's measures differ in that they often come abruptly, without announcement, acknowledgement or diplomatic negotiation. They are based not on international law but on selective enforcement of China's domestic laws and regulations, which Xi treats not as constraints but as tools to enhance his power.[14]

There has been, and continues to be, growing pushback against Beijing's tactics, including from governments in Canada and Australia, which continue to stand their ground amid rifts with China, despite the economic consequences.[15] But for smaller countries, there is limited scope for retaliation, and few can afford to bypass the opportunities that BRI financing and projects present or trade with China offers.

For these countries, the best hope is to ally themselves with larger countries or country groupings, such as the European Union (EU). In a boost to Lithuania, the European Commission recently proposed a new anti-coercion legal instrument that would empower the Commission to act on behalf of the Union against non-EU entities threatening or applying economic sanctions to member states.[16] Potential responses to coercive actions include increasing trade restrictions, suspending tariff concessions and imposing new or higher customs duties.

As the European Commission's action suggests, China may discover that the costs of its growing use of coercive economic power outweigh the gains. China's arbitrary use of economic measures to punish foreign firms and governments during political disagreements makes it an unreliable partner. While engaging with China pragmatically, countries will inevitably shift their supply chains as necessary to eliminate vulnerabilities to Chinese economic coercion in strategic areas.[17]

The Chinese economy got where it is today because, from roughly 1998–2005, the government developed a consistent framework whereby the economy's various components supported one another towards the single end goal of economic growth. However, in recent years the unpredictability arising from economic coercion has resulted in inefficiencies. When the government, without warning, banned Australian coal and domestic coal prices rose, price ceilings prevented power companies from passing on the added costs, driving many out of business.

So long as China persists on its current path of economic coercion, look out for further inefficiencies to arise and Chinese economic growth rates to drop even more rapidly than they have in recent years. The country may also find fewer takers for its BRI programmes while facing greater anti-Chinese sentiment in countries burdened with Chinese debt and projects that serve China's interests more than their own.

A recent glimpse of China's developing approach to BRI countries appeared in its dealings with Sri Lanka's debt crisis. During a visit to Sri Lanka by Chinese Minister of Foreign Affairs Wang Yi in early January 2022 President Gotabaya Rajapaksa requested a restructuring of Sri Lanka's debt to China and a concessional scheme for its imports from the country to help to ease its current macroeconomic crisis.[18] Sri Lanka's foreign exchange reserves had fallen to dangerous levels, thereby hindering its ability to pay for imports and raising the risk of a sovereign debt default.

China's ambassador to Sri Lanka stated that China would like to resume negotiations with Sri Lanka over an FTA. Sri Lanka, concerned about the harm that the FTA might inflict on domestic firms, stalled the discussions for years.[19] Ultimately, China will help Sri Lanka but only in ways that serve its interests. It may restructure Sri Lanka's debt and consider a concessional trade credit scheme but will expect Sri Lanka to show enthusiasm over resuming FTA talks and to remain committed to China-funded infrastructure projects in Sri Lanka that further Chinese economic and strategic goals perhaps significantly more than Sri Lanka's. Sri Lanka fast-tracked the FTA in March 2022.[20]

As with Sri Lanka, the main leverage China will have over countries in which it has BRI programmes is their indebtedness. Recent research suggests that Chinese loan contracts with foreign countries often include uncommon conditions, such as an obligation to keep the contents of the contract secret.[21] Other stipulations prioritize repayment of the Chinese loan ahead of other creditors, and clauses which 'potentially allow the lenders to influence debtors' domestic and foreign policies' that 'could limit the sovereign debtor's crisis management options and complicate debt renegotiation'.[22]

Notes

1 S. J. Liebowitz and Stephen E. Margolis, 'Path Dependence, Lock-in, and History', University of Dallas. https://personal.utdallas.edu/~liebowit/paths.html (accessed 27 May 2022).

2 Kristine Sabillo, 'Classic Theories of Economic Growth and Development', Academia.edu, 2 June 2014. www.academia.edu/5335721/Classic_Theories_of_Economic_Growth_and_Development.

3 Wang Xinsong, 'One Belt, One Road's Governance Deficit Problem', *Foreign Affairs*, 17 November 2017. www.foreignaffairs.com/articles/east-asia/2017-11-17/one-belt-one-roads-governance-deficit-problem.

4 Mercy A. Kuo, 'China's BRI Lending: $385 Billion in "Hidden Debts"', *The Diplomat*, 29 November 2021. https://thediplomat.com/2021/11/chinas-bri-lending-385-billion-in-hidden-debts/.

5 Hal Brands and Jake Sullivan, 'China Has Two Paths to Global Domination', Carnegie Endowment for International Peace, 22 May 2020. https:// carnegieendowment.org/2020/05/22/china-has-two-paths-to-global-domina tion-pub-81908.

6 The following draws heavily on Robert Looney, 'China Flexes its Economic Muscles', *Milken Institute Review*, 16 February 2022. www.milk enreview.org/articles/china-flexes-its-economic-muscles

7 Abraham M. Denmark and Lucas Myers (eds), '2020–21 Wilson China Fellowship: Essays on the Rise of China and Its Implications', Wilson Center, 2021. www.wilsoncenter.org/sites/default/files/media/uploads/docu ments/ASIA-210304%20-%20The%20Wilson%20China%20Fellowship%20 report%20-%20web.pdf.

8 Looney, 'China Flexes its Economic Muscles'.

9 Richard Javad, '"Hide Your Strength, Bide Your Time"', *Al Jazeera*, 7 December 2014. www.aljazeera.com/opinions/2014/11/21/hide-your-streng th-bide-your-time.

10 Stephen S. Roach, 'No Middle Income Trap for China', Project Syndicate, 28 March 2019. www.project-syndicate.org/commentary/china-no-middle-income-trap-by-stephen-s–roach-2019-03?utm_term=&utm_campaign=& utm_source=adwords&utm_medium=ppc&hsa_acc=1220154768&hsa_ca m=12374283753&hsa_grp=117511853986&hsa_ad=499567080219&hsa_sr c=g&hsa_tgt=aud-1249316000637%3Adsa-19959388920&hsa_kw=&hsa_ mt=&hsa_net=adwords&hsa_ver=3&gclid=CjwKCAiAlfqOBhAeEiwAYi 43Fy8dR0zXAFqN5pGeMhaS_PQz50zEoMzlIWDMYNerSIgSexIcC1X OqhoCZb4QAvD_BwE.

11 Thomas Colson, 'China Threatened to Send Lithuania to the "Garbage Bin of History" after It Stood up to Beijing by Strengthening Ties with Taiwan', *Business Insider*, 23 December 2021. www.businessinsider.com/china-threaten s-lithuania-with garbage-bin-of-history-for-taiwan-office-2021-12.

12 Johns Hopkins School of Advanced International Studies, 'Global Debt Relief Dashboard'. www.sais-cari.org/debt-relief (accessed 27 May 2022).

13 Chad P. Bown and Melina Kolb, 'Trump's Trade War Timeline: An up-to-Date Guide', PIIE, 10 May 2022. www.piie.com/blogs/trade-investment-p olicy-watch/trump-trade-war-china-date-guide.

14 Congressional Research Service, 'Understanding China's Political System', 20 March 2013. www.everycrsreport.com/reports/R41007.html.

15 *Al Jazeera*, 'Canada's Trudeau Hits China on Human Rights, "Coercive Diplomacy"', 14 October 2020. www.aljazeera.com/news/2020/10/14/cana das-trudeau-hits-china-on-human-rights-coercive-diplomacy.

16 European Commission, 'EU Strengthens Protection against Economic Coercion'. https://ec.europa.eu/commission/presscorner/detail/en/ip_21_6642 (accessed 27 May 2022).

17 Jeffrey Wilson, 'China and Supply Chain Vulnerabilities', Perth USAsia Centre, 24 March 2021. https://perthusasia.edu.au/blog/china-and-supp ly-chain-vulnerabilities.

18 Uditha Jayasinghe, 'Sri Lanka's President Asks China to Restructure Debt Repayments', Reuters, 10 January 2022. www.reuters.com/markets/rates-bonds/ sri-lankas-president-asks-china-restructure-debt-repayments-2022-01-09/.

19 Keshala Dias, 'China-Sri Lanka FTA Talks Stalled', *Bilaterals*, 2 June 2018. www.bilaterals.org/?china-sri-lanka-fta-talks-stalled&lang=es.

20 *Newsfirst*, 'China-Sri Lanka FTA to be Fast-tracked', 13 March 2022. www.newsfirst.lk/2022/03/13/china-sri-lanka-fta-to-be-fast-tracked/.
21 Anna Gelpern, Sebastian Horn, Scott Morris, Brad Parks and Christoph Trebesch, 'How China Lends: A Rare Look into 100 Debt Contracts with Foreign Governments', March 2021. www.cgdev.org/sites/default/files/how-china-lends-rare-look-100-debt-contracts-foreign-governments.pdf.
22 Ibid.

Appendix A: The Governance/Transport Infrastructure Quality Relationship

Because of the short period that the Belt and Road Initiative (BRI) has been in effect and thus limited time series observations, little statistical work currently exists on its impact. The vagueness concerning which projects are BRI and those which are not, is also a factor. The Chinese themselves do not have a master schedule of projects and their cost. As a result, we lack a clear understanding of why BRI programmes appear to be more successful in some countries than in others.

Still, some generalizations using indirect measures have emerged from the literature. One longstanding criticism of the People's Republic of China's assistance programmes, in contrast to those of the West, is the lack of governance improvement as a requirement for funding. The Chinese rarely specify improved rule of law or anti-corruption initiatives as a condition for making BRI investments and loans.

One interesting question is the extent to which improvements in the quality of a country's infrastructure can occur despite the lack of corresponding improvements in governance. If corruption is rampant, can a country significantly enhance the quality of its infrastructure by simply spending more money on construction projects? Fortunately, the World Bank data sets contain detailed information on governance and infrastructure quality.

The World Bank's Worldwide Governance Indicators[1] include data on the six primary components of governance, namely voice and accountability, political stability and absence of violence/terrorism, government effectiveness, regulatory quality, rule of law and control of corruption. The series covers the period 1996–2019, with annual data from 2002 onwards. The World Bank Logistic Performance Index[2] has infrastructure quality as one of its components. The data are for 2007–18, with data for the even-numbered years from 2010. The Bank ranks countries on this index from 1 through 160.

Linear regression analysis was performed[3] to see the extent to which improved governance led to improved infrastructure (while causation between governance and infrastructure is not established, it seems highly unlikely that improved infrastructure would lead to enhanced governance). The two dates selected for analysis were 2012 – pre-BRI – and 2018, the last date for which data are available after the BRI came into effect.

For 2012 the regression results were as follows:

$$1\ INF = 152.1 - 1.8\ GOV$$
$$(15.2)^{**}\ (-6.2)^{**}\ r2\ (adj) = 0.545$$

Where INF is the World Bank's country ranking for infrastructure quality with 1 denoting the best. GOV is the average of the World Bank's six governance dimensions noted above. The summary statistic, r2(adj), is the adjusted r2, while ** signifies significance at the 95% level. GOV is the country's average governance percentile, ranking from 0 (the lowest) to 100 (the highest). The minus sign on the GOV term therefore shows that better governance is associated with higher levels of infrastructure quality.

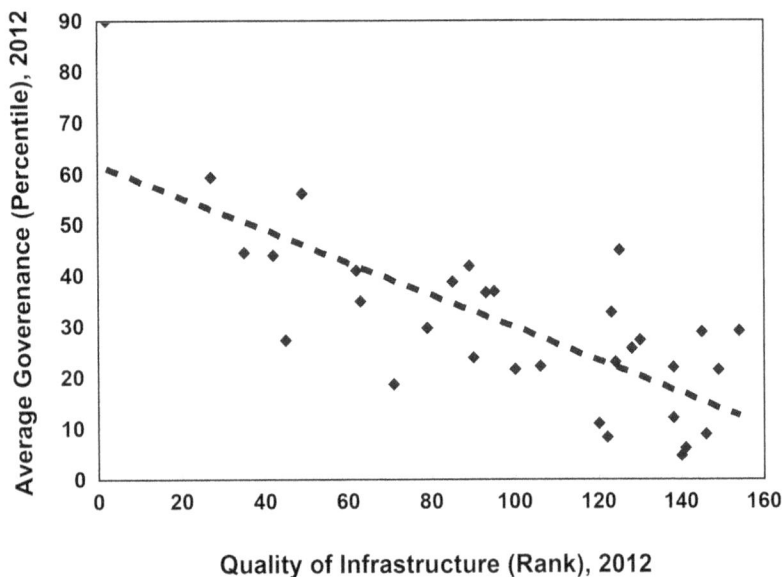

Quality of Infrastructure (Rank), 2012

Figure A.1 Governance/Infrastructure Regression 2012
Source: compiled by the author.

Dummy variables were tested for regional differences but were statistically insignificant in the regression equation. The results from equation 1 are presented in Figure A.1 with countries falling into two groups – underachievers (those to the right of the regression line) and overachievers (those to the left) in infrastructure quality given their level of governance.

For 2018 the regression analysis was expanded to consider developments in 2012. Specifically, did deviations from the 2012 governance/infrastructure equation impact the 2018 regression equation? For 2018 the results were:

$$2 \text{ INF} = 137.8 - 1.4 \text{ GOV}$$
$$(12.1)^{**} \; (-4.7)^{**} \; r2 \text{ (adj)} = 0.429$$

The results (Figure A.2) show a looser relationship between infrastructure in governance than in 2012. An interpretation is that since BRI infrastructure programmes do not have a governance component, they can enable countries to have a higher quality infrastructure, given their level of infrastructure, than would normally be the case.

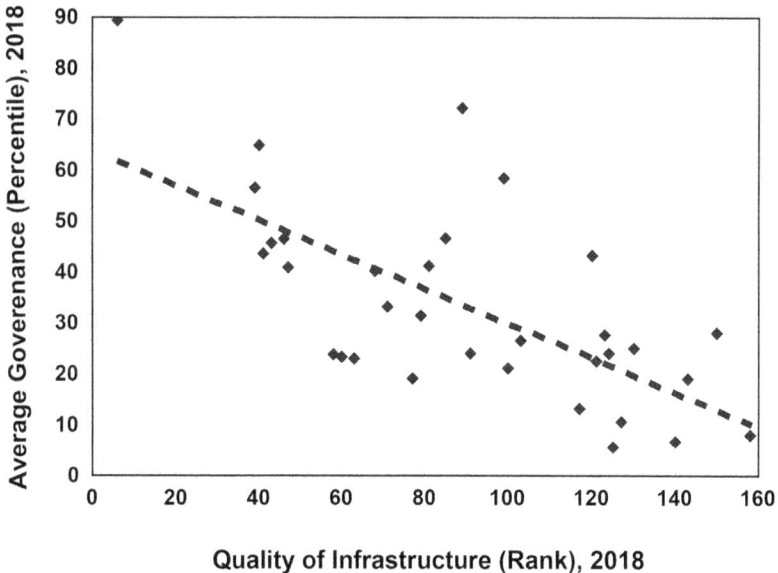

Figure A.2 Governance/Infrastructure Regression 2018
Source: compiled by the author.

A final equation links infrastructure quality in 2018 to that existing in 2012:

$$3 \text{ INF} = 151.2\text{–}1.5 \text{ GOV} - 20.4 \text{ RESID}$$
$$(12.2)^{**} \ (-5.2)^{**} \ (-2.2)^{**} \ r2(\text{adj}) = 0.497$$

Where RESID is the country's residual value (deviation from regression line in equation 1). Since 2012 underachievers (actual infrastructure quality – estimated infrastructure quality) have positive residuals and overachievers have negative residuals, the minus sign on the RESID term suggests that an equilibrating infrastructure/governance relationship is in effect. In other words, countries that underachieved in 2012, everything else being equal, will have lower INF values (higher rankings) in 2018. Similarly, countries that overachieved in 2012 will have, everything else being equal, lower INF values (lower rankings) in 2018.

Since BRI programmes rarely have a governance component but are centred on physical accumulation, we can assume that countries that greatly underachieved in 2018 are likely to have the greatest chance of improved infrastructure associated with current BRI programmes. Those who overachieved in 2018 might find that further infrastructure quality improvements were challenging because they lacked an adequate governance/institutional foundation.

Notes

1 The World Bank, Worldwide Governance Indicators (Washington: World Bank, 2022). http://info.worldbank.org/governance/wgi/.
2 The World Bank, Logistic Performance Index, (Washington: World Bank, 2018). https://lpi.worldbank.org/.
3 Regression analysis was performed using IBM, SPSS Statistical Software.

Appendix B: Data Sources

Unless otherwise specified, the following sources provided the data used throughout the volume.

The International Monetary Fund for data on the economy such as gross domestic product, per capita incomes, government expenditures, government revenues, government debt, aggregate investment and savings, and the current account.[1]

The American Enterprise Institute (AEI) for information on total Chinese investment and construction by country. The AEI identifies investments as BRI-type and non-BRI.[2]

The United Nations Conference on Trade and Investment (UNCTAD) for figures on foreign direct investment (FDI).[3]

The World Bank for governance statistics by country. The figure for total governance used throughout the volume is the yearly average of the Bank's six governance dimensions: voice and accountability, political stability and absence of violence/terrorism, government effectiveness, regulatory quality, rule of law and control of corruption.[4]

The World Bank for data on the quality of transport infrastructure.[5]

Statista for data on Chinese FDI yearly flows and the stock of Chinese FDI by country.[6]

The Heritage Foundation for data on economic freedom and its components.[7]

Notes

1 International Monetary Fund (IMF), World Economic Outlook Database (Washington, DC: IMF, October 2021). www.imf.org/en/Publications/ WEO/weo-database/2021/October.
2 American Enterprise Institute (AEI), *China Global Investment Tracker* (Washington, DC: AEI, continually updated). www.aei.org/china-globa l-investment-tracker/.

3 United Nations Conference on Trade and Development (UNCTAD), *World Investment Report 2021* (New York: United Nations, 2021). https://unctad.org/webflyer/world-investment-report-2021.

4 The World Bank, Worldwide Governance Indicators (Washington, DC: World Bank, 2022). http://info.worldbank.org/governance/wgi/.

5 The World Bank, Logistic Performance Index (Washington, DC: World Bank, 2018). https://lpi.worldbank.org/.

6 Statista. www.statista.com/.

7 The Heritage Foundation, *2022 Index of Economic Freedom* (Washington, DC: Heritage Foundation, 2022). www.heritage.org/index/about.

Appendix C: Notes on the BRI in Central Asia

Central Asia is critical to the People's Republic of China's Belt and Road Initiative (BRI) land routes to Europe, with two significant branches passing through the region. The Republics of Central Asia, namely Kazakhstan, Uzbekistan, the Kyrgyz Republic (Kyrgyzstan) and Tajikistan, see their economic potential as being enhanced by the BRI. However, Turkmenistan, because of its neutrality, did not join the BRI. They hope to use it to leverage their existing strengths and regain some growth momentum lost after 2015.

All four countries roughly follow (Figure C.1) the transport infrastructure quality and governance pattern identified in Appendix A, with Tajikistan and Uzbekistan overachieving significantly and Kyrgyzstan slightly. Kazakhstan was an underachiever, with its infrastructure quality somewhat lower than that associated with its level of governance. Chinese BRI projects will probably have their most significant impact on transport infrastructure quality in Kazakhstan, followed by Kyrgyzstan. Unless governance levels improve significantly in Uzbekistan and Tajikistan, their BRI projects will face strong headwinds.

In this setting, China's goals for the region are both strategic and economic.[1] Strategically, building infrastructure is critical for improving stability in a chronically unstable neighbouring region. China's economic objectives for Central Asia are to establish the region as a transit centre for trade with Europe and the Middle East, exporting manufactured goods to the area by creating new markets there, and importing oil, gas and electricity. However, both objectives face strong headwinds due to several shocks since 2019. First, there were the debilitating effects of the coronavirus COVID-19 pandemic. Second, an ongoing energy crisis developed in 2021.[2] The third is the damaging effects of the Russian Federation's invasion of Ukraine.[3]

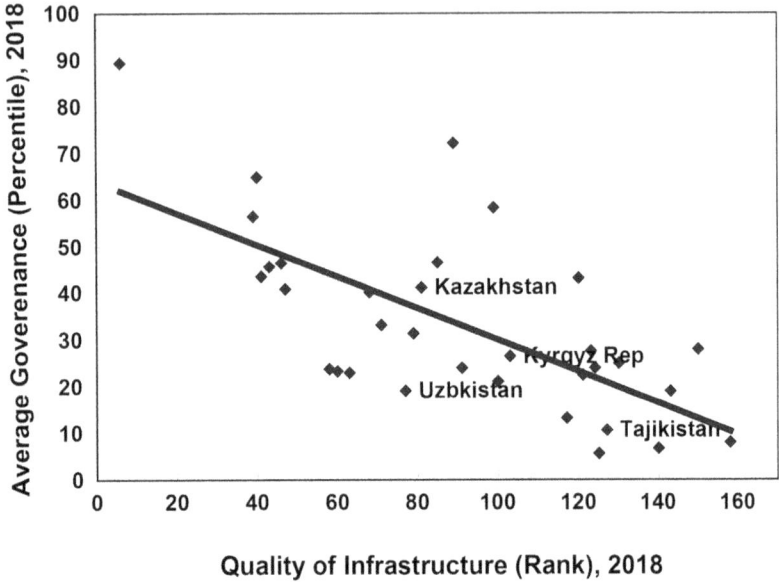

Figure C.1 Central Asia: Governance/Transport Infrastructure Quality
Relationship, 2018
Note: The solid line represents the governance/infrastructure trend.
Source: Governance: World Bank, Worldwide Governance Indicators
Database; Infrastructure: World Bank, Logistics Performance Index Database.

Of these the shock and ramifications of Russia's invasion of Ukraine
may turn out to be the most significant. The Central Asian economies
have many more global connections than in the 1990s, but Russia remains
a significant partner in import and export terms. For many of these
states – especially lower-income countries such as Kyrgyzstan and Tajikistan – workers' remittances from Russia are an essential component of the
countries' balance of payments, helping to sustain domestic demand.

Following the imposition of crippling sanctions, the Russian economy
may enter a prolonged recession. Shocks from the Russian economy
will vary depending on the extent of reliance on Russia, the openness
of the economy, and natural resource endowment, mainly in terms of
hydrocarbon assets and gold. BRI activity will probably continue,
though, until the invasion's uncertain outcome may eventually force

both China and its Central Asian partners to rethink the viability of large projects. For China, a severe recession in Europe and increasing domestic indebtedness may force the country to re-evaluate its whole BRI programme.

Notes

1 Andrew Scobell, Ely Ratner and Michael Beckley, 'China's Strategy toward South and Central Asia', RAND Corporation, 11 August 2014. www.rand. org/pubs/research_reports/RR525.html.
2 Robert Looney, 'Power Shortages in Central Asia's Lands of Abundant Energy', *Milken Institute Review*, 15 April 2022. www.milkenreview.org/arti cles/power-shortages-in-central-asias-lands-of-abundant-energy.
3 Mohammadbagher Forough, 'What Will Russia's Invasion of Ukraine Mean for China's Belt and Road?' *The Diplomat*, 23 March 2022. https:// thediplomat.com/2022/03/what-will-russias-invasion-of-ukraine-mean-for-c hinas-belt-and-road/.

Selected Bibliography

Ali, S. Mahmud (2020) *China's Belt and Road Vision: Geoeconomics and Geopolitics,* Cham: Springer.

Berlie, Jean A. (2019) *China's Globalization and the Belt and Road Initiative,* New York: Palgrave Macmillan.

Chan, Hing Kai, Faith Ka Shun Chan and David O'Brien (2020) *International Flows in the Belt and Road Initiative Context: Business, People, History and Geography,* New York: Palgrave Macmillan.

Chong, Alan and Quang Minh Pham (eds) (2020) *Critical Reflections on China's Belt & Road Initiative,* New York: Palgrave Macmillan.

Clarke, Michael, Matthew Sussex and Nick Bisley (eds) (2020) *The Belt and Road Initiative and the Future of Regional Order in the Indo-Pacific,* Lanham, MD: Lexington Books.

Cockburn, John and Yazid Dissou, Jean-Yves Duclos and Luca Tiberti (eds) (2013) *Infrastructure and Economic Growth in Asia,* Cham: Springer

Fulton, Jonathan (ed.) (2020) *Regions in the Belt and Road Initiative,* London: Routledge.

Garlick, Jeremy (2020) *The Impact of China's Belt and Road Initiative: From Asia to Europe,* London: Routledge.

Gomez, Edmund Terence, Siew Yean Tam, Ran Li and Kee Cheok Cheong (2020) *China in Malaysia: State-Business Relations and the New Order of Investment Flows,* New York: Palgrave Macmillan.

Kohli, Harinder S., Johannes F. Linn and Leo M. Zucker (eds) (2020) *China's Belt and Road Initiative: Potential Transformation of Central Asia and the South Caucasus,* Los Angeles, CA: SAGE.

Leandro, Francisco Jose B. S. and Paulo Afonso B. Duarte (2020) *The Belt and Road Initiative: An Old Archetype of a New Development Model,* New York: Palgrave Macmillan.

Lim, Alvin Cheng-Hin and Frank Cibulks (eds) (2019) *China and Southeast Asia in the Xi Jinping Era,* Lanham, MD: Lexington books.

Ploberger, Christian (2020) *Political Economic Perspectives of China's Belt and Road Initiative: Reshaping Regional Integration,* London: Routledge.

Rana, Pradumna B.. and Xianbali, Ji (2020) *China's Belt and Road Initiative: Impacts on Asia and Policy Agenda Initiative*, New York: Palgrave Macmillan.

Tapiero, Eddie (2019) *The Silk Road in Panama: A Strategic Prospective Scenario between the Americas and China*, Panama City: Self-published.

Index

Page numbers in italics refer to figures.

For Product Safety Concerns and Information please contact our EU
representative GPSR@taylorandfrancis.com
Taylor & Francis Verlag GmbH, Kaufingerstraße 24, 80331 München, Germany

www.ingramcontent.com/pod-product-compliance
Lightning Source LLC
Chambersburg PA
CBHW061313220326
41599CB00026B/4862